MARXIST THEORY AND SOCIALIST STATES

MARXIST THEORY AND SOCIALIST STATES

NILANJANA MAJUMDAR

Publications

KALPAZ PUBLICATIONS

DELHI-110052

Marxist Theory and Socialist States

Rs. 750

ISBN: 81-7835-429-2

Published in 2005 in India by
Kalpaz Publications,
C-30, Satyawati Nagar, Delhi-110052
E-mail : Kalpaz@hotmail.com

Laser Typesetting at : Master Computers, Delhi
Printed at : Salasar Imaging System, Delhi

Contents

Preface

This work is concerned with the inadequacies of Marxist theory and socialist practice in former socialist societies within their own paradigm and framework, respectively. I believe in the continued relevance of Marxian analysis and practice. I do not, though subscribe dichotomy for socialist project. It regards the possibilities of renewal in socialist societies and Marxian theory as tangible, though, these attempts failed in the context of the challenge that cybernetic capitalism posed to these societies in term of scientific revolution and its challenges.

I was inspired to get this published as a result of the encouragement and suggestion of Professor Arun Patnaik, Central University, Hyderabad, the external examiner of my M. Phil work that I pursued at the Centre for Political Studies, Jawaharlal Nehru University, New Delhi. I am thankful to Professor Rakesh Gupta for his patient guidance and empathy during the execution of this work. It was a learning experience to work under him. I am thankful to the staffs of JNU library, Nehru Memorial and Museum Library and library of Presidency College of Kolkata.

I am grateful to my husband, Sayon, for standing by me in this endeavour. All members of my family have been a source of encouragement.

Nilanjana Majumdar

Introduction

One of the most important aspects of Marxism which explained transition from one phase to another is historical materialism–the central body of doctrine, which is also referred to as the materialist conception of history, that forms the social-scientific core of Marxist theory. Engels had credited Marx for being the originator of the term historical materialism. Marx had put forward his theory of Historical Materialism in *The German Ideology* and also in *A Contribution to the Critique of Political Economy, Theses on Feuerbach, Capital Volume 1 and 2*, Engels Labour in the transition from Ape to Man and *Anti Duhring*. He had quite often in his writings said that the economic structure is the actual base for all society, and politics in most cases just the superstructure which is heavily indebted to the base in a dialectical relationship, though.

The economic structure according to Marx comprises of forces, relations, and also the means of production of which the first two were the most important. Tom Bottomore writes that "As the society's productive forces develop, they clash with existing production relations, which now fetter their growth. Then begins an epoch of social revolution as this contradiction divides society and as people become, in a more or less ideological form, conscious of this conflict and fights it out. The conflict is resolved in favour of the productive forces, and new, higher relations of production, whose material pre-conditions have matured in the womb of the old society, emerge which better accommodate the continued growth of society's productive capacity."[1]

The basic principle of the new scientific world outlook, which Marx had formulated in the "Theses on Feuerbach"[2], was developed in the German Ideology. The German Ideology is the continuation in new form of previous works by Marx and Engels, mainly of the Economic and Philosophic Manuscripts of 1844, and the Holy Family and in the end assimilates the ideas contained in them. First of all Marx and Engels constituted the real living people, their activity and material conditions which they find already existing, and the ones produced by their activity, as the "premises" of the materialist conception of history. Thus, what is underlined here is the historic character of the material conditions themselves, which are increasingly influenced by the people's activity, or, the species being.

None of the philosophers before Marx had put so great an importance to 'men' as had been done by Marx. However, Feuerbach was the first philosopher who had concentrated on man as such. But even in that case it was in the form of 'man,' as an individual in abstraction, never in the collective and never historically. In his Theses on Feuerbach, Marx put forward the materialist conception of 'the essence of man.' In opposition to Feuerbach, who had only an abstract conception of 'man' in isolation from social relations and historical reality, Marx emphasised that real men could only be understood as products of social relations. Marx then went much further than Feuerbach in critical comprehension of religion and the ways of overcoming it. He pointed out that it was not enough to understand the earthly basis of religion. The condition for eliminating religion, the "Theses" underline, is the revolutionary elimination of the social contradictions which give rise to it.

For Marx 'men' should be at the centre of all discussion. Any change in the socio-economic-political structure would be brought about keeping in mind that men are the centre of almost everything.[3] Marx believed in the species being. In a polemical article in 1844, Marx wrote "Social revolution concentrates on the whole because it is... a protest of man against dehumanised life, because its point of departure is the particular, real individual, because it is the protest of the individual against his isolation from the community which is the true community of men, that is the essence of man. Whatever may be the topic of discussion—be it the class struggle or the laws that govern history—it is the real, concrete individual, the true maker of history that remains the foundation of all analysis; for he is the true object of action. For Marx the point of departure was always the individuals and in that sense defying ontology.

This concern for men was the aspect which prompted Marx to bring about a change in the lives of men. Particularly important in this respect was the eleventh thesis, which says: "The philosophers have only interpreted the world in various ways; the point is to change it"[4] The world cannot be changed by merely changing our notions of it, by theoretically criticising what exists; it must be effective action, material revolutionary practice. The Theses concisely formulates the fundamental difference of Marxist philosophy from all earlier philosophy, including pre-Marxian materialism and Utopian socialism. It concentrates into a single sentence the effective, transforming character of the revolutionary theory created by Marx and Engels, its inseparable connection with revolutionary practice.

In *The German Ideology*[5] Marx and Engels not only developed in all its aspects the thesis of the decisive role of the material production in the life of society, which they had already formulated in their previous works, they also revealed for the first time the dialectics of the development of the productive forces and the relations of production. This most important discovery was formulated here as the dialectics of the productive forces and the form of intercourse. It illuminated the whole conceptual system of historical materialism and made it possible to expound the substance of the materialist way of understanding history as an integral scientific conception.

Marx from here goes on to show that how the lives of men had remained unchanged even though the relations of production had changed from one period to another. This discovery can be reduced to the following propositions. The productive forces determine the form of social relations. At a certain stage of development, the productive forces came into contradiction with the existing social relations. Social revolutions are only in the position to bring about changes in such a scenario. In the place of the previous social relations, which has become fetter, a new one is evolved which corresponds to the most developed productive forces. Subsequently, this new form of social relations in its turn ceases to correspond to the developing productive forces, turns into their fetter and is replaced by an ensuing, historically more progressive form of social relations. Thus in the course of the entire historical development a link of continuity is established between successive stages and this is how change in the form of a spiral takes place in society.

The discovery of the laws of social development provided the key to the scientific understanding of the entire historical process. It served as the point of departure for the scientific periodisation of history. Lenin commented that Marx's historical materialism was a great achievement in scientific thinking.

In the German ideology Marx and Engels investigated the basic determinants of the sequence of phases in the historical development of social production. They showed that the outward expression of the level of development of the productive forces is always to be found in that of the division of labour. The transition from primary historical relations to the ensuing stage in social development was determined by the development of the productive forces, resulting in the transition from an initial, natural division of labour to the social division of labour in the form which is expressed in the division of society into classes.

Along with the social division of labour there develop such derivative historical phenomena as private property, the state and the 'estrangement" of social activity. Just as the natural division of labour in primitive society determines the first, tribal (family) form of property so the increasing social division of labour determines the further development and change of the forms of property. The second form of property is the "ancient communal and state property", the third form is "feudal or estate property" and the fourth is "bourgeois property". The singling out and analysis of forms of property which successively replace one another and dominate at different stages of historical development provided the basis for the scientific Marxist theory of the social formations, the successive replacement of which is the principal feature of the whole historical process.

Marx and Engels examined the last, the bourgeois, form of private property in greater detail than the other historical forms of property, tracing its transition from the guild-system to manufacture and large-scale industry. This was the first time that these two principal stages in the development of bourgeois society, the manufacture period and the period of large-scale industry, had been singled out and analysed. At this point of time Marx discusses primitive accumulation.

Marx defines and analyses primitive accumulation in Capital I, pt. VII. Having examined the laws of development of production by capital, he is concerned with the process by which capitalism is itself historically established. His understanding of capitalism is a precondition for this, as is his more general analysis of mode of production. This follows from the necessary focus upon how one set of class relations of production becomes transformed into another. In particular, how is it that a property-less class of wage-labourers, the proletariat, becomes confronted by a class of capitalists who monopolise the means of production?

Marx's answer is disarmingly simple. Since pre-capitalist relations of production are predominantly agricultural, the peasantry having possession of the principle means of production, namely land, capitalism can only be created by dispossessing the peasantry of the land. Accordingly the origins of capitalism are to be found in the transformation of relations of production of land. The freeing of the peasantry from land is the source of wage labourers both for agricultural capital and for industry.[6]

The German Ideology expounds the basic features of future communist society—the abolition of private property, of the class division of labour and classes themselves, the transformation of production and all the social relations and the disappearance of the state, the instrument of class domination. People's own activity will cease to confront them as a power alien to them.

This transition from one historical phase to another could also be explained in terms of Dialectical materialism. It is considered as the philosophy of Marxism—the main theories of which are scientific laws of completely general type which govern nature, society and thought. It had given a philosophic background to historical materialism and has shown that history indeed moves in this particular fashion as dialectics prove that there actually exist laws of motion in the world. Marx and Engel's dialectical materialism had an imprint of Hegel's thought on it minus his Idealism.

What distinguished Hegel's mode of thinking from that of all other philosophers was the exceptional historical sense underlying it. However, abstract and idealist the form employed, the development of his ideas always runs parallel to the development of world history, and the latter is indeed supposed to be only the proof of the former. Although this reversed the actual relation and stood it on its head, yet the real content was invariably incorporated in his philosophy, especially since Hegel—unlike his pupils—did not rely on ignorance, but was one of the most erudite thinkers of all time. He was the first to try to demonstrate that there is development, an intrinsic coherence in history, and however strange some things in this philosophy of history may seem to us now; the grandeur of the basic conception is still admirable today[7].

Marx was and is the only one who could undertake the work of extracting from the Hegelian logic the kernel containing Hegel's real discoveries in this field, and establishing the dialectical method, divested of its idealist trappings, in the simple form in which it becomes the only correct mode of the development of thought. The working out of the method which underlies Marx's critique of political economy is, we think, a result hardly less significant than the basic materialist outlook.

One important aspect that could be discerned in whole of Marx and Engels writings is the fact that society would change and the focus is on change. Social revolutions would bring about socialism, after capitalism.

The application of materialist world outlook to social questions leads to three guiding principles, which historical materialism employs in the understanding of social affairs:

(1) That society in its development is regulated by objective laws discoverable by science.

(2) That views and institutions, political, ideological and cultural developments, arise on the basis of development of the material life of society;

(3) That ideas and institutions which thus arise on the basis of conditions of material life play an active role in the development of material life.[8]

If one applies these three to the existing socialist societies, we are confronted with the problem of opening up of a pandora's box from within Marxist theorisation. Old and young Marx, Marx Vs Engels, Lenin's modifications (if not vulgarisations), Mao's theorisation on New Democracy and continuous revolution, Dimitrov's People's Democracies, Gramsci's Passive Revolution and concepts of hegemony, Stalin's distortions, Trotsky's Permanent Revolution and the whole tradition of Critical Marxism make their appearance to refute or retain the possibility of socialist revolutions in countries where they took place, the path they followed and theorisations they attempted. It appears that the phenomenon of break-up of Hegelian thought in young and old Hegelians and their many versions repeated itself with the body of Marxian thought as well as the experience of the socialist societies practice and theorisations.

There are plural ways of comprehending this unique phenomenon–both from within Marxism as also from without. Some, like Immanuel Wallerstein may call the experiment as failed liberal experiment. Others like Francis Fukuyama may call it failure of Marxism and victory of Hegelianism. Still others consider it the victory of the Great Game that Cold War launched since the Truman doctrine and the victory of the one world system, under the Bush Administration. Could one exclaim this is blooming of hundred flowers?

The Marxian terrain needs to be further explored as far as transitions in society are considered. For Marx transitions themselves are not ideal types as anything would be for Max Weber. The three principles underlined by Maurice Cornforth suggest in the interplay of dynamic forces under changed circumstances, whereas Engels would say contradictions sublate. Let us go a little further; the fetish of commodity existed only under capitalism though commodity production did exist since slavery. Contradictions related to fetishism of commodities would create their own social formation and own transition. Similarly the primary stage of scientific socialism scantily sketched by Marx may have same principles of political economy but extremely different contexts and conjunctures. While it is clear that the continuation of the State will remain, it is by no means humanely possible to lay down the dynamics of its genesis of revolution, factors for its continuation, perpetuation or decay.

Let us take an example, did the elucidation of principles by Marx anticipate, let alone experience or theorise upon, the role of civil war in transition to socialism. It happened after the revolution in Soviet Russia and before the revolution in China. What impact this would have on the socialist state is not found in any of Marx's writings. What one finds though is that reaction would not voluntarily surrender power. Let us take another example that of the role of the monopolies. Marx had only hinted about it in his book on capital. Lenin developed Marxian interpretation of Finance Capital. He, who lived to see Mussolini, could define fascism as the most violent form of capitalist rule. He could not anticipate the virulent hatred of finance capital in the form of the world war that used WMD's of the time and during which circumstances East European societies were liberated from Nazism by the Red Army. What impact this would have on state and society of people's democracies needed to be theorised upon despite Lenin's writings. Gramsci's Prison Note Books can raise the issue of hegemony in the Italian context but could not have been a guide to practice either in Italy or elsewhere. Were these passive revolutions, late socialism creating dichotony of State and civil society?

Conditions of socialist transformation could not be concretely worked out and theorised upon. That this was attempted, there is no doubt. The theory of stages as opposed to continuous revolutions suggests it. There is a whole range of issues linked with transitions in these societies. These could relate to fetishisation of class, nation, bureaucracy, state, distribution, personality, of industrialisation, principles of reward, creation of material conditions for transitions for say electricity to mechanical power to micro-electronic and nuclear power, party and the withering away of the state itself. These societies were faced with innumerable problems and produced blueprints from reform packages to revolutionary changes from within the Marxian Leninist framework and from without, either initiatively or creatively. What would have happened is a surmise that the Chinese leadership's modernisation results explain. What did happen was that some interpretations of Gorbachev's Leninist reform endeavour failed for within Marxism there was very little to guide practice at that stage in a condition where the world was more than what is denoted by proletarian internationalism.

Marx noted the emergence of the bourgeois state and civil society in his writing titled On the Jewish Question. He had, as per Poulantzas, rejected the presumed dichotomy between the two since he did not give the idea of the class nature of the state, He stipulated the possibility of the State being autonomous in certain conjunctures during the period of transition to the capitalist mode of production, as in case of dictatorships and Bonapartism. He linked this fact up with a certain balance inn the class struggle and not the dichotomous State and Civil Society relationship as Gramsci had subsequently done it. After the revolution the State retained its class nature, as birth marks but changed its character from a representative of the minority of the bourgeoisie to the majority of the producers in the city and the country-side along with the middle classes. If we posit the Gramscian dichotomy then we recognise the right of the bourgeois to oppose the State after the revolution. This is precisely what did not happen as gentlemanly as is assumed by the State and civil society paradigm. It happened in the form of the civil wars/ liberation from fascism as a result of war that marked the beginning of socialist construction, distorted by the external factors.

The Gramscian argument would make us assume that the socialist state is also independent of the Civil Society and to look at it in this fashion would be to give it an immutability that is not the substance of Marxist-Leninist prescriptions for the withering away of the State. The theoretical construct in that case would become a fetish and dangerously so. The Socialist State would have to be turned into an institution of autonomy from the struggles and civil society as an institution will become the vehicle of socialism. Theories on the State and Society relationship differ in the impact of the State and civil Society even in the European context. The role of Civil Society depends of specific political culture and this differed within Western European countries as much as between West and East European countries, It is suggested that generally in countries of Eastern Europe there is neo-patrimonial culture. This implies that people expect that the initiative for change comes from the State, Further the argument that it is with a robust civil society that democracy can be brought in has also to be taken in the context of the bourgeois society where fascism was threatening democracy. It is not clear if that argument can be transplanted in another mode of production. That would assume a universal value of bourgeois democracy with which Marx and Lenin had dispensed with in their concept of smashing of the state machinery.

We do recognise that the socialist societies that came into existence had oppositions from within and without and that these had their class nature. In that context were the distortions introduced that we have analysed. The critiques that follow are examples of the continuation of older ideology as well as penetration of the other in the imperfect construction of the socialist order. In that sense the State and civil society dichotomy came into analysis of the critics, How far would it be possible to introduce the concept of civil society is not clear. Within the Marxist framework Gorbachev attempted to reformulate the theory given the crisis of these societies as a result of socialist industrialisation and emergence of new social strata. This strata demanded new social compact and that is precisely what the Gorbachevan attempt was within the Leninist and socialist framework, It failed, though for reasons of Stalinisation. Failure has been a phenomenon in Marx's own time. He had posited the revolution on the shoulders of the English working class but found it sleeping. He did stipulate the coming to power to the working class once adult franchise was introduced. This did happen in the form of the Labour party coming to power. In case of the socialist society the Stalin phenomenon did spoiled the party.

References

1. Tom Bottomore, *Dictionary of Marxist Thought*, Blackwell Publishers, England, 1983, p. 207.

2. Karl Marx, 'Theses on Feuerbach', Collected Works, Vol. 5, Progress Publishers Moscow, 1976.

3. Adam Schaff, *Marxism and the Human Individual*, McGraw Hill Book Company, New York, 1970.

4. Karl Marx, 'Theses on Feuerbach', *Collected Works, Vol. 5*, Progress Publishers, Moscow, 1976, p. 5.

5. Karl Marx, 'The German Ideology', *Collected Works, Vol. 5*, Progress Publishers, Moscow, 1976.

6. Tom Bottomore, *Dictionary of Marxist Thought*, Blackwell Publishers, England, 1983, p. 393.

7. Karl Marx, 'A Contribution to the Critique of Political Economy', *Collected Works, Vol. 16*, Progress Publishers, Moscow, 1980.

8. Maurice Cornforth, *Dialectical Materialism Vol. 2*, Lawrence and Wishart, London, 1953.

1

Problems of Transitions in Socialist Societies

> All the writings of Marx, Engels and Lenin are directed in one way or the other to the question: how and why societies change? But in no way is it a theory of how societies have changed in the past or how are they changing under our eyes. It's analyses are aimed at making it possible to control change in accordance with human needs and ideals on the basis of a genuine understanding of what the actual possibilities are.
>
> —*Howard Selsam.*[1]

The term change has immense importance in all spheres of a human being's life. Change rules out the chance of any system reaching any point of stagnation and losing its way amidst it towards a better world. It is man's eternal endeavour to reach out for something new and better everyday, always. To achieve something higher and greater; to reach a point where one can claim to have attained salvation. This salvation however could come in different forms and colour in various people's thoughts and ideas. For some it could be realising

The Almighty in one self and for some it could be to leave the world a better place than what they found it to be. For Marx, Engels and their followers, it was the second and in the process they wanted to find or form a better world. In the process of change from one system to another, anything goes through a transition–a period which retains the birthmarks of the system preceding it and yet, shows the prospects of a new future.

Marx realised that it was the common-man who needed the change most and more so the working class. To bring about any difference to their lives it was important to bring about a change in the political lives of the people concerned, thus the political system needed change at the beginning–a change from capitalism to communism. Situations where political changes towards a better world do not come about naturally, Marx believed that it needs a revolution to do the same. Transition, or a shift, in Marxist ideology could be brought about through revolution. Thus revolutions have occupied a very important position in Marxist ideology. Another aspect which have become equally important in the understanding of Marxist ideas on change is the nature of the transitional stage, or the stage that comes right after capitalism but when the goal for attaining something better have not yet been reached. Marx had conceptualised on the nature of the transitional stage too. But it was Lenin who had to deal with the idea of bringing about a revolution and answer to the demands of a transitional stage, practically, since he is credited to have brought about the first socialist revolution in any country in Russia in October 1917.

This chapter tries to look into the thoughts of Marx and his followers regarding this change and transition and situations that arose in the process.

In order to understand change it would be pertinent on our part to understand dialectical materialism, as had been developed by Marx and Engels. Marx, in this case says that he is heavily indebted to Hegel, although his ideas are an entire opposite of Hegelian dialectics, though Della Volpe[2] thinks he borrows heavily from him. To Marx, to put it simply, there is a motion and mutation of matter in a dialectical way. Materialism, of course, was not Marx's unique philosophical invention. The philosophic concept 'materialism' in no sense means the reduction of all human activity to crude matter, and inanimate stuff. In the area of philosophy, materialism, according to Marx and Engels means only that life and their thinking matter have their origins in non-thinking matter that under favourable conditions, inorganic produced organic life. Applied to history, materialism means only that, before men can have government, religion, or philosophies, they must have food, shelter and on much of the earth–clothing, in other words, material prerequisites of life. By historical, Marx and Engels mean that human existence can be understood only as a process of social development. Everything in our lives is part of a continuous pattern of social movement and social change. Thus, there can be no adequate explanation of any question facing man unless that question is viewed historically. Men are their own masters to the extent material circumstances allow them to be. So are heroes if they cognise and contribute to the changing circumstance creatively. Criticality, change and creativity is the core of Marxism, says Karl Korsch. Marx put his theory of change on an objective analysis of capitalist dialectics in contrast to the then Utopian socialists.[3]

The coincidence of the changing of circumstances and of human activity can be conceived and rationally understood only as revolutionising practice of a species being that denies ontology of communist in terms of changing class relations.

Throughout their wide ranging studies of history and the events of their own day, Marx and Engels gave detailed attention to the theoretical and practical problems of politics and revolution. Lenin, under the new conditions of the imperialist stage of capitalism, greatly enriched and extended this theory, making it the foundation of the Russian Revolution he led. Marx was the first to project a theory of revolution from a materialist and scientific point of view. Even the best of earlier approaches to this question (e.g. Montesquieu's *Spirit of the Laws*, or Thomas Paine's *The Rights of Man*) based themselves on some version of an ideal 'human nature' to which government is supposed to conform, or else like Rousseau, they posited a 'mythical social contract' between an abstract 'government' and an equally abstract 'people.' Revolution, it was believed, was necessitated by the violation of the 'contract' by the government or by its failure to conform to 'human nature.' The Theory of Critical Realism, and Zola, suffered some similar notion of the natural, according to Lukacs. Marx took the subject out of this realm of abstraction and placed it where it belonged–on the ground of real people living in real society i.e. in a mode of production.

Marxist theory begins with the recognition that social revolutions are neither aberrations nor accidents–they are the essence of social movement. At the same time they are not teleological. Knowing that no social formation is permanent, Marxism does not look on revolutions as inevitable calamitous interruptions of the slow peaceful evolution of the status quo, rather it is seen as a fact of political life that makes or mars a transition to a new society when situations of contradictions take place. The struggle for individual existence in social context assumes new forms of antagonistic and non-antagonistic contradictions in Mao and need for social pluralism in socialist state according to Burlatski. The journey from being unconscious part of nature to its manipulation in terms of genetic engineering, to give one example, and social control another, has produced changing modes of production as part of revolutionising practice in terms of social organisation, class solidarity and a sense of creative being that the Marxist paradigm proclaimed and promised. The relationship of necessity and freedom kept changing hands and new social contradictions created new logic to comprehend and transcend in socialist society. The new social contradictions and the failure to transcend them led to the modification of the claim that history begins with Marxism. The purposive activity produced an implosion in existing socialist states.

The implosion has raised the issue of removal of human alienation through human emancipation and again in existing socialist societies. This implosion was the product of new socialist classes incubated in a new kind of state but not the implosion of necessity and freedom dialectic. It put on the agenda a paucity of theorisation on transition itself in post capitalist societies. After the proletarian revolution where to go and how, became a complicated issue not only because of the specific internal or external objective circumstance but equally because of a lacuna in Marxist theory of transition.

In *A Contribution to the Critique of Political Economy*, both Marx and Engels speak of a revolutionary process whose components are economic, civilising and political. Though the components are interlocked, they make their appearance in a fixed sequence[4]. The meaning which Marx gives to the revolution always depends on the context in which he uses it. Sometimes he uses it to designate the upheaval, but often it means the whole revolutionary process, which is, the economic, civilising and political moments taken together. Marxist statements enable us to infer with certainty that each and every revolutionary action must accord with the social conditions which are present in any given phase of the historical process. The discussion of the relative merits and the new forms of revolutionary action was continued by the second generation of Marxists in all countries[5].

The problem of transition from the kingdom of necessity to the kingdom of freedom is linked to the role the working class will play. The Proletariat will transform itself from class-in-itself to class-for-itself. For Marx the class conscious proletariat will form the dictatorship of the Proletariat after overthrowing capitalism in a particular country. The issue is how to work out the new state.

Marx's first reference to 'the dictatorship of the proletariat' occurs in the third of a trilogy of articles which he wrote for his journal *Neue Rheinische Zeitung-Politisch-Oekonomisch Revue* in 1850, and subsequently which were assembled under the title *The Class Struggles in France*, 1848-50. The term is here employed by Marx in the context of an exposition of what, for him, was entailed by revolutionary socialism:

> ...the declaration of the permanence of the revolution, the class dictatorship of the proletariat as the necessary transition point to the abolition of class distinctions generally, to the abolition of all the relations of production on which they rest, to the abolition of all the social relations that correspond to these relations of production, to the revolutionising of all the ideas that result from these social relations.[6]

In April 1850, a month after Marx's writing of this article, the concept of the dictatorship of the proletariat was incorporated into the first of the six statutes of the *Universal Society of Communist Revolutionaries*, among the principle figures of which were numbered, in addition to Marx and Engels.

Without doubt, the most significant effect which the experience of the Commune had on the way in which Marx and Engels conceptualised the transition to socialism was that they no longer presented the establishment of the dictatorship of the proletariat and the disappearance of the state as two separate and distinct stages within the transition period. In his account of the Commune, as has already been noted, Marx emphasised that the political power which the proletariat substituted for the bourgeois state was fundamentally different in character from the power which it supplanted; the establishment of the Commune was therefore 'a revolution against the state itself'.

Santiago Carrillo writes that in a the time of Marx and Engels the working class was only a small minority and so the dictatorship of the proletariat was required as it would help the proletariat control state power. He considered the term therefore as just a synonym for 'consolidating the hegemony, the social domination of the proletariat.'[7]

Marx, at the last part of his life paid much attention to Russia, which was at that point in time going through an economic transition. He was quite aware of the conditions that marred the development of capitalism in Russia. Marx assessed many elements of capitalism in Russia's agriculture[8]. By as early as the 1870s he was quite sure that Russia was closing in on a revolution in the country. He believed that a revolution in the country would be bourgeois-democratic in nature, and it would aim at abolishing autocracy in the country. But even then Marx believed that the West would have a proletarian revolution first and with its assistance Russia could also go for one, either by bypassing capitalism in the country or by shortening its life-span in the country. The bypassing will take place on the basis of the Russian Commune, said Marx.

However, Marx had written in his 1877 letter that it would be possible for Russia to initiate the transition to socialism without having to go through the vagaries of capitalism in the country. In the preface to the Russian edition of the *Manifesto of the Communist Party*, Marx and Engels had given their joint conclusion:

> If the Russian revolution becomes the signal for a proletarian revolution in the West, so that both complement each other, the Russian common ownership of land may serve as the starting point of the communist development.

Trotsky, on the other hand, viewed the transition of society from capitalism to socialism, postulated by Marxism, as an immense succession of socio-economic and political upheavals leading to the establishment of an international classless and stateless society. No single phase of this revolution, whatever its social character or geographic limitation, can be regarded as self-contained or self-sufficient. Trotsky went on to point out that because of its industrial and cultural backwardness and poverty, Russia could only begin the socialist revolution but could not achieve or complete it except in association and co-operation with the western industrial countries. The Russian revolution he considered would be a prelude to a series of western Revolutions. Both internationally as well as nationally the revolution would be "Permanent".[9]

Trotsky's idea of 'permanent revolution got widespread support from a large group of intellectuals from various parts of the world as the 'embodiment of true Marxism'. Trotsky all along maintained that 'socialism in one country' is an error. In his *'Three Concepts of the Russian Revolution'*, Trotsky sided with Lenin against either the Populists or the Mensheviks when he put forward the slogan of a democratic dictatorship of the proletariat and peasantry in the hope that a revolution under this banner would give an impulse for a socialist victory in the West, which would make possible a rapid transition to socialism in Russia.[10]

Trotsky expressed no doubts regarding the working class character of the Soviet state. The state still continued to control the means of production but, unfortunately the political power were in the hands of the bureaucrats. An expected counter revolution by the bourgeois could only be avoided if the Bolshevik party took appropriate measures to organise themselves properly.

Trotsky blamed the delay in the world revolution as one of the reasons why the bureaucracy has been able to become such a big unwanted force in the country. The theory of 'socialism in one country' dealt the final blow in the coffin. It took away the hope for the Russian Proletariat to get some support from the world. He had time and again blamed the Russian bureaucracy as the force behind the defeat of the world proletarian revolution.

Among the second generation Marxists, Kautsky, in his theory of transition from capitalism to socialism concentrates more on working class consciousness as he focuses on the role that capitalism plays in developing consciousness, rather than on the breakdown of the state. The working class cannot prematurely stage a revolution. It does so only when objective conditions are ripe for them. Kautsky's understanding of revolution encompasses tactics of peaceful change of social democracy even though he realised that reform may not lead to revolution.

Kautsky's focus on the political consciousness as necessity of Revolution finds a resonance in Gorbachev. When Gorbachev came to the Central Committee and became General Secretary, the Party was struggling with the issue of transition from extensive to intensive agriculture and from machine tool industry to the high technology based production system. The Party was incapable of comprehending the whole gamut of issues that this would entail–namely the role of Leninism, reform of the party, transformation of the market, labour laws, change of social relations of production in the city and the countryside on meritocracy rather than solidarity, etc. In that context, there were underground movements like the Novosibirsk Report, and quite a few of these found expressions in Gorbachev's book, *Perestroika, New Thinking.* The consciousness of a new phase of revolution in the form of transition from lower to higher stages of revolution and a whole range of new political movements was an issue that the CPSU was unable to come to grips with[11].

We now come to Rosa Luxemburg[12]. The accumulation of Capital, according to Rosa Luxemburg, will go on increasing, as long as the capitalists find a place to sell their commodity, in internal as well as external markets, i.e., the colonies. She believed in the breakdown of capitalism through revolution and not through the process of reform. Reforms have relevance, only if they add to revolutionary movement. Rosa says that the intelligentsia should be the ones who would impart consciousness to the party. So spontaneity is stressed, but not of the Leninist variety. Unlike Lenin, she discounts the national question. As a result of her emphasis on spontaneity, she attempted a revolution under the Spartacus League in Germany. Her fetish on the denial of national question made her misread World War–I since she considered that the Polish Question had modified the imperial character of the war.

Rosa's thesis of accumulation of capital under changed conditions amounts to Brzezinski's thesis on limits of Soviet revolution. He had maintained that the Soviet Union will not be able to transit from first stage of scientific revolution to the second stage of the scientific revolution. Rosa's thesis of accumulation of capital can be applied to socialist division of labour within the Soviet Union and Warsaw pact powers. This division reached a plateau of growth by the mid-70s and continued to be so with minor spurts of marginal increase. The Stalinist State was an overgrowth and a distorted one owing to the problem of socialist primitive accumulation of Preobryzinski, as noted by Jean Ellenstein[13].

The exhaustion of the State, despite Khrushchev's Spring, can be seen from the fact that the system remained partially petrified and failed to allow for spontaneous political activity as part of socialist pluralism. While participation increased and so did education of newer sections of society, autonomous political participation did not in the Soviet case, and worse still, in Eastern Europe, especially its more advanced parts like Poland, Czech Republic and Hungary. Very early on, the populations of these countries gave notice of autonomous political activity, especially with Dübcek[14], in Czechoslovakia in 1969, Vaclav Havel[15], Tamara Deutscher and Ro Medvedev in Russia, Solidarity under Walesa[16], Rudolph Bahro in GDR and a whole host of artists and intellectuals who kept getting arrested and freed under general amnesty during Khrushchev and Gorbachev's time. They failed since they remained spontaneous and individualistic. It is only when Yevtushenko[17] became part of

New Thinking that spontaneity became meaningful. This of course cannot be said of Solzhenitsyn[18]. Yevtushenko was proud of being a Ukrainian and Solzenitsyn of some archaic rightwing form of Slav identity ghoary past.

Once again we notice that Rosa Luxembourg goes wrong on the National Question. The right of Nations to self determination granted by Leninist State had its other in subsequent developments, especially in late 70's and 80's in Ukraine, Azerbaijan, Kazakhstan, Georgia, Moldova, Chechnya and the Baltic republics. This led to the CPSU to hold a special conference on the national question in the 1980's. What is significant to note is that a nation forming process and arrival of nationhood are distinct phases of the same European historical process, where there were only eight developed nation-states in the 19th century[19]. Even now, the national question remains in the Russian Federation, which is a multi-ethnic state. Basically Lenin was right that the question of the nation cannot be solved on the basis of spontaneity. It has to be linked to bourgeois or proletarian dimension. Hence this also involves greater social interaction and identification of the individual with the community.

This became the condition of the transitory state that Marx called the period of political transition period, in which the state can be no other than the revolutionary dictatorship of the proletariat. *Lenin and Leninism* in the hands of Stalin and *Long Live Leninism* in the hands of Mao Tze Dong were theorisations about this state and how to arrive at it. Lenin's concept of political organisation, revolutionary tactics, War Communism, new peaceful agrarian relations were steps in that direction.

Isaac Deutscher[20] tries to find an answer to the question whether the party, which ruled Soviet Union, is the same as that of the one which ruled Russia in 1917, whether the continuity has remained or whether it has been preserved in outward form only. Deutscher answers in the negative.

He does not see any reason, historical or otherwise as to why the party would be the same. Deutscher writes that in any case "within the framework of the revolution's continuity sharp breaks have occurred'. Unlike Lenin, Deutscher does not show any sign of confidence in the Russian working class and considered them as 'not inherently revolutionary.' The reason why Russia still had a socialist revolution is not because, according to him, Russia's productive forces had advanced just far enough under the old regime to burst the social structure and its political superstructure. Deutscher speaks in line with Trotsky that the masses will have to play a conscious and a direct role in bringing about a revolution, a task which the Russian working class was not fit to take up. He attributes the bringing about of the revolution in the country to the East, for example the Decembrists, many of them had been young officers in the Russian occupation troops in Paris. Deutscher finds a strange continuity in the outbreak of the revolution in Russia in the fact that the 'epicentre' of the revolution have moved from west to east as if Russia did not have anything indigenous to start off a revolution in its own soil and that the revolution would take place in Russia was preconceived.

The fact that Deutscher felt that Russia was not the place where a socialist revolution could get started is reflected in most of his writings. According to him, although the urban working class supported the revolution whole heartedly, yet, their number was too small. But the revolution broke out and it was precisely because both the bourgeois and the socialist revolutions had taken place at the same time in Russia as a result of which the working class and the peasant joined hands in Russia thereby helping Lenin's cause. This also turned out to be the greatest weakness of the Russian revolution and thus the country suffered from all the problems of bringing about a revolution in a backward country.

Another point where, according to Deutscher the Russian Revolution have failed in its objective of carrying the revolution forward, to carry it beyond the boundaries of Russia. Lenin had claimed to have broken the chain of imperialism in the country, but Deutscher finds him guilty of not being able to break the chain in other parts of the world. He considered the Russian revolution as not something Russia's own but something which the entire world can claim to be theirs. The fact that it failed to transform into a world phenomena is also because the revolution have taken place in a backward country like Russia which was not ready for socialism at that point of time.

Let us now take a look at what position the Western Marxists take regarding bringing about a revolution in Russia. Perry Anderson in 'Considerations on Western Marxism'[21] have cited that in the aftermath of the Second World War various changes had taken place in the world political scene like 'no reversions to military or police dictatorships in the major West European countries, stable parliamentary democracy, based on fully universal suffrage, no catastrophic slumps of the twenties and thirties.' In the light of this there arose a group of Marxist scholars whose work could be distinctly separated from the generation before. The Western Marxists inverted the trajectory of Marx's thought by contributing first on economics or politics and then on philosophy itself. No philosopher within the Marxist tradition ever claimed that the main or the ultimate aim of historical materialism was a theory of knowledge. According to Anderson 'the peculiar esotericism of Western Marxist theory was to assume manifold forms: in Lukacs, Gramsci, Benjamin, Della Volpe etc'. On the question of success of the Russian revolution Anderson too considers that had the revolution of 1917 taken place in some other industrialised country of the West, socialism would have been a successful phenomena round the globe. Because of her economic backwardness, primarily, Russia has not been able to transmit it. Thus there is a deep sense of despair in the writings of Perry Anderson and the other contemporary Marxist authors-a sense of loss. The fact that socialism did not advance beyond the territorial boundaries of Russia, 'restabilisation of imperialism', and Stalinisation brought about a significant change in the equation of Marxist theory and proletarian practice, where the latter got supplemented with bourgeois theory. According to Perry Anderson with the victory of socialism in one country, theory gradually contracted into national compartments, sealed off from each other by comparative indifference and ignorance.

> ...the dominant framework of Marxist discussion underwent a fundamental change... Various Western Marxist scholars, however, have not really dealt with the fact, whether or not Russia could get socialism, at length. For, most of them dealt with the various theoretical aspects[22].

Scholars like Lukacs believed that merely accumulating facts, will not lead to the understanding of 'social totality'[23]. Hence Marx's theory of revolution and socialism can be based only on a global understanding of society that cannot be achieved by any detailed, factual analysis. "That is why opportunists and revisionists always appeal to facts, knowing that there is no logical transition from facts to the revolutionary transformation of society." The unity of the object and subject of history, of the cognitive and normative aspects of consciousness, is, Lukacs argues, the most precious legacy of Hegelianism to Marxism. Hegel could not have discovered the identity of the object and subject in history itself, as there was no real historical basis for it. Lukacs criticised the laws of dialectics of Engels and says that it loses its revolutionary character and the unity of theory and practice can be conceived only in a contemplative bourgeois, reified sense-the technical exploitation of the world as it exists not the collective subject taking possession of the world by revolutionary action.

Pre-Marxist philosophy with its dichotomy between knowledge and praxis was obliged to see the world as a collection of crystallised 'data', and praxis as a set of arbitrary ethical precepts and technical devices. By contrast, when, as in the class consciousness of the proletariat, the subjects self awareness coincides with the knowledge of the whole-when social being is recognised as man made and subject to conscious regulation by the organised community-then the dichotomy ceases to exist and the dilemma of empiricism versus utopianism is resolved.

Western Marxism found it's another expression in the form of Critical theory. Critical Theory, Perry Anderson writes, 'is an inconsistent attempt to preserve Marxism without accepting its identification with the proletariat and without recognising the class or the party criteria of truth, but also without seeking a solution of the difficulties that arise when Marxism is truncated.'[24] This theory does not try to find any answer, as a traditional does to the existing laws of society, nor does it try to explain the causes or circumstances behind the Russian revolution.

Erich Fromm identified the problem of alienation affecting all social classes.[25] He suggested as a way out of alienation a faith in the human capacity for friendship and cooperation. In this context he considered the capitalist society to have creative possibilities in human beings but have resulted in powerful destructive elements because of competition and conflict. He was critical of totalitarian doctrines and communist regimes which do not have Marxist humanistic vision, the visions included voluntary solidarity, freedom from constraint and irrational authority.

Santiago Carrillo writes that socialism triumphed first in countries which were primarily agricultural in nature, as 'the revolutionary vanguard was able to combine the class contradictions with all kinds of contradictions peculiar to imperialism'. Carrillo thinks that if socialism had triumphed in any advanced countries the results would have been remarkably different. He writes that the results would have been 'tangible and attractive'. His faith in it prompts him to write that socialism would not have faced the so-called distortions that have taken place in it.[26]

After Marx and Engels, Lenin tried to carry out the work of the masters in his own way. Lenin being one of the many, who were actually instrumental in bringing about a revolution in Russia, therefore it now becomes indispensable to look into his ideas quite closely too. E.H. Carr, the historian of Soviet Russia, explained the uniqueness of the Russian Revolution, and by implication Lenin's contribution to it in these terms: "The Russian Revolution was the first great revolution in history to be deliberately planned and made. It was this element of self consciousness, which gave the Russian Revolution its unique place in modern history."[27] Lenin had discussed the idea of bringing about socialism in Russia in a number of places. He, however, was not the only one who contemplated a revolution in Russia. Before him, the Slavophiles, the Narodniks, Chernychevsky and others had also tried to bring about a change in the country. Chernychevsky accepted the basic values of liberalism, 'Europeanisation' of Russia, the overthrow of the autocracy, political freedom, universal education, and emancipation of the peasants.[28] He especially, had a profound influence on Lenin. Lenin had discussed the prospects of a revolution in Russia and as to how it would come about with a number of contemporary Marxists like Plekhanov, the Mensheviks, Trotsky and even Rosa Luxemburg, Karl Kautsky and others. Lenin had also written in length, to discuss the Russian condition and transition from a capitalist country to a socialist one. He believed that Russia was a capitalist country and thus socialism could be brought in that country.

"The Russian empire at the turn of the century was a backward European country, but nonetheless a great power." This is how Alec Nove expresses Russia before 1917. The working class was forming and have not been formed in some large modern factories which were brought up with the help of foreign capital, and foreign specialists. But, the bulk of the population consisted of peasants. Contrary to the Slavophiles Lenin hoped to form a dictatorship of the proletariat. The Slavophiles were looking for a solution based on peasant communal tradition. But the question remained how to make it available in 'peasant' Russia? Nove writes 'Indeed, as we shall see, most of them had still not made the mental transformation when the revolution broke out. Yet the communal institutions were decaying, were permeated by market relations.'[29] Against the Mensheviks idea of Russia being developing as towards a bourgeois revolution to overthrow the Tsar, Lenin argued in the opposite.

Lenin could see in the peasants a potential revolutionary as although the peasants were backward and confused, they still wanted their lands which were owned by the great landlords and the church. Lenin indeed had a strong belief that in case their demands were met most of the peasants would even start opposing socialism, yet, there would always be a considerable number of them who would join hands with the working class to serve their cause of bringing about socialism in the country.

Lenin believed[30] that Russia had already gone the capitalist way. In 1896, Lenin was writing *The Development of Capitalism in Russia.*[31] During this time in July of the same year 30,000 St. Petersburg textile workers went on strike. Lenin's analysis of capitalism in Russia, according to James D. White was different in scope from that of his predecessors. Lenin had all through shown in his book that Russia was actually a capitalist country if one considers it from strictly Marx's point of view. He argued that a home market had already been created for Russian commodities. The second section of the book deals with the differentiation of the peasantry, and is an attempt to demonstrate that the inequalities among peasant bourgeoisie on the one hand and a peasant proletariat on the other. The third section is concerned with Russian industry, and surveys the three main types of industry to be found in Russia at the end of the nineteenth century. These are handicraft industries, in which workers are brought together within a single establishment, and modern machine industry, where division of labour have taken place and industry has finally become separated from agriculture. The conclusion is that Russia has become a capitalist country, though one, which is relatively less, advanced.

Lenin's book *The Development of Capitalism in Russia* is considered as one of the fullest and best documented and best argued examination of the crucial period of the evolution of capitalism out of feudalism in the literature of Marxism. But James D. White considered it as a 'very poor guide to the social and economic situation in Russia at the time'.[32] It was not only Lenin who had argued that capitalism had developed in Russia. Marx had also showed as to how capitalism had developed in Russia in as early as in the 1870s. Marx had emphasised on an essential element in the development of capitalism in Russia. For him, the replacement of traditional social bonds by civil society is good enough indicator to suggest that capitalism had taken over in Russia. Lenin's commentaries on statistics showing the distribution of land, livestock, and other resources between peasant families in the various parts of the country show that there had been an emergence on one hand of a wealthy group of peasants destined to form an agrarian bourgeoisie and on the other of a stratum of poor peasants, well on the way of becoming a proletariat. Marx too had noted the emergence of differences in economic status among the Russian peasantry, but had not regarded this as central to the problem of how capital began to circulate in the country.

He had also envisaged the Russian revolution as a world revolution. Russia could be one of the weakest links in the world imperialist chain but if this weakest link could be broken then the revolutions in the Western economies would also follow and probably these countries would come up to save Russia. Lenin also considered the Menshevik point of waiting for a situation to ripe as a mere heresy. According to him one has to make use of the situation available and then use it to one's own convenience as noted by Nove.[33] Again, imperialism which Lenin considered, as the highest form of capitalism (contrary to Kautsky's viewpoint) in his book *Imperialism: The Highest Stage of Capitalism,*[34] said was surprisingly prevalent in Russia. Russia indeed was an imperialistic power. With the Bolshevik revolution of 1917, it is said that Lenin could break the weakest link in the chain of capitalism in Russia. Lenin considered World War I as an imperialistic war that could be solved in a revolutionary way. As a result of this he diverted his attention for a while towards the colonised nations of the east and 'made it as much a business of the Communist International as that in the imperialist countries.'

Contrary to the position taken by Trotsky, Lenin not only considered Russia as a fertile ground for any working class movement, but that the movement would still be considered a success even if it did not immediately spread to the advanced capitalist countries of the west. He writes:

> "The Russian working-class, is able to wage its economic and political struggle alone."[35] Lenin writes this shortly before the Russian revolution of 1905 in an article published in 1925.This statement of Lenin's echoes the fact that he believed that a socialist revolution can be successful in a backward country like Russia. His strong belief contradicts the position taken either by the Trotskyites or the Western Marxists like Perry Anderson.

Again in an article which was written not before 1899, Lenin asked "What are the main questions that arise in the application to Russia of the programme common to all Social Democrats?" The essence of this programme he writes is to organise class struggle and the ultimate aim being gaining political power by the proletariat and the establishment of socialist society. Class struggle for him becomes complete only when economic struggle join hand with political struggle, which was absolutely necessary in contemporary Tsarist Russia.

Lenin said that "between capitalism and communism there lies a definite transition period which must combine features and properties of both these forms of social economy."[36] Since the definite stage of socialism is different from that of either capitalism or communism, it is important to find socialism quite firmly on the ground. In this particular stage the proletariat becomes the ruling class and it could be called the dictatorship of the proletariat and it wields state power. Socialism also means "abolition of classes".... "This protracted transition will involve transformation of individual and petty property into production, into large scale social production".[37] In the period of revolutionary transformation of capitalism to communism, a corresponding period of political transition would be marked by the revolutionary dictatorship of the proletariat, says Marx. This means that the state will continue to exist right till the time when socialism has grown into communism.[38]

However, he did not stop before acknowledging the fact that the socio-economic conditions in Russia were different from that of the advanced capitalist countries of the West and so would be the nature of the Dictatorship of the Proletariat but that should not in any way become a disadvantage for bringing about a socialist revolution in Russia.[39] But despite this, the basic forces and the basic forms of social economy were the same in Russia, as in any capitalist country, so that the peculiarities can apply to what is of lesser importance. Lenin had also identified the basic form of social–economy as capitalism, petty commodity production, and communism. The basic forces are the bourgeoisie and the petty bourgeoisie.

> "The economic system of Russia in the era of the dictatorship of the proletariat represents the struggle of labour, united on communist principles on the scale of a vast state and making its first steps-the struggle against petty commodity production and the capitalism which still persists and against that which is newly arising on the basis of petty commodity production."

After the October Revolution of 1917, while assessing the economic conditions of Russia, Lenin, had mentioned that Russia is going through a transition and was striving to bring about socialism in the country and that it had not yet reached the most coveted form of political, social or economic life. In this transitional phase in the country, fragments of both capitalism and socialism lingered on. It had (a) patriarchal, i.e. to a considerable extent natural peasant farming,(b) small commodity production,(c) private capitalism,(d) state capitalism,(e) socialism. The petty bourgeoisie was the most common element in the Russian social structure and they had most fiercely opposed state-socialism.

Socialism for him was inconceivable without large scale engineering, without planned state organisation, without electrification of Russia and without the proletariat being the ruler of the state.

In Russia, according to Lenin, labour was united communistically insofar as, first, private ownership of the means of production was abolished, and secondly, the proletarian state power organised large scale production on state-owned land and in state owned enterprises on a national scale distributed labour-power among the various branches of production and the various enterprises and distributed among the working people large quantities of consumption articles which belonged to the state.[40]

Socialism meant for him, the abolition of all classes. Lenin realised that the first task of overthrowing the landowners and the capitalists have been implemented, but the most difficult task of aligning the factory-worker and the peasantry and turning them all into workers have been realised.

Lenin's best known and most extended treatment of the dictatorship of the proletariat and the transition period is to be found in his 1917 text *The State and Revolution*, written immediately before the Bolshevik Party's seizure of power.

Lenin argued that the proletariat must, on seising power, smash and destroy the existing state apparatus, as the political form, in which was inscribed its own socio-economic subjugation.

The proletarian revolution, Colletti writes, therefore is not only the transfer of power from one class to another, but constitutes also the replacement of one type of power by another, both aspects being necessarily interlinked 'because the working class that seizes power is the working class that governs itself.'[41]

The bourgeois state apparatus, Lenin argued in *The State and Revolution*, would actually be supplanted by 'something which was no longer the state proper,' that is, by 'a state so constituted that it begins to wither away immediately, and cannot but wither away,' the essence of this change being 'a gigantic replacement of certain institutions of a fundamentally different type.' Although, again following Marx and Engels, he maintained that the new proletariat state would consist of 'the proletariat armed and organised as the ruling class,' there are few indications in their work as to what would be the specific form (as opposed to the general character) of the institutions of proletarian rule. Lenin did suggest, however, that under the dictatorship of the proletariat

...the people can suppress the exploiters even with a very simple "machine", almost without a "machine", without a special apparatus, by the simple organisation of the armed people.

In *The Immediate Tasks of the Soviet Government*, Lenin wrote that 'Soviet power is nothing but an organisational form of the dictatorship of the proletariat, dictatorship of the advanced class, which raises to a new democracy and to independent participation in the administration of the state tens upon tens of millions of working and exploited people, who by their own experience learn to regard the disciplined and class-conscious vanguard of the proletariat as their most reliable leader.[42]

In his *Letter to American Workers*, Lenin described the soviets as 'a new and higher type of democracy, a form of the proletarian dictatorship, a means of administering the state without the bourgeoisie and against the bourgeoisie'.

In its first phase, or first stage, communism cannot as yet be fully mature economically and entirely free from traditions or vestiges of capitalism. Hence the interesting phenomenon that communism in its first phase retains "the narrow horizon of bourgeois right." Of course, bourgeois right in regard to the distribution of consumer goods inevitably presupposes the existence of the bourgeois state, for right is nothing without an apparatus capable of enforcing the observance of the standards of right.

Lenin did not mean by this that the capitalist state as such survives during the transition period, but referred rather to the dual role in which the proletarian state apparatus was necessarily cast in its enforcement of differentials within the sphere of distribution simultaneously with its safeguarding of the collective ownership of the means of production.

Lenin's conceptualisation of transition went beyond that of Marx and Engels. In an article written on the second anniversary of the October Revolution, he averted that 'Theoretically, there can be no doubt that between capitalism and communism there lies a definite transition period which must combine the features and properties of both these forms of social economy. This transition period has to be a period of struggle between dying capitalism and nascent communism-or, in other words, between capitalism which has been defeated but not destroyed and communism which has been born but is still very feeble.'

In *What is To Be Done?* Lenin explained that a socialist consciousness could only be introduced into the workers movement from outside by the intellectuals[43]. In the third chapter of the same book Lenin argued that showing the problems of the working class people is merely a trade union activity. The true function of the social democrats would be to represent the working class in relation to all classes in society and state, rather than the working class. In the fourth chapter of the same book Lenin wrote that revolutionary activity requires some kind of organisation and it would not be wise to chalk out a revolution without discussing the organisation part in detail.

The split of the Social Democratic Party into two fractions had taken even the participants in the Congress by surprise. To justify their respective positions both Martov and Lenin produced pamphlets which in their turn served to intensify their polemic. *'What is To Be done?'* is also concerned with the relationship between the workers and the intelligentsia.

Economic matters were not in Lenin's mind immediately after the revolution of 1905. He was more concerned with the questions of the state and its role he had assigned to the Soviets. *The April Theses* stated that the revolution was at a transitional stage. Since there was a lack of class consciousness and organisation, the proletariat had allowed the political power to pass into the hands of the bourgeoisie. In the second stage, however, the power would pass into the hands of the poor proletariat. Lenin declined any support whatsoever, to the Provincial Government.

In the fourth chapter of the same book Lenin mentioned that power in Russia should pass over temporarily to the Soviets. He feared that the Mensheviks might continue work against that aspect as they supported the Provincial Government. In agrarian policy Lenin considered that more emphasis should be placed on the Soviets of Agricultural Labourers Deputies. All landed estates should be confiscated and placed at the disposal of these agrarian soviets. As far as economic policies are concerned, the theses demanded the immediate amalgamation of all banks in the country into a single bank, the activities of which were monitored by the Soviet of Workers' Deputies. This according to White shows the influence of Hilferding and his conception of finance capital. Hilferding had believed that control of chief banks in the country would make it possible to regulate the entire economy.

The importance of Lenin's *April Theses* as the document in which the Bolshevik strategy for 1917 was laid down has encouraged some mythology to grow up. According to Trotsky Lenin had come around in believing that a socialist revolution was possible in Russia, while he wrote the *The April Theses*, which Trotsky considered was in a way accepting his ideas on 'permanent revolution'. Some of the main themes in *'The State and Revolution'* were already discussed in *'The April Theses'*. But unlike *'The State and Revolution'* the soviets received great importance in the *'The April Theses'*.

The April Theses gave a reasonably precise statement of how the proletariat would gain power and what institutions would enable it to do so, *State and Revolution* is much vague on this issue, and according to White is a very poor guide to how the Bolsheviks came to power.[44]

At the beginning of September Lenin believed he could see an opportunity for compromise with the Menshevik and SR parties which controlled the Soviet. At the end of September Lenin began to agitate within the Bolshevik party for an insurrection to overthrow the Provincial Government. Lenin insisted that the Provincial Government should be overthrown and that the Bolsheviks should not wait until the Second Congress of the Soviets take place.

There were a number of ways in which Russia was a different country from that of the others around. It was a country whose resources were snapped by almost three years of war. The economy was disintegrating under the strain, with industry, agriculture and transport approaching a state of crisis. The country had lost an immense expanse of territory as a result of German advance, and refugees from the occupied territories retreated into the Russian heartland to share the deprivation and despair of the settled population. The Russia in which the February revolution had taken place was one in which quite exceptional circumstances prevailed. No writings of theoreticians have stipulated that there will be imperialist encirclement, civil war demanding war communism which in turn led to NEP, collectivisation and industrialisation in the context of the threat of the World War II, as to how Europe would respond to fascism and the nature of transitions of socialism to East European countries in the post World War II phase.

The existing socialist societies were confronted with problems related to internal dynamics and external pressures. Both created a mosaic of problems that could not be resolved within the existing Marxian theorisation on transition to socialism and subsequent social change. One of the most important problems which were confronted in the Socialist Societies was that of political alienation. The true origin of the term alienation as developed by Marx is to be found in the German tradition. Hegel must take credit for having clearly described this situation for the first time. He says that the spirit is self alienation: the discipline of culture and civilisation. In the course of development man discovered that the world of culture and society is not simply a part of the cultural order but his own creation; yet at the same time he realised he is not the master of the world, which he had come to recognise as his own work. Thus the world of culture received "Its existence by self-consciousness of its own accord relinquishing itself and giving up its essentiality..." and this process led eventually to the "alienation of personality." In the *Phenomenology of the Mind*, Ludwig Feuerbach also speaks of alienation. For him religion is a projection of human self consciousness. He understands this projection as an alienation of the self. Hence all human perfections are alienated from the subject man. After Feuerbach Marx talks in his Theses on Feuerbach about historical and not abstract man that the former had.

Marx speaks of alienation in bourgeois society, in the *Economic and Political Manuscripts of 1844*. He applies this theory to the situation of the proletariat and hence by implication to bourgeoisie society in its entirety. Here private property is traced back to 'alienated externalised labour,' that is to a productive activity in which 'Man' de-realises himself rather than as in all genuinely creative activities, realising himself in his deepest potential. This linked to surplus value and that to class struggle and socialism.

The significance of the October Revolution, the backwardness of the Russian people, the liberality of discussion within the Communist Party, the strategy of Industrial Development, the New Economic Policy, i.e. introduction of one man management and entrepreneurship within the socialist state, the rights of self determination, were relevant in all phases of Soviet history, despite the political vicissitudes of Stalin's terror, Khrushchev's Spring, Brezhnev's part-petrification and Gorbachev's crisis management.

The crisis, which emerged in Russia, indicates the resonance of some of these positions taken by Marxists, though under different conditions. Kautsky's thesis of peaceful transition suggests that incremental change could have led to socialism. This finds an echo in Gorbachev's attempt to introduce political democracy : perestroika. Old national anti-Stalinist heroes, restructure Soviet State through banishing party institutions and introducing new political focus of activity. The difference between Kautsky and Gorbachev lay in the fact that the new middle class which emerged in Russia is not the same as the German working class during Kautsky's time–the obvious difference being that one was the product of Bismarkian nationalism and the other of Soviet industrialism. The new middle class was committed to socialism and meritocracy, while the working class was committed to solidarity and bonuses which formed the backbone of the CPSU. In case of Bismarck the state was a product of an alliance of *junkerdom* and the capitalist class and the working class was a victim of the sentiment that new state would give them space to change.

Gorbachev's Perestroika, although critical of Lenin's specific solution of the time, e.g. War communism or principles of democratic centralism, upheld Lenin's fundamental principles (e.g. NEP, socialism and need to transform the party by fighting bureaucracy). Here we find that Gorbachev was faced with a major lacuna in Marxian theory. None of the Marxist scholars of the late 19th and early 20th century could have possibly visualised the problems, paradoxes and predilections within a socialist society. To take an example, that existing socialist societies started discussing questions of future economic and political strategy in Hungary and Poland in the '50s, in Czechoslovakia in the '60s and in Poland, East Europe, China and Russia in the '80s and '90s. The question of political economy of socialism and nature of political economy of socialism–and nature of political rule were discussed thoroughly within the framework of the problems of alienation (Oscar Lange[45] on economy. Mikhailovich on humanism underlined philosophic anthropology and Dubcek on political reform).

The problem of alienation leads to the kind of issues discussed in the Frankfurt School. It is an issue that young Marx talked about for many 'Western Marxists'. Bahro talks about political alienation in existing socialist societies[46]. Stark images come to mind from 1985–1991. In Bucharest pregnant women protested against Ceausescu.[47] He had barricaded the streets. They were raising slogans asking the soldiers to hit them in the stomach with the riffe butts as they would not be able to feed the newborn. In the German Democratic Republic, pregnant women, who were supposed to wear an identity card to show that they were pregnant, were hit by the police when they were demonstrating against Honecker's[48] regime. Nightlong vigils in different parts of Eastern Europe under the aegis of the Church, the round table conference in Germany and the Breakdown of the Berlin

Wall reminds one of the issues of alienation that was raised in *The Dolls House* by Kierkegaard.[49] It is an old problem which had haunted philosophers ever since, but especially in socialist societies now. In the play the main protagonist got alienated from the riches of the society.

Political alienation is linked to a lack of theory of transition within socialism. We hear of New Democracy transiting to proletariat dictatorship after the Cultural Revolution in China. We hear of War Communism transiting to NEP to Socialism to people's State to developed socialism to crisis of Socialism in Soviet Union. All these indicate that socialist leadership which claimed scienticity did not have a socialist theory of transition as part of their Marxian legacy in existing socialist states. Marx's writings on France, the then Germany, England and Russia give routes of transition to socialism. They do not give us a theory of transition from one stage / phase to another within socialism. What one can do is to reassert Marx's insight into transition: "Men make their own history, but they do not make it just as they please; they do not make it under circumstances chosen by them, but under circumstances directly encountered, given and transmitted from the past".[50]

Currently cybernetic revolution overtook the socialist world and sucked the science and technology research base of the third world. Globalisation ruined the possibilities of primitive accumulation in Zaire and sucked the South-east Asian economies into flush capitalism. The Socialist world was penetrated by the communication revolution and progressive thought moved in the direction of genealogy, deconstruction and post-modernity. The stagnant economies of the socialist world had to find valiant answers to this phase of greater penetration and stablisation of finance capital. Marxian theory and practice needed new constructs to deal with new contradictions and new theorisations. Gorbachev and Deng did attempt precisely this. The first failed and the second allowed capitalism to creep in.

References

1. Howard Selsam, David Goldway, Harry Martel; *Dynamics of Social Change*, International Publishers, London,1970.

2. Della Volpe; *Rousseau and Marx*, Lawrence and Wishart, London, 1978.

3. Frederick Engels; *Anti Duhring: Herr Eugen Duhring's Revolution in Science*, Foreign Languages Publishing House, Moscow, 1954.

4. Karl Marx; "*A Contribution to the Critique of Political Economy*" in Collected Works Vol. 16; Progress Publishers, Moscow, 1980.

5. Encyclopedia of Marxism and Communism, Vol. 7.

6. Paul Bellis, *Marxism and the U.S.S.R.*, The Macmillan Press Ltd. London, 1979.

7. Santiago Carrillo, *Euro Communism and the State*, Lawrence and Wishart, London, 1977, p. 150.

8. P.N. Fedoseyev et. al. *Karl Marx: A Biography*; Progress Publishers, Moscow, 1973.

9. David L Sills (ed.); *International Encyclopaedia of Social Sciences Vol. 15*, The Macmillan Company & Free Press, New York, 1972.

10. Leszek Kolakowski, *Main Currents of Marxism Vol. 2*, Clarendon Press, Oxford, 1978.

11. Geoffrey Hosking, *The Beginning of Independent Political Activity in Post Communist Societies*, 1995.

12. *op. cit.*

13. Jean Ellenstein, *The Stalin Phenomena*, Trans. Peter Latham, Laurence & Wishart, London, 1976.

14. Dubcek, Alexander : first secretary of the Communist Party of Czechoslovakia (Jan. 5, 1968, to April 17, 1969) whose liberal reforms led to the Soviet invasion and occupation of Czechoslovakia in August 1968.

15. Havel, Vaclav : prominent Czech playwright, poet, and political dissident, who, after the fall of communism, was president of Czechoslovakia from December 1989 to July 1992 and president of the Czech Republic from January 1993.

16. Walesa, Lech: labour activist who helped form and led (1980–90) communist Poland's first independent trade union, Solidarity. The charismatic leader of millions of Polish workers, he went on to become the President of Poland (1990–95) and received the Nobel Prize for Peace in 1983.

17. Yevtushenko, Yevgeny Aleksandrovich: poet and spokesman for the younger post-Stalin generation of Ukranian poets, whose internationally publicised demands for greater artistic freedom and for a literature based on aesthetic rather than political standards signalled an easing of Soviet control over artists in the late 1950s and '60s. famous for his poem titled Zima Junction.

18. Solzhenitsyn, Aleksandr Isayevich Russian novelist and historian who was awarded the Nobel Prize for Literature for 1970, for the novel *Gulag Archipelago.*

19. Miroslav Hroch, "Nationalism in Central and Eastern Europe *in Anthony D. Smith,* edited, *Nationalism, Critical Concepts in Political Science, Vol. 2*, Routledge, London.

20. Isaac Deutscher, *Russia, Unfinished Revolution: Russia 1917–1967*, Oxford University Press, London, 1967.

21. Perry Anderson, *Considerations in Western Marxism*, NLB, London, 1976.

22. *Ibid.*

23. *op. cit.*

24. *op. cit.*

25. Leszek Kolakowski, *Main Currents of Marxism Vol. 3*, Clarendon Press, Oxford, 1978.

26. Santiago Carrillo, *EuroCommunism and the State*, Lawrence and Wishart, London, 1977, p. 153.

27. E.H. Carr, *1917: Before and After*, Macmillan, London, 1969, pp. 8-9.

28. Leszek Kolakowski, *Main Currents of Marxism Vol. 1*, *op. cit.*

29. Alec Nove, *Stalinism and After*, George Allen and Unwin Publishers Limited, London, 1975.

30. James D. White, *Lenin: The Practice and Theory of Revolution*, Palgrave Publishers, New York, 2001.

31. V.I. Lenin, "The Development of Capitalism in Russia", *Collected Works, Vol. 3*, Progress Publishers, Moscow, 1960.

32. *op. cit.*

33. *op. cit.*

34. V.I. Lenin, *"Imperialism: The Highest Stage of Capitalism"*, *Collected Works, Vol. 22*, Progress Publishers, Moscow, 1964.

35. *Ibid.*

36. V.I. Lenin, *"Economics and Politics in the Era of Dictatorship of the Proletariat," Collected Works, Vol. 30*, Progress Publishers, Moscow, p. 107.

37. Rakesh Gupta, *Soviet Policies in the Eighties*, Patriot Publishers, New Delhi, 1987.

38. *Ibid.* p. 2.

39. V. I. Lenin; *Two Tactics of Social Democracy in the Democratic Revolution; Collected Works Vol. 27*, Progress Publishers, Moscow, 1961.

40. V.I. Lenin, *Economics and Politics in the Dictatorship of the Proletariat, Collected Works, Vol. 30*, Progress Publishers, Moscow, 1965.

41. Lucio Colletti, *From Rousseau to Lenin: Studies in Ideology and Society*, Trans. John Merrington and Judith White, Oxford University Press, Oxford, 1976.

42. V.I. Lenin, *The Immediate Tasks of the Soviet Government; Collected Works, Vol. 27*, Progress Publishers, Moscow, 1965, p. 422.

43. V.I. Lenin, *What is to be Done?, Collected Works, Vol. 5*, Progress Publishers, Moscow, 1961.

44. James D. White, *op. cit.*, p. 143.

45. Oskar Lange & Fred M Taylor, *On the Economic Theory of Socialism*, Tata McGraw Hill Publisher Co., New Delhi; 1976.

46. Rudolph Barho; *The Alternative in Eastern Europe*, NLB, U.S.A., 1978.

47. Ceausescu, Nicolae : Communist official who was leader of Romania from 1965 until he was overthrown and killed in a revolution in 1989.

48. Honecker, Erich : communist official who, as first secretary of East Germany's Socialist Unity Party of Germany (Sozialistische Einheitspartei Deutschlands, or SED), was East Germany's leader

from 1971 until he fell from power in 1989 in the wake of the democratic reforms sweeping eastern Europe.

49. *SØren Aabye Kierkegaard*: Danish religious philosopher and critic of rationalism, regarded as the founder of existentialist philosophy. He is famous for his critique of systematic rational philosophy, particularly Hegelianism.

50. Quoted in B.N. Arora, *Lenin: The Stuff He Was Made Of* Vol. XLI, No. 18, Perspective publication Pvt Ltd, April 19, 2003, p. 27.

2

Critical Issues of East Europe–I

Marx had written that the state after the revolution, in the dictatorship of the Proletariat retains bourgeois birthmarks and yet has to create conditions of its withering away. This meant that the state determine the quantum of individual's contribution to society and the reward in return. This function of the state, as an alien institution, remains in all capitalist societies. The difference within the socialist state is that it is not the class agency of the propertied. Rather it is the committee of the majority, i.e., workers, peasants and the middle classes. Dictatorship of the proletariat had dual aspect of destroying state machinery as Marx observed in the Gotha Programme and at the same time prescribed setting up in its place organs of power of the working class as Lenin reasserted later in the context of the Russian Revolution as well.

The purpose of the State is to develop the material conditions of life through the scientific revolution so that necessity of the State is overcome and the freedom of the individual as a species being is attained. Between the two a theory of transition needed to be worked out on the basis of Marx's dialectics and actual material conditions.

In the first phase it creates conditions of consolidation of socialist states and then the problems that it generates lead these states to crisis and the need for renewal. It is here that they collapse.

The October Revolution of 1917 brought the Bolsheviks to power giving a chance to Lenin and his comrades to test Marxist theories practically in U.S.S.R. A number of communist parties came into existence during this time, but it was only in and around 1945 that a number of communist governments were formed in many parts of the globe, primarily in the East of Europe. Although many scholars, argue that the East European countries installing communist governments in their respective countries is nothing but the result of the imperialistic design of the Soviet Union during the cold war, but that is disputed. What we do know for certain is that these East European countries have their own tales to tell, their giant failures, but also amidst that their stories of accomplishments and endeavours. So for the purpose of highlighting their successes some of the East European countries like Czechoslovakia, East Germany, Hungary, and Poland have been taken considered in this chapter. We need to note that they shared an anti-fascist sentiment apart from internal dynamics.

Czechoslovakia

Czechoslovakia under Communist rule is characterised by a history of alternate periods of success and failures. The fate of Czechoslovakia was in many cases intimately linked with the nature of a regime and its governance in the Soviet Union.

Czechoslovakia's re-emergence from its hibernation[1], as a sovereign state, as a result of Allied policies, to find itself within the Soviet sphere of influence—a fact that had to be taken into account in any post war reconstruction. Thus, the political and economic organisation of post war Czechoslovakia was largely influenced by the result of negotiations between Beneš[2] and KSC[3] exiles in Moscow.

The Third Republic came into being in April 1945. Its government installed at Kosice on April 4 and moved to Prague in May, was a National Front coalition in which three socialist parties—KSC, Czechoslovak Social Democratic Party, and Czechoslovak National Socialist Party—predominated. The Slovak Populist Party was banned as collaborators with the Nazis. Other conservative yet democratic parties, such as the Republican Party of Farmers and Peasants, were prevented from resuming activities in the post war period. Certain acceptable non-socialist parties were included in the coalition; among them were the Catholic People's Party (in Moravia) and the Slovak Democratic Party.

Beneš anticipated that the democratic process would restore a more equitable distribution of power but at the same time he had negotiated the Soviet alliance, and had hoped to establish Czechoslovakia as a "bridge" between East and West, capable of maintaining contacts with both sides. The popular enthusiasm evoked by the Soviet armies of liberation benefited the KSC. Czechoslovaks, bitterly disappointed by the West at Munich, responded favourably to both the KSC and the Soviet alliance. Communists secured strong representation in the popularly elected national committees, the new organs of local administration. The KSC organised and centralised the trade union movement; of 120 representatives to the Central Council of Trade Unions, 94 were communists. The party worked to acquire a mass membership, including peasants and the petite bourgeoisie, as well as the proletariat. Between May 1945 and May 1946, KSC membership grew from 27,000 to over 1.1 million, showing that there was a popular support for the KSC among the people.

In the May 1946 election, the KSC won a plurality of 38 per cent of the vote. The communists, although, held only a minority of portfolios, they were able to gain control over such key ministries, thereby being able to dominate over the Opposition and create a situation for eventual takeover.

In February 1948, Czechoslovakia became a "people's democracy"—a preliminary step toward socialism and, ultimately, communism. The country also started to witness the impact of Stalinisation in the Soviet Union. Dissident elements were purged from all levels of society, including the Catholic Church (by 1960 KSC membership has been reduced to 1.4 million.)

The Ninth-of-May Constitution provided for the nationalisation of all commercial and industrial enterprises having more than fifty employees. The non-agricultural private sector was nearly eliminated. Private ownership of land was limited to fifty hectares. The remnants of private enterprise and independent farming were permitted to carry on only as a temporary concession to the petite bourgeoisie and the peasantry. The Czechoslovak economy was subjected to a succession of five-year plans.

Following the Soviet example, Czechoslovakia began emphasising the rapid development of heavy industry. The industrial sector was reorganised with an emphasis on metallurgy, heavy machinery, and coal mining. Production was concentrated in larger units; the more than 350,000 units of the pre-war period were reduced to about 1,700 units by 1958. Industrial output reportedly increased 233s between 1948 and 1959; employment in industry, 44 per cent. The speed of industrialisation was particularly accelerated in Slovakia, where production increased 347 per cent and employment, 70 per cent. Although Czechoslovakia's industrial growth of 170 per cent between 1948 and 1957 was impressive, it was far exceeded by that of Japan (300 per cent) and the Federal Republic of Germany (almost 300 per cent) and more than equalled by Austria and Greece. For the 1954-59 period, Czechoslovak industrial growth was equalled by France and Italy.

Industrial growth in Czechoslovakia required substantial additional labour. Czechoslovaks were subjected to long hours and long workweeks to meet production quotas. Part-time, volunteer labour—students and white-collar workers—was drafted in massive numbers. Labour productivity, however, was not significantly increased, nor was production costs reduced.

The Ninth-of-May Constitution declared the government's intention to collectivise agriculture. In February 1949, the National Assembly adopted the Unified Agricultural Cooperatives Act. Cooperatives were to be founded on a voluntary basis; formal title to land was left vested in the original owners. The imposition of high compulsory quotas, however, forced peasants to collectivise in order to increase efficiency and facilitate mechanisation. Discriminatory policies were employed to bring about the ruin of recalcitrant kulaks (wealthy peasants). Collectivisation was near completion by 1960. Sixteen per cent of all farmland (obtained from collaborators and kulaks) had been turned into state farms.

The 1960 Constitution declared the victory of "socialism" and proclaimed the Czechoslovak Socialist Republic. The ambiguous precept of "democratic centralism"—power emanating from the people but bound by the authority of higher organs—was made a formal part of constitutional law. The President, the Cabinet, the Slovak National Council, and the local governments were made responsible to the National Assembly. The National Assembly, however, continued it's rubber-stamp approval of KSC policies. All private enterprises using hired labour were abolished. Comprehensive economic planning was reaffirmed. The Bill of Rights emphasised economic and social rights, e.g., the right to work, leisure, health care, and education. Civil rights, however, were deemphasised. The judiciary was combined with the prosecuting branch; all judges were committed to the protection of the socialist State and the education of citizens in loyalty to the cause of socialism.

But one of the most significant instances of success in the history of Czechoslovakia under communist rule could be seen during the reform period. Although, again during this period one does not find any economic or social indicator to assess the success level but one does find that efforts have been made to amend some of the measures of the government in Czechoslovakia and address those issues in the country. Again, as have been stated right at the beginning, this reform movement in Czechoslovakia had a clear relationship with the political situation in U.S.S.R during that time. The reforms in Czechoslovakia, were to a great extent brought about by the de-Stalinisation process which came into being by 1956.

De-Stalinisation had a late start in Czechoslovakia. The KSC leadership virtually ignored the Soviet thaw announced by Nikita Khrushchev in 1956 at the Twentieth Congress of the Communist Party of the Soviet Union. In Czechoslovakia that April, at the Second Writers' Congress, several authors criticised acts of political repression and attempted to gain control of the writers' congress. The writers' rebellion was suppressed, however, and the conservatives retained control. Students in Prague and Bratislava demonstrated on May Day of 1956, demanding freedom of speech and access to the western press. The Novotny[4] regime condemned these activities and introduced a policy of neo-Stalinism. The 1958 KSC Party Congress formalised the continuation of Stalinism.

The National Front and the possibility of opposition

It was recognised at an early stage that the National Front had become no more than a formality, still another 'transmission belt.' It consisted of the various mass organisations and the remodelled remnants of certain political parties from the 1945-8 period. If the mass organisations were nothing but transmission belts for the Party, the political parties had even less of a role to play. In 1959, in accordance with the Party Central Committee resolution, the National Front itself had been placed under the direction of the Party. A number of Party theoreticians and the leader ship itself shared to some degree the fears of the conservatives that the Party could not maintain its position in a genuinely pluralist system. While the Party agreed to become a partner with the various elements of the National Front and to permit them independence and a voice in policy formulation, it was not willing to permit a competitor for power.[5]

Democratic Centralism was redefined, placing a stronger emphasis on democracy.[6] The leading role of the KSC was reaffirmed but limited. In consequence, the National Assembly was promised increased legislative responsibility. The Slovak executive (Board of Commissioners) and legislature (Slovak National Council) were assured that they could assist the central government in program planning and assume responsibility for program implementation in Slovakia. The regional, district, and local national committees were to be permitted a degree of autonomy. The KSC agreed to refrain from superseding the authority of economic and social organisations. Party control in cultural policy, however, was reaffirmed.

January 1967 was the date for full implementation of the reform program. Novotny and his supporters hesitated, introducing amendments to reinforce central control: Pressure from the reformists was stepped up. Slovaks pressed for federalisation. Economists called for complete enterprise autonomy and economic responsiveness to the market mechanism. The Fourth Writers' Congress adopted a resolution calling for rehabilitation of the Czechoslovak literary tradition and the establishment of free contact with Western culture. The Novotny regime responded with repressive measures.

At the October 30-31 meeting of the KSC Central Committee, Alexander Dubcek, a moderate reformer, challenged Novotny. As university students in Prague demonstrated in support of the liberals, Novotny appealed to Moscow for assistance. On December 8, Soviet leader Leonid Brezhnev arrived in Prague but did not support Novotny.

The Soviet leadership was alarmed. In mid-July a Warsaw Pact conference was held without Czechoslovak participation. The Warsaw Pact nations drafted a letter to the KSC leadership referring to the manifesto as an "organisational and political platform of counterrevolution." Pact members demanded the re-imposition of censorship, the banning of new political parties and clubs, and the repression of "rightist" forces within the party.

Soviet leader Brezhnev hesitated to intervene militarily in Czechoslovakia. Dubcek's Action Program proposed a "new model of socialism"—"democratic" and "national." Significantly, however, Dubcek did not challenge Czechoslovak commitment to the Warsaw Pact. In the early spring of 1968, the Soviet leadership adopted a wait-and-see attitude. By midsummer, however, two camps had formed: advocates and opponents of military intervention.

The generalised resistance caused the Soviet Union to abandon its original plan to oust Dubcek.

Dubcek remained in office only until April 1969. Anti-Soviet demonstrations, following Czechoslovakia's victory over the Soviet team in the World Ice Hockey Championships in March, precipitated Soviet pressures for a KSC Presidium reorganisation. Gustav Husak (a centrist) was named first secretary (title changed to general secretary in 1971).

In the early 1960s, the Czechoslovak economy severely stagnated. The industrial growth rate was the lowest in Eastern Europe. Food imports strained the balance of payments. Pressures both from Moscow and from within the party precipitated a reform movement. In 1963 reform-minded Communist intellectuals produced a proliferation of critical articles. Criticism of economic planning merged with more generalised protests against KSC bureaucratic control and ideological conformity. The KSC leadership responded. The purge trials of 1949-54 were reviewed, for example, and some of those purged were rehabilitated. Some hardliners were removed from top levels of government and replaced by younger, more liberal communists. Jozef Lenart replaced Prime Minister Vilam Siroky. The KSC organised committees to review economic policy.

In 1965 the party approved the New Economic Model, which had been drafted under the direction of economist and theoretician Ota Sik. The program called for a second, intensive stage of economic development, emphasising technological and managerial improvements. Central planning would be limited to overall production and investment indexes as well as price and wage guidelines. Management personnel would be involved in decision making. Production would be market oriented and geared toward profitability. Prices would respond to supply and demand. Wage differentials would be introduced.

The KSC "Theses" of December 1965 presented the party response to the call for political reform. By taking these basic decisions in 1962, the Party did indeed open the floodgates to demands and criticisms which led ultimately to a revolutionary reform programme. According to Galia Golan, "Everything from the economic system and the social services, to the misrepresentations of T.G. Masaryk and Kafka in Communist histories, and the lack of contact with the West, came under fire. Demands for change were made concerning almost every aspect of the prevailing model of Socialism, including the dictatorship of the Party and the all pervasive nature of political-class considerations"[7].

There was a significant change in the feasibility of dictatorship of the proletariat in the country. Czechoslovakian theoreticians asserted that socialist societies too was composed of various 'strata' or groups, although not classes in the Marxist sense of the term since all had the same relation to the means of production in a socialist society. These groups not only existed but brought with them conflicting interests which could well serve as the motor of society. The dictatorship of the proletariat was not, therefore, the suitable form of government for such a society for there was hardly any need for a dictatorship of one class over the other when in fact classes have been eliminated.[8]

Economic Reforms

The economic reforms were to place the economy on a market-determined, profit basis as distinct from the former plan-directed, volume-oriented system. Enterprises are to be independent, not only from directives and quotas but also from state support. They were to be dependent upon their gross income to cover their expenses, including wages. In this way the enterprise would be forced to gear production, in structure, costs and assortment, to the demands of the market, for only from its profits would it cover its costs. Unsuccessful enterprises were to close. This dependence of an enterprise on its own means was intended to provide an incentive for workers, as well as for increased productivity and technological advance, since wages were to be paid out of the gross income. A bonus system would also be introduced for special contributions to the increased income of the enterprise. Investments were to be financed partially by the plant's own resources and partially by the plant's own resources and partially with the help of credits from the state bank. These credits were to be awarded on the basis of the economic effectiveness of the project and the ability of the enterprise to repay, with more or less fixed interest rates.[9]

Wages were to be differentiated according to the workers' tasks and merit, instead of the former system of wage-equalisation. While the level of wages was to depend on the success or failure of the plant, prices were to be flexible, depending upon the market. The market must be competitive, with foreign as well as domestic products. The roles of the state, the central authorities, and the plan were to be clearly delineated and limited to guidance. Neither the government nor the Party was to interfere in plant operations or in the basic planning of the enterprise. The enterprise was to be free to choose its own suppliers and to determine its own yearly operational plan. The state was to limit itself to long-term plans designed principally to predict trends in supply, demand, costs and resources, so as to provide overall long-range coordination for the economy as a whole.[10]

The key to the whole system was the rule of the market mechanism. Economic values and instruments were to replace administrative direction and arbitrary indices. A free competitive market, responsive to the world market, would direct the enterprise towards greater labour productivity, technological progress, and satisfaction of demands. These criteria were to be applied to every enterprise in Czechoslovakia, not only to industry, internal and external trade, and services, but to the social and cultural spheres as well, although details were to be worked out with regard to state subsidies and guarantees for certain 'non-productive' sectors.

Reforms in Health and Education

A minor reform in health system gave patients the right to choose their own doctors, even if they were located in another district. The educational reform was much more significant, for it was conceived to eliminate a large number of Soviet design practices which had destroyed the once exemplary quality of the Czechoslovak educational system. At the higher education level, reforms reintroduced entrance examinations and pre-Communist degree titles and eliminated the cadre system. The cultural world too underwent reform. Without formally riding themselves the state censor, the intellectuals continuously expanded the boundaries within which they could publish. The change was clearly felt in press, radio, television, films theatres and also books.[11]

Reforms in Politico-governmental Sphere

The reform could not help but affect the political-governmental sphere as well. Reforms were introduced in the legal and judiciary systems designed to give defendants greater rights and protection: the all powerful Soviet-type prosecutor-general was downgraded in favour of greater rights for the defence attorney. The government itself was reformed to accommodate the economic reforms and to improve the quality and nature of its work. Government organs, from the Cabinet down to the locally elected National Committees, were given greater responsibility and independence-on the top level, independence from the party; on the lower levels, from the centre.

They argued for a federal system, and, thus, they too accepted the formerly debated conclusion that only political reform, in their sense a new Constitution, could assuage their grievances.

The major elements of the economic reforms were reviewed, on a number of open platforms with an eye towards the revival of the spirit of the reformers' programme. Together with declarations on the need for swift, thorough and genuine implementation of the reform, those elements of the reform most connected with the idea of democratisation were increasingly singled out. It was repeatedly pointed out that the market could not work if there were not genuine enterprise independence which would permit greater responsibility and, therefore, initiative for the enterprise, as well as the sink-or swim element, so necessary if the market were to determine the fate of an enterprise. There were those, such as Slovak economist Eugen Lobl, who had long been criticising the new economic model for its organisation of the economy into associations and trusts, i.e. basically monopolistic units which restricted the freedom of enterprise and of the market. Lobl continued this argument, favouring the end to monopolies and the creation of a market of competing enterprises. In order for plants to be competitive, he maintained, they would have to be independent to the extent of receiving the profits they earned and bearing their own losses even to the point of closure. If economic criteria were thus to operate, enterprise independence should be further ensured by permitting enterprises to amalgamate or separate according to economic, rather than administrative demands. If these were taken to its logical conclusion, one must permit the founding of small enterprises, preferably private, the flexibility and speedy adaptability of which were suitable for such spheres as hand-production etc.

Lobl maintained that an obstacle to the competitive market he envisaged was the concept of specialisation which predominated in Czechoslovakia, i.e. the idea of one enterprise, one product. He pointed out in Kulturny Zivot of 9 February 1968 that Philips produced a whole range of products from refrigerators to television sets and even the old Bata shoe company had produced a whole range of rubber products and operated their own export-import firms. Enforced specialisation provided a measure of restriction on the enterprise, limiting it as to what it could or could not produce no matter what the enterprise directors' own economic calculations or initiatives were. A second, and presumably more critical, obstacle, according to Lobl, was the association directorate or management board devised by Sik. This in Lobl's eyes was nothing but 'superfluous' a 'bulky bureaucratic administrative barrier' which hampered development. Arguing that every cooperative, including consumer cooperatives, should be an independent enterprise, Lobl asserted that there should be no central management. If so desired, enterprises could establish 'superior organisations' to handle such things as wholesale purchasing, market research and so forth, but these organisations should play no role in management.

A third obstacle to enterprise independence and, therefore to a competitive market, according to Lobl, was the foreign trade monopoly. While in the pre-1968 reforms direct enterprise participation in the foreign trade had been urged, the furthest the reformers had gotten in this area was the decision announced in December 1966 to create joint-stock companies of producers together with foreign trade enterprises, and to permit limited foreign currency bonuses for certain plants. Even joint-stock companies still prevented independent enterprise decisions on what the enterprise need import and what it would export, and they still shielded the enterprise from the pressures of the world market.

Many argued in favour of enterprise independence, some directly criticising the association directorate system, other's referring more vaguely to carry-overs from the former directive system and the need for changes in institutions. Sik blamed mainly the state and the economic institutions for the failure of the system to work as he had planned. His original intention had been that the ministries should concentrate on legislation relevant to their fields and refrain from making economic policy. What was needed in Sik's view, was some central economic authority. This policy centre would direct national income policy, through economic measures, in the interests of protecting the consumer and stimulating competition. 'Democratisation of the economy' was to be applied within the enterprises, as well, in the form of greater worker participation in management. The idea has been raised in earlier years, yet, they had been rejected as premature for the then current state of the economy. The nucleus for worker management body had been created in the form of production committees, which were gradually to receive a certain voice in the administration of the enterprise, but the pre-1968 programme had not specifically envisaged autonomy for these bodies. Sik attacked the former system of selecting managers, arguing that it was impossible for a central body or ministry to select a manager. He urged that the representatives of workers, together with specialists decide on managers, 'in a public selection procedure'. Demands for inner enterprise democracy in agriculture were also raised, particularly at one of the dramatic events of the early days of the revival: the seventh congress of the cooperative farms (JZD) meaning thereby that members of the collectives have the right freely to elect or recall their chairman. Collective farms were to have received autonomy under the reforms-at least in so far as planning their own production and deliveries according to the market, based on contracts. Moreover, the functioning of the market was even more seriously limited in agriculture than in industry, not only by the bureaucratic function of the DAA, but by restrictions, exceptions, and 'temporary measures', such as subsidies, grants, taxes, and redistribution to help weaker farms which had appeared even as part of the reform[12].

Enterprise Independence and the Market

The Party's new programme, the Action Programme, called for an end to 'administrative measures and the measures restricting the implementation of the economic reforms. The Programme asserted that 'enterprises confronted with a demanding market must be granted the freedom to decide on all problems concerning the immediate management of the enterprise and its operation, and they must be enabled to react in a creative manner to the demands of the market. The party programme stipulated, however, that the new policy of voluntary association should not be implemented until the government have set up appropriate regulations, so as to avoid the possible chaos of immediate departures from existing associations and trusts, or disruption of scheduled production. These restrictions at least presumed rather than administrative criteria for association, even if full independence from the central authorities were not achieved. More important, the association or trust itself was to have a different function and character. This new character and function evolved from the new role envisaged for the government in the economy, and, as the idea of enterprise independence vis-à-vis the government became more certain, to retain the associations and trusts as organisational units became superfluous. According to the Action Programme, the government would be limited, as originally envisaged by the reforms, to general economic policy, long-term planning, and protecting the consumer's interests. To do this without suppressing the various actors on the market specifically the enterprises, a reorganisation of the government's economic organs was introduced, the purpose of which was to limit the power of the economic ministries by subordinating them to an over-all economic policy board. While it would appear contradictory to establish still another central organ, what was supposed to be a drive to limit central control, the logic of the move was to remove the various economic ministries to policy decisions, and to provide a measure of control over the powerful monopolies which these ministries constituted.

However, one of the problems encountered in earlier 1964 attempts to permit private enterprise, on a very limited scale, in the service sector, was the large degree of scepticism and fear on the part of prospective private owners. People would have to be convinced that they would not risk political or economic discrimination (higher purchase prices, taxes, etc.).[13]

Foreign Trade

Reforms in the sphere of foreign trade concerned three issues: organisation of foreign trade; prices and the achievement of convertible currency; and orientation of trade. This organisational change did not provide the entire answer to the gap between domestic production and the influence of the world market. The Action Programme called for creation of conditions that would make the Czechoslovak crown convertible, such as an adjustment of prices so as to bring domestic prices more in line with world prices. The convertibility of the crown, which in itself was the result of the isolation of the domestic market, in turn provided an obstacle to Czechoslovakia's possibility of trading on the world market. The issue of convertibility, while most directly connected with price policy and domestic reform, involved also the related issue of trade orientation and Czechoslovakia's ability to compete on the world market. The lack of convertible currency and the hard currency reserves limited Czechoslovakia to trading primarily with soft currency areas, and because even within these areas there existed no convertibility, barter trading was the rule. The issue of currency-orientation was also the result of political considerations, for the lack of hard-currency reserves meant that trade with the West would need credits–in part long-term credits–which were politically undesirable. For political reasons trade with the Communist countries was desirable, but this trade was not always economically beneficial to Czechoslovakia.

The orientation of Czechoslovak trade was debated in the period of revival, for, together with the recognised need for a large hard currency credit, this appeared to be the major obstacle left to the desired connection of the domestic market with the world standards. The issue did not start as an effort to gain economic independence, to disengage from the Eastern bloc, from CEMA or the Soviet Union. The demands for a change in trade orientation were born of economic, not political considerations; if the placing of trade on an economic rather than political basis could have meant a continuation of almost exclusive eastern orientation, the reformers probably would have favoured it.

It appeared that Czechoslovakia hoped to solve at least part of its problems within the framework of CEMA, particularly through a reform of CEMA, as Sik himself proclaimed at the March rally.

The Action Program asserted that, in addition to continued CEMA cooperation, Prague would 'also actively encourage the development of economic relations with any other country in the world that is interested, on the basis of equality of rights and mutual benefits and without discrimination.'

A sample of this new policy was the founding of a joint Yugoslav-Czechoslovak bank to provide the currency convertibility for increased trade and cooperation agreed upon between the two countries even before 1968. In the spirit of the new policy, Prague opened talks with Austria. She also began to show interest in renewed membership in the International Monetary Fund and the International Bank for Reconstruction and Development. Perhaps more controversially, Prague began looking for a hard currency loan. But most of these statements were later denied by the Czechoslovak officials, who were anxious to play down the political aspects of such moves, particularly in view of growing Soviet sensitivity on the subject. None of these moves, however, need have been at the expense of Czechoslovakia's allies or loyalty to the Soviet bloc, for even Western credits, Czechoslovakia was likely to continue to turn to the USSR as a vital soft currency supplier of raw materials and a major market for manufactured goods. One might have assumed that if Moscow was seriously concerned that western credits might lead Czechoslovakia to assume a more independent economic position vis-à-vis the East, it would have itself hastened to grant the loan when approached. The issue was not simple from the Russian point of view. To refuse the loan outright or try to use it as a lever to gain concessions from Prague risked pushing the Czechs into western arms; to grant only part of the loan would not have eliminated Czechoslovakia's need to seek credits in the West. On the other hand Soviet Union had never granted a hard currency loan of anything approaching this size to any of her allies. Czechoslovakia had in 1957 received a Soviet gold loan of $13.5 million, and the largest such loan granted by USSR to date was $85 million (to East Germany also in 1957). The only loan of this size ever granted to Czechoslovakia by the USSR was in soft currency. Thus it was not clear whether USSR could afford such a loan.

It is difficult to determined to what extent there were genuine Soviet fears of a change in Czechoslovakia's trade orientation, to what extent such fears were justified, and to what extent the Soviet Union created the very situation it claimed to fear through its own pressures and interference. On the other hand, there were countless statements by Dubcek and other leading officials attesting to continued loyalty to CEMA, plus the very real economic basis for Czechoslovak cooperation with the Soviet Union and CEMA.

During this time effort was also being made to put to rest the Czech-Slovak crisis in Czechoslovakia.[14]

Slovakia

Dubcek had been a supporter of the economic reform programme before 1968, but this support had been somewhat equivocal insofar as economic reform in Slovakia was concerned. In late 1967 he had proposed that subsidies and other such aid be provided by the state for Slovak enterprises-despite the principles of the new economic system-because of the disadvantaged position of Slovak enterprises if unfettered competition and the profitability criteria were introduced. Dubcek's position was, not unexpectedly, reflected in the Action Program. Otherwise, the argument went, the federalisation of the country, sought by the Slovaks, could not be genuinely effected, for it would perpetuate the gap between the two nations. Moreover, it was a fact that earlier political decisions to raise the economic level of Slovakia had often conflicted with sound economic policy; thus left alone, Dubcek's apprehensions, existing Slovak enterprises could not survive economically. It was on this basis that the Action Program urged that the new economic system be worked out in such a way in order to permit Slovakia to participate on 'an equal level.'

In keeping with this thinking, the economic policy directive issued in August 1968 provided for a number of 'special' measures for Slovakia: exemptions from taxes for certain enterprises, maintenance of previously established favourable credit conditions, and subsidies. Specifically tax exemptions might be granted to enterprises which would suffer serious strain as a result of the introduction of the new economic system.[15]

Reactions to the Reforms

The economic reforms had something of a political football in the time of Novotny and particularly in the early months of 1968. Among the political implications of the reform, evident in the pre-1968 efforts to introduce the program, were the fear of Party appointees that they would lose their jobs if economic qualifications were given a priority; and the fear of the conservatives that the economic reforms would necessitate political reforms, and diminished power and control in the hands of the central organs, specifically the Party. The workers had responded half-heartedly to the economic reforms, and Novotny had long exploited worker disdain for intellectuals to set the former against the reform movement and, thereby, prevent the formation of a powerful alliance against his continued rule.

In response to the conservative attacks on the economic reforms, Dubcek frankly decried the efforts to split the intellectuals and the workers and offered the workers a chance finally to 'implement' their interests through democratisation. One such freedom which helped to convert the workers to the idea of reform was the new possibility of going out on strike. There were a number of short strikes, reported by the Czechoslovak media, from March through the summer, protesting such things as unprofitable production lines, poor wages, and unpopular or inefficient managers; many more strikes were threatened. The interesting thing about the 1968 strikes, however was not only that they were objectively-sometimes even sympathetically-reported by the official state and Party media, but that they often had the support of the local Party committee and sometimes even achieved their goals. Dubcek himself did not reject the idea of strike, though he termed it as the maximum method of exerting pressure. Thus the legality of the strikes was not questioned.

Yet another way in which worker opposition to the reforms was to be overcome was the promise of welfare benefits for those adversely affected by the introduction of the reforms. It was promised that progress would not be at the expense of workers' security, for the government would see to jobs, retraining and support for released workers. It was not these promises of improved or increased welfare benefits that marked the revolutionary aspect of the policy towards workers, however. Although the conservatives strove to stir up worker opposition on just such specific issues as these, the essential point was the democratisation of the process: the right for workers to have a decisive say in matters concerning them.[16]

Mass Organisations

The trade union movement was relatively slow to respond to the new situation in Prague at the beginning of 1968, and the former line predominated for close to three months. There were numerous efforts towards change in this role in the 1963-67 period, but, even after January, ROH chairman proclaimed that the major role of the trade union was to unconditionally serve 'socialism' and rally the masses around the regimes' economic programme through propaganda and education, with the aim of 'contributing to the strengthening of ideological unity.'

The need for reform was recognised by the Party and eventually, even at the highest levels of the ROH. Dubcek criticised the former role of the ROH and called for a change in the unions' function and orientation so as to 'create free scope for the implementation of the workers' specific interest through the trade union organisation.

A necessary step in the democratisation of the trade union movement was the granting of independence with regard to the Party, demanded within the context of the new role for all mass organisations. Once independent of the Party, the trade union movement was to return to the original function of the trade unions in a democracy: representation and defence of the interests of the working people. The relationship between the trade union organisations and the new enterprise councils was outlined in an ROH statement published on 5th July 1968. Democratisation of the inner life and structure of the movement itself was also sought and included the following demands: democratic elections at all levels, including election of the ROH chairman by an all-state congress leaders exclusively responsible to the membership, i.e. subject to control from lower organisations, which in turn would mean better informed lower organs and decentralisation in favour of the basic organisations so that the members could see and control the management of their contributions.[17]

The Leading Role of the Party

The very earliest discussions in 1968 on the Party's role did little more than affirm points conceded earlier, for example, the idea that the leading role of the Party did not mean that the Party should interfere in day to day matters of the economy and management. This was a principle implicit to the economic reforms. The Party should provide no more than a programmatic statement and, also, create conditions for the settlement of conflicts which might arise as a result of leaving matters to the various groups in society.[18]

Political Reform and the Government

Popular participation was seen as a necessary, perhaps the best, guarantee against concentration of power. Dubcek often emphasised that democratisation could only be accomplished and maintained with a high degree of public involvement and participation of the people. Czechoslovakia, as many, were to point out, 'In the past... belonged among the countries with the most developed parliamentary democracy.' Yet under the Communists the elected organs had become a mere formality. Basic to any reform of the elected organ was the resolution of a fundamental contradiction. According to the Constitution, and reiterated by a Party resolution in May 1964, the National Assembly was the supreme organ of state power in the country. Yet the Assembly was subordinate to the Party not only in practice but even by explicit order of the 1966 Party statutes.

The Action Program endorsed most of these suggestions, calling for a National Assembly 'which will truly make laws and decide important questions, and not just approve draft submitted to it.' Suggestions prepared by Mlynar's committee for discussion at the Fourteenth Party Congress included a radical change in the National Assembly which would resemble the structure introduced in Yugoslavia. In addition to a chamber of deputies from the two major nations, there might be chambers selected along professional lines and elected by the enterprises or institutions engaged in these professions, e.g. an industrial chamber, an agricultural chamber, and so forth having control over bills relating to their specific fields. This proposal was envisaged for adoption probably only after federalisation and workers council had taken root.

The National Committees were dealt with only in general terms. Although the local representatives of the state organs of power, their primary function, according to the Action Program, was to provide local self-administration.

It was clear to most that the success of the changes planned for the elected organs would be dependent upon the method of representation or, specifically on election procedures. The then current system was criticised, from the first stages of the procedure to the last, and demands were heard for an entirely new electoral law. Another suggestion was to publicise the work of the election commissions so that people might know the deadline for proposing candidates, and such practices as predetermining the number of women, of Slovaks, of youth and so forth to be among the candidates, might be eliminated. The fact that the election commissions determined the order of candidates on the ballot was considered a serious obstacle to democracy, for although there were more candidates on the list had positions, as a result of the 1964-67 electoral laws, the order of the candidates, not the number of votes they received determined who would be elected. Indeed, it was pointed out, the very act of voting had become a mere formality: one did not know anything of the candidates, one could not really determine who would be elected, and one could not actually do anything at the polls because of the custom of demonstrative voting. Suggestions for the introduction of popular election would have meant a change in the Constitution and Czechoslovakia tradition; they apparently did not receive much support.[19]

Developments since 1968 need to be understood. In that year, a formerly near Unitarian State became a federation of two republics.[20] This arrangement, according to some led to the break-up of Czech and Slovakia in the 1990's. This was the only realised and accepted outcome by the Soviet Union of the Prague Spring of 1968. The change improved Slovakia's status while at the same time weakening the political standing of the Czechs. An external but not negligible feature of the situation allowed a Slovak–Gustav Husak–to become President of the federal republic, and more importantly, the leading man in the radically purged Communist Party of

Czechoslovakia. An unusual constitutional system of an asymmetric sort was established, with the central federal government on the one hand and the government of the Slovak republic on the other. There was no Czech government; only a not very influential Parliament, the Czech National Council. All important institutions were organised in a similarly asymmetric way. Moreover the principle of parity was introduced in all federal institutions, though the Slovaks were only one-third of the Federation's population. In the economic sphere, Slovakia's rapid industrialisation continued after the Soviet invasion in 1968; that meant relatively higher investments in the Slovak Republic than in the Czech regions. During the whole period between 1945 and the end of the 1980's, Slovakia registered an unusually rapid rate of industrialisation and urbanisation; differences between both parts of Czechoslovakia rapidly disappeared. For Slovakia, this was a period of great social change, with modernisation, high mobility and obviously improved standard of living. The situation of the Western part of the Federation, principally Bohemia, was different: Bohemia changed from being a core area of Central Europe into becoming a periphery of the Soviet bloc on its Western most borders. The Western parts of Czechoslovakia decayed, population stagnated; the industrial structure became obsolete; the environment was damaged, and health conditions deteriorated.

In Slovakia the Husak regime, slightly more liberal than in the Czech region, managed a certain cultural development, at least institutionally, in the years 1969-89. The latent political tension between the two parts of the Federation was suppressed as much as possible by the Soviets themselves as well as the local regime installed by the Soviets; still, tension existed under the surface.

In a relatively short time, however, in the first half of 1990, in the ideological vacuum accompanying the collapse of the communist Supra-Gemeinschaft and its ideology, the situation in Slovakia began to change.

Only centrists and the conservatives led by Bilak continued in the Presidium. A program of "normalisation"—

the restoration of continuity with the pre-reform period—was initiated. Normalisation entailed thoroughgoing political repression and the return to ideological conformity. A new purge cleansed the Czechoslovak leadership of all reformist elements. Of the 115 members of the KSC Central Committee, 54 were replaced.

In May 1971, party chief Husak announced at the official Fourteenth Party Congress—the 1968 Fourteenth Party Congress had been abrogated—that "normalisation" had been completed and that all that remained was for the party to consolidate its gains. Husak's policy was to maintain a rigid status quo; for the next fifteen years even key personnel of the party and government remained the same. In 1975 Husak added the position of President to his post as party chief. He and other party leaders faced the task of rebuilding general party membership after the purges of 1969-71. By 1983 membership had returned to 1.6 million, about the same as in 1960.

Dissent and Independent Activity

Through the 1970s and 1980s, the regime's emphasis on obedience, conformity, and the preservation of the status quo was challenged by individuals and organised groups aspiring to independent thinking and activity. Although only a few such activities could be deemed political by Western standards, the regime viewed any independent action, no matter how innocuous, as a defiance of the party's control over all aspects of Czechoslovak life. The regime's response to such activity was harassment, persecution, and, in some instances, imprisonment.

The first organised Opposition emerged under the umbrella of Charter 77. On January 6, 1977, a manifesto called Charter 77 appeared in West German newspapers. The document was immediately translated and reprinted throughout the world. The original manifesto reportedly was signed by 243 persons; among them were artists, former public officials, and other prominent figures, such as Zdenek

Mlynar, secretary of the KSC Central Committee in 1968; Vaclav Slavik, a Central Committee member in 1968; and Vaculik, author of "Two Thousand Words." Charter 77 defined itself as "a loose, informal, and open community of people" concerned with the protection of civil and human rights. It denied oppositional intent and based its defence of rights on legally binding international documents signed by the Czechoslovak government and on guarantees of civil rights contained in the Czechoslovak Constitution.

In the context of international detente, Czechoslovakia had signed the United Nations Covenant on Economic, Social, and Cultural Rights and the Covenant on Civil and Political Rights in 1968. In 1975 these were ratified by the Federal Assembly, which, according to the Constitution of 1960, is the highest legislative organisation. The Helsinki Conference on Security and Cooperation in Europe's Final Act (also known as the Helsinki Accords), signed by Czechoslovakia in 1975, also included guarantees of human rights.

The Charter 77 group declared its objectives to be the following: to draw attention to individual cases of human rights infringements; to suggest remedies; to make general proposals to strengthen rights and freedoms and the mechanisms designed to protect them; and to act as intermediary in situations of conflict. The Charter had over 800 signatures by the end of 1977, including workers and youth; by 1985 nearly 1,200 Czechoslovaks had signed the Charter.

The Husak regime, which claimed that all rights derive from the state and that international covenants are subject to the internal jurisdiction of the state, responded with fury to the Charter. The text was never published in the official media. Signatories were arrested and interrogated; dismissal from employment often followed. The Czechoslovak press launched vicious attacks against the Charter. The public was mobilised to sign either individual condemnations or various forms of "anti-Charters."

Closely associated with Charter 77, the Committee for the Defence of the Unjustly Persecuted (Vybor na obranu nespravedlive stihanych—VONS) was formed in 1978 with the specific goal of documenting individual cases of government persecution and human rights violations. Between 1978 and 1984, VONS issued 409 communiqués concerning individuals prosecuted or harassed.

On a larger scale, independent activity was expressed through underground writing and publishing. Because of the decentralised nature of underground writing, it is difficult to estimate its extent or impact. Some observers state that hundreds of books, journals, essays, and short stories were published and distributed. In the mid-1980s, several samizdat publishing houses were in operation. The best known was Edice Petlice (Padlock Editions), which had published more than 250 volumes. There were a number of clandestine religious publishing houses that published journals in photocopy or printed form.

Hungary

The Hungarian Communist Party which was formed on November 4, 1918 in a Moscow hotel saw a swift rise to power with its membership rising to 30,000 to 40,000 members, by February 1919. The Hungarian Soviet Republic was proclaimed on March 21, 1919. However, a militantly anticommunist authoritarian government composed of military officers entered Budapest.

In the aftermath of World War II, Hungary followed Soviet Union's way in its political, social, and economic system. After the Soviet Red Army invaded Hungary in September 1944, Laszlo Rajik, a former student Communist leader's organisation emerged from hiding, and the Muscovites returned to their homeland. Rakosi's close ties with the Soviet occupiers enhanced his influence within the party. Between the invasion and the end of the war, party membership rose significantly. Although party rolls listed only about 3,000 names in November 1944, membership had swelled to about 500,000 by October 1945.

In the immediate post-war period, the government pursued economic reconstruction and land reform in war shattered Hungary by gradual nationalisation of mines, electric plants, the four largest concerns in heavy industry, and the ten largest banks. In 1945 the government also carried out a radical land reform, expropriating all holdings larger than fifty-seven hectares and distributing them to the country's poorest peasants. Nevertheless, the peasants received portions barely large enough for self-sufficiency. Finally, the government introduced a new currency—the forint—to help curb high inflation.[21]

Rakosi's Rule

With the death of Stalin in 1953 and ongoing De-Stalinisation the Soviet Union showed more flexible policies in the Eastern European countries, which they named as the New Course. Rakosi and Imre Nagy were summoned to Moscow. Although Rakosi retained his position as the party chief, yet Imre Nagy was made the Prime Minister of Hungary.

Nagy charted his New Course for Hungary's drifting economy in a speech before the Central Committee, which gave the plan unanimous approval. Hungary ceased collectivisation of agriculture, allowed peasants to leave the collective farms, cancelled the collective farms' compulsory production quotas, and raised government prices for deliveries. Government financial support and guarantees were extended to private producers, investment in the farm sector jumped 20 per cent in the 1953-54 period, and peasants were able to increase the size of their private plots. The number of peasants on collective farms thus shrank by half between October and December 1953. Nagy also slashed investment in heavy industry by 41.1 per cent in 1953-54 and shifted resources to light industry and the production of consumer goods. However, Nagy failed to fundamentally alter the planning system and neglected to introduce incentives to replace compulsory plan targets, resulting in a poorer record of plan fulfilment after 1953 than before. In 1954 Soviet leaders who favoured economic policies akin to Nagy's lost a Kremlin power struggle. Rakosi seized the opportunity to attack Nagy as a right-wing deviationist and to criticise shortcomings in the economy. Nagy was forced to resign from the Government in April 1955 and was later expelled from the Politburo, Central Committee, and finally the party itself. Thus, the Central Committee that had lauded the New Course in June 1953 unanimously condemned its architect less than two years later.

The Revolution of 1956 discredited Hungary's Stalinist political and economic system and sent a clear warning to the leadership that popular tolerance for its policies had limits, and that if these limits were exceeded, popular reaction could threaten communist control. In response, regime leaders decided to formulate economic policies leading to an improvement of the population's standard of living. Pragmatism and reform gradually became the watchwords in economic policy-making, especially after 1960, and policymakers began relying on economists and other specialists rather than ideologists in the formation of economic policies. The result was a series of reforms that modified Hungary's rigid, centrally planned economy and eventually introduced elements of a free market, creating a concoction sometimes called "goulash communism".

In late 1956, the party named a committee of mostly reform-minded experts to examine Hungary's economic system and make proposals for its revision. The committee's report marked the first step on Hungary's road to economic reform. Its proposals presaged many of the changes implemented a decade later, including elimination of administrative direction of the economy, introduction of greater enterprise autonomy, cooperation between private and collective sectors in agriculture, economic regulation using price and credit policies, and central planning focused only on long-term objectives. However, the committee's proposals were never really implemented. Some observers suggested that the party had solidified its power so quickly that it no longer needed to enact such drastic measures; others claimed that Soviet leaders opposed such reform until they ensured that the party (on November 1, 1956, renamed the Hungarian Socialist Workers' Party–HSWP) had consolidated its power and demonstrated a clear need for a fundamental economic change. During the chaos of the revolution in 1956, Hungary's collective farms lost about two-thirds of their members. Many left to become private farmers. In July 1957, Kadar appeased hard-liners in Hungary and abroad by agreeing to re-collectivise agriculture, and in early 1959 the drive began in earnest. The regime combined force and economic coercion with persuasion and incentives to drive peasants back to the collective farms. The government abolished compulsory production quotas and delivery obligations and substituted voluntary contracts at good prices. It also permitted profit-sharing schemes and programs to promote technical innovation. The regime allowed peasants to retain sizeable private plots and ample livestock and to choose between collective or cooperative farms. The farms also received substantial government investments. As a result, Hungary became the only country with a centrally planned economy where crop output increased as a result of collectivisation.[22]

Kadar's pragmatic approach to the rural economy yielded substantial political and economic dividend in the years to come. As beneficiaries, from the late 1960 onwards, of sizeable state investments in modern agricultural technology and trained labour, the cooperatives repaid the politicians by making Hungary–alone in Eastern Europe–self sufficient in food production. Though the agricultural operations were not particularly efficient by Western European standards, the basic staples, hail rain or storm was always there in the well stocked Hungarian food stores. Whereas periodic meat and food shortages helped, from time to time, destabilise some regimes of the region, the 'goulash' part of Hungary's communism became a model of consumerist legitimacy under state socialism.[23]

The long-term political consequences of bringing the rural economy back into the socialist fold were contradictory, On the one hand, the appointment and often decade-long tenure of county HSWP first secretaries and those of their state administrative opposite numbers, the county council chairmen, created a semblance of political stability. On the other hand, the situation thus created was ready-made for the rise of semiautonomous fiefdoms of the county.[24]

Social mobility is a key element in the overall process of modernisation. Economic development is the principal cause 'driving' social mobility–'creating space' in blue collar occupations by means of the development of industry; in white-collar administrative, technical, and professional job strata by means of the need for a larger administrative/ expert stratum; and typically reducing the need, relative and absolute, due to mechanisation, for labour in agriculture and so on.[25]

From the time it came to power in 1948-9, the Hungarian party sought to restructure the society to make it more responsive to the regime's developmental goals and political-ideological objectives. The massive promotion of additional blue-collar workers, 60,000 in 1948 alone, and by the early 1980s, 210,000, to executive and managerial positions were important steps in the forty-year process of creating a new ruling elite that was both 'red' and 'expert.'

Following the 1956 revolution the regime needed a highly skilled labour force to supply industry, agriculture, science, education, trade, commerce, and public administration with specialists and skilled workers of all kinds. The political leadership's solution to the dilemma of 'modernisation versus security' was ingenious. A key element in Kádár's break with Stalinist precedents was the implementation of the partial and later complete, removal of class backgrounds as decisive factor in the admission policies in universities and colleges. In doing so, the regime made amends for the sins of the Rákosi era and laid the groundwork, from the mid-1960s on, for the restoration of merit-based mobility opportunity for all Hungarians.

As Walter Connor explained, 'education has been central in the process of status inheritance and attainment.' According to a 1973 survey of students in three types of secondary schools by father's occupation and secondary-school background before and after 1941, one discerns evidence of both continuity and change. Those belonging to the top executive and intellectual categories had preserved their traditional share in high-quality academic high-school programmes; those at the lower rungs of the occupational hierarchy had made remarkable progress.

According to another, 1977 survey on the participation of 20-year olds in higher education according to father's occupation, much of the socially more diversified pattern of secondary-school enrolments spilled over into the higher education category as well. Because this survey made no distinction between universities and the admittedly less demanding colleges, one may assume that most of those from culturally disadvantaged social backgrounds ended up in colleges rather than in universities. These changes were evidence of the significant expansion of the pool of highly trained personnel and ultimately for the breakdown of the traditional intelligentsia's overwhelming ly favourable mobility opportunities. Withal, the children of those without inherited educational advantages still faced handicaps in the early 1970s.

The result of a 1977 national survey bespeak much progress and new opportunities for offspring of non-intelligentsia and white collar groups.[26]

Young person's chance of entering into the upper-white-collar (intelligentsia) group, by parental social status is delineated[27].

Father's social status in 1938	*Offspring's Chance*				
	In 1939	*In 1949*	*In 1957*	*In 1963*	*In 1975*
Men					
Executive and upper white-collar	107.4	73.4	23.8	17.1	19.5
Other white-collar	31.2	24.8	9.9	8.2	8.8
Craftman, small businessman	5.6	5.0	3.1	2.6	2.9
Skilled worker	2.8	3.0	2.9	2.7	3.4
Semi-skilled worker	1.6	3.1	1.8	1.6	1.8
Unskilled worker	1.8	2.1	0.9	0.8	0.8
Women					
Executive and upper white-collar	308.8	273.0	61.0	28.7	25.0
Other white-collar	49.0	38.0	20.0	10.7	10.9
Craftsman, small businessman	12.0	20.0	6.8	5.0	4.8
Skilled worker	8.0	4.0	4.8	3.9	4.1
Semi-skilled worker	3.0	4.0	3.8	2.3	2.4
Unskilled worker	1.0	8.0	2.8	1.7	1.8

Note: Chance for a female child of an unskilled worker in 1939 = 1.

Apart from the general tendency of enhanced mobility opportunities, that is of chances of becoming a diploma-holding intellectual, for children of blue collar families, women made important strides toward overcoming traditional handicaps due to gender and social origin.

Cadre stability was an important characteristic of the Hungarian Politburo in the Kadar era. With the exception of

Kadar (thirty-two years at the helm), and the marathon-length services of Sandar Gasper (twenty-nine years), Karoly Nemeth (twenty-five years), Jeno Fock (twenty-three years), and Gyula Kallai (twenty years), the average length of a Politburo's members tenure was three terms, or about fifteen years. Under Kadar, only six Politburo members were removed "out of cycle" from this body and transferred to non-party positions or pensioned off: Gyorgy Marosan in 1962, Lajos Feher and Rezso Nyers in 1975, Bela Biszku in 1978, Istvan Huszar in 1980, and Lajos Mehes in 1985.[28]

By 1962 more than 95 per cent of all farmland had been collectivised either in the form of state farms or cooperatives. The collectivisation drive deflected the hard-liners' criticism of Kadar for his advocacy of reform, and problems with the program's implementation, including excessive coercion of the peasants, later helped Kadar oust the hard-line agriculture minister.

By the early 1960s, Hungary was ripe for a political shake-up. Khrushchev had consolidated his position in the Kremlin and had begun a second wave of de-Stalinisation, thus leading Kadar to believe that the Soviet leadership would support political changes in Hungary. Soon Hungary became the leader of the reform movement within the Soviet alliance system. Kadar intended to provide the regime with some legitimacy and political stability based on solid economic performance. The Soviet Union demonstrated its support with its decision to withdraw its advisers to the Hungarian government.

During the 1960s, the government gave high priority to expanding the industrial sector's engineering and chemical branches. Production of buses, machine tools, precision instruments, and telecommunications equipment received the most attention in the engineering sector. The chemical sector focused on artificial-fertilizer, plastic, and synthetic-fibre production. The Hungarian and Comecon[29] markets were the government's primary targets, and the policies resulted in increased imports of energy, raw materials, and semi finished goods.

As part of this "alliance policy," in 1961 he denounced the practice of making party membership a prerequisite for jobs demanding specialisation and technical expertise. Kadar sought to remove opportunists who had joined the party solely for the status and economic benefits that membership conferred. Rather, Kadar wanted to open the government and economic enterprises to talented people who were prepared to cooperate without adhering to party discipline or compromising their political beliefs.

Plans for reforming the centrally planned economy steadily took shape after the Eighth Party Congress of the HSWP in November 1962. Central Committee Secretary Rezso Nyers, who supported a comprehensive reform rather than continued piecemeal adjustments to the economic system, took charge of economic affairs. The regime also appointed committees to prepare reform proposals. Khrushchev's ouster in October 1964 failed to weaken Hungary's desire for reform. Kadar responded to the change in the Kremlin by affirming that "the political attitude of the HSWP and the government of the Hungarian People's Republic has not changed one iota, nor will it change." In December 1964, a Central Committee plenum approved the basic concept of economic reform and formed a committee to provide fundamental guidelines.

Economic problems also continued to underscore the need for reform. Agricultural output fell by 5.5 per cent. In addition, the government increased production quotas, cut wages, and announced price hikes. Popular discontent rose as a result. In May 1966, the Central Committee approved a sweeping reform package known as the New Economic Mechanism (NEM). Although many of its elements could be phased in during a preparation period, the central features of the reform could be implemented only with the introduction of a new price system, which was set for January 1, 1968. With the NEM, the government sought to overcome the inefficiencies of central planning, to motivate talented and skilled people to work harder and produce more, to make Hungary's products competitive in foreign markets, especially in the West, and, above all, to create the prosperity that would ensure political stability.

The NEM decentralised decision making and made profit, rather than plan fulfilment, the enterprises' main goal. Instead of setting plan targets and allocating supplies, the government was to influence enterprise activity only through indirect financial, fiscal, and price instruments known as "economic regulators." The NEM introduced a profit tax and allowed enterprises to make their own decisions concerning output, marketing, and sales. Subsidies were eliminated for most goods except basic raw materials. The government decentralised allocation of capital and supply and partially decentralised foreign trade and investment decision making. The economy's focus moved away from heavy industry to light industry and modernisation of the infrastructure. Finally, agricultural collectives gained the freedom to make investment decisions. The NEM's initial results were positive. In the 1968-70 period, plan fulfilment was more successful than in previous years. The standard of living rose as production and trade increased. Product variety broadened, sales increased faster than production, inventory backlogs declined, and the trade balance with both East and West improved. In practice, however, the reform was not as sweeping as planned. Enterprises continued to bargain with government authorities for resources from central funds and sought preferential treatment. The reform also failed to dismantle the highly concentrated industrial structure, which was originally established to facilitate central planning and which inhibited competition under the NEM.

The Kadar regime gave serious attention to implementing the NEM from 1968 to 1972. In 1971, however, counter-reform forces were gathering strength and calling for the return of central controls. The opposition arose from government and party bureaucrats and was supported by large enterprises and some workers. The bureaucrats perceived the NEM as a threat to their privileged positions. The large enterprises saw their income drop after the introduction of the NEM and were troubled by competition for materials and labour from smaller enterprises. Disaffected workers who were on the payrolls of outdated, inefficient industries resented the higher incomes earned by workers in more modern firms. This opposition successfully reversed the reform a few months after Moscow expressed reservations about the NEM and concern about "petit bourgeois tendencies" in Hungary.

In November 1972, the Central Committee introduced a package of extraordinary measures to recentralise part of the economy, but the regime did not formally abandon the NEM. Fifty large enterprises, which produced about 50 per cent of Hungary's industrial output and 60 per cent of its exports, came under direct ministerial supervision, supported by special subsidies. New restrictions applied to small enterprises and agricultural producers. Wages rose, prices came under central control, and the regime introduced price supports. In the following years, the government also merged many profitable small firms with large enterprises.

In 1979 and 1980, the government implemented a number of institutional reforms. The new reforms abolished branch ministries and replaced them with a single Ministry of Industry intended to act as a policy-formulating body without direct authority over enterprises. Large enterprises were broken up into smaller firms. In 1982 the government legalised the formation of small private firms, including restaurants, small shops, and service companies, and it permitted workers to lease enterprise equipment, use it on their own time, and keep the earnings from their products. In 1984 the regime introduced new forms of enterprise management, including supervisory councils that would include worker-elected representatives. New financial institutions also emerged, and a 1983 government decree allowed enterprises, cooperatives, financial institutions, and local governments to issue bonds.

In the early and mid-1980s, Kadar had encouraged a limited amount of political liberalisation. The HSWP maintained its monopoly on political power, but the norms of democratic centralism were looser than in other countries of Eastern Europe. County party secretaries acquired the freedom to make decisions of local importance, including control of personnel. The government again exhorted delegates of the National Assembly to scrutinise laws and government policies more critically. In 1983 a new electoral law required a minimum of two candidates for each national and local constituency in general elections. Trade unions began to defend workers' interests more energetically. Journalists were urged to expose low-and mid-level corruption and abuse of power, although they could not criticise the regime's basic tenets. The leadership also bolstered economic reforms of the early 1980s with a foreign policy geared to a greater degree than before on trade with the West, and it maintained this course during the deterioration of superpower relations in the early 1980s. Thus, the economic reforms of the late 1960s had also come to provoke a measure of political reform and changes in foreign policy. These new departures were inspired in large measure by Hungarian nationalism, a force that had long encouraged Hungarians to control their own destiny and to resist the hegemony of their larger, more powerful neighbours.

Hungary's post-war social transformation from a predominantly rural and traditional society into a mainly urbanised and largely modern society began with an immense social benefit. The war, the Holocaust, the flight of the ancient regimes' civil servants, and expulsion of ethnic Germans deprived Hungary of important human resources. The effects, even fifty years later, had not been fully overcome. A review of the demographic data on the distribution of the population among the capital city and other towns with more than 5,000 inhabitants revealed important trends and anomalies. The change in the respective population ratios for communities with fewer than 5,000 inhabitants from 43.7 per cent (1949) to 30.5 per cent (1990) and the corresponding growth of larger communities from 56.3 per cent to 69.5 per cent in this period represented the overall trend of the rural exodus to the cities. The net beneficiaries of this process had been the mid-size, 50,000 to 100,000, and the large, more than 100,000, cities that grew two-and fourfold, respectively, between 1950 and 1990.

In the same period the number of farmers in the labour force declined from 53.6 per cent to 22.3 per cent. Some of the rural migrants settled in towns and cities and became unskilled or semi-skilled workers in factories and construction sites; some settled in the new 'socialist' industrial centres. An elusive component of the rural population was the growing army of commuting peasant workers. The process of daily or weekly commuting from villages to urban centres began with the economic refugees of the regime's first collectivisation drive in the early 1950s. However, the movement of rural people gained momentum from an annual number of 638,000 (1960) to 977,000 (1970) and 1,218,000 (1980). This mobile labour force mainly of people under 40 (68.2 per cent of commuters in 1970) gave the initial impetus to the birth of the second economy in Hungary. Saving from work in factories was invested in new village houses and in small-business ventures like vegetable growing greenhouses and contract life-stock raising. Indeed, as shown by Ivan Szelenyi and associates, these village entrepreneurs catalysed the rebirth of rural civil society in the 1970s and the 1980s.

The unresolved conflict of interest between the capital and the counties had a decisive bearing on the relationship between the central and the provincial party apparat. The main counter-trend to Budapest's economic and cultural domination was the dynamic increase in population from 6.4 per cent (1949) to 19.3 per cent (1990) of provincial cities with more than 50,000 inhabitants. In these rapidly growing communities, probably, more so than elsewhere, the state was always behind with the delivery of essential resources.

Therefore, this was where the communities' unmet needs (housing, services, and consumer goods) and the local elites' demands for discretionary resource allocations coalesced over time and helped shape local and regional political agendas in the multi-candidate parliamentary election in 1985.

In terms of educational attainment, Hungarian society was quite backward at the time of communist takeover. To be sure, this dismal situation was wholly congruent wit the cultural matrix–a small educated elite and a large poorly educated mass component–of pre-war Hungary. Indeed, in 1949, 69.7 per cent of the 15–29 age-group had formal education of less than eight grades, By 1980 this figure had declined to 5.1 per cent. Against this background of humble beginnings, the regime's educational record had been quite impressive. In 1980, of the 15–29 age group, 37.9 per cent completed only eight grades; 30.7 per cent vocational high school; 29.5 per cent academic high school, and 9.8 per cent, university or college at their highest level of formal education. In fact, in 1981, of the under-30 population, 46.1 per cent were enrolled as full-time students from kindergarten through to university level–for a 1984 total of 2,387,400.

The population's continued upgrading of educational qualifications continued unabated through the 1980s. The virtual elimination of illiteracy (the 93,100 'unschooled,' most likely rural Gypsy, cluster is the sole exception) and the growth in the number of high-school and post-secondary school graduates to 6.7 and 2.9 per cent, respectively, are solid evidence of progress in this area.

Thanks to the regime's policies that granted equal access to higher education for men and women, the number of female professionals increased fifteen-fold between 1949 to 1990. In fact, at most of the fifty-seven faculties of Hungary's universities in the 1980s, the majority of students were women. Although women were still kept out of high positions in the party and government, several professions, including law, medicine, the humanities, and many fields of science and engineering, became feminised to a considerable extent.

The Educational Reform Law of 1961 established a three-tier system of secondary education and two main tracks of higher education. At the age of 14 and upon completion of eighth grade, a student could continue in (a) an academic high school (referred to as *gimnázium* in Hungarian), (b) a vocational–trade or commercial–high school, or (c) an industrial or agricultural vocational secondary school, or they could (d) stay at home and start working at the age of 16.

A graduate of an academic high school was eligible to apply for admission to any university or college. A graduate of a vocational high school *could not* enter a university, but only a college (*fõiskola* or college). His or her alternative option was to take a job as a skilled worker's apprentice and join the blue-collar labour force.[30]

Although comparative data are relatively difficult to obtain, it appears that as late as 1981, Hungary led the way in East Europe in the growth of social consumption of assorted benefits, while the rate of private–cash-based–consumption showed a more modest rate of growth between 1977 and 1983.

Social and private consumption, Eastern Europe, 1983[31]

Country	*Social Consumption*	*Private Consumption*
Bulgaria	119.6	111.9
Czechoslovakia	115.2	110.0
GDR	122.9	112.6
Hungary (1981)	128.3	113.2
Poland	114.3	98.9
Romania	104.3	115.3

Note. 1977 = 100.

The planned construction of 1.5 million apartments between 1960 and 1975 was the centrepiece of Kádárist regime's program to provide the working people of Hungary with affordable modern housing. The scarcity of available housing, particularly for people under 35, was a burning issue for members of the post-1956 generation.

Of the four possible ways–rental from the local council, a service flat from one's place of employment, building and purchase of an apartment or a one-family house, and inheritance–of acquiring a roof over one's head, the first two were the more frequent solutions. However, both placed the aspiring tenants or home-owner I the position of deferential petitioner vis-à-vis the local authorities, the immediate employer (together with the workplace party and trade union secretaries), who were empowered to assign housing, or to approve requests for interest-free loans for the applicant[32].

In addition to age–and probably more so than party membership–position in the occupational hierarchy was a critical factor that helped improve one's access to housing. It appears that the less costly solution, that is, the acquisition of a rent-controlled apartment from the local council, was more readily available to executives and intellectuals than to those at the bottom of the occupational hierarchy.

Data presented in György Konrád and Iván Szelényi's pioneering study on housing conditions in four provincial cities in the late 1960s demonstrate the endemic nature of bureaucratic mal-distribution of publicly owned housing resources by criteria that were very different from those propounded by the political regime. In any case, most younger people, of whom 62.9 per cent had no 'independent entitlement' to housing, as well as half of the 'over-40' age cohort, had to make do, often well into their 50's with living in their parents' home.

Family entitlement to housing, by occupation or profession of principal breadwinner, Hungarian provincial cities, 1968.[33]

Occupation or profession	*Independent leaseholder*	*Owner of apartment*	*Neither owner nor leaseholder*	*Sample families*
	N = 956	*N = 943*	*N = 242*	*N = 2141*
Executive	58.9	34.4	6.7	90
Mid-level white-collar	59.4	31.2	9.4	128
Technician	46.9	44.5	8.6	254
Office worker	53.7	34.6	11.7	112
Service sector employee	50.6	34.4	15.0	73
Skilled worker	40.1	48.7	11.2	474
Semiskilled worker	40.6	46.8	12.6	271
Unskilled worker	35.8	52.1	12.1	217
Agricultural manual	8.4	91.6	0.0	36
Retired white-collar	58.5	32.3	9.2	99
Retired manual	44.7	48.6	6.7	387
Percentage	44.7	44.0	11.3	—

Note: Cities, Pécs and Szeged.

In Hungary restructuring was not confined to the economy only, and it has already spread to other institutions. While mass organisations and special interest groups exercised more influence in the 1980's than before, their intercourse with high level political decision making agencies noticeably increased recently. This gained graphic expression since the 1985 parliamentary elections and culminated in the September 1987 session of the Assembly. With regard to the government program of economic reconstruction and the tax laws and the National Trade Union (SzOT) and the peoples Front (HNF) expressed reservations and differences of opinion; while accepting the programmes at the moment, they pledged to work for their own policy in the long run. It is official policy that 'without the trade unions there cannot be major political decision making in Hungary today', however, the SzOT remains under the party's ultimate oversight. The above measures represent a substantial adaptation of the entire political system and the party's role in it; naturally it is controversial and has its opponents. Conservative forces were still present in the Hungarian political fora, including the political apparatus and the government bureaucracy, and might attempt to prevent the successful implementation of the political reforms. This danger prompted several warnings in the Parliament. However, the solution of the economic crisis necessitates political reforms; without which it cannot succeed, and it is expected that the anti reformists would remain isolated. It is crucial for the regime that the harsh economic reconstruction measures be balanced with political reforms, support was needed for the same political decision makers who admittedly committed the post mistakes and still ask for more public confidence to remedy them.[34]

East Germany

After World War II Germany's fate was decided at the Yalta Conference[35], held in February 1945, where the country was actually divided by the United States, Britain, and the Soviet Union. The Soviet occupation zone followed the path shown by the Soviet Union An SMAD decree of June 10, granted permission for the formation of the anti fascist democratic political parties in the Soviet zone; and elections were scheduled for October 1946. In undivided Berlin, the SPD had polled 48.7 per cent thus scoring a major electoral victory.

The SMAD introduced an economic reform program and simultaneously arranged for German war reparations to the Soviet Union. Military industries and those owned by the state, by Nazi activists, and by war criminals were confiscated. These industries amounted to approximately 60 per cent of total industrial production in the Soviet zone. Most heavy industry (constituting 20 per cent of total production) was claimed by the Soviet Union as reparations, and Soviet joint stock companies (Sowjetische Aktiengesellschaften–SAGs) were formed. The remaining confiscated industrial property was nationalised, leaving 40 per cent of total industrial production to private enterprise. The agrarian reform expropriated all land belonging to former Nazis and war criminals and generally limited ownership to 100 hectares. Some 500 Junker estates were converted into collective people's farms, and more than 3 million hectares were distributed among 500,000 peasant farmers, agricultural labourers, and refugees.

The years 1949 to 1955 were a period of Stalinisation, during which East Germany was politically consolidated as an authoritarian Soviet-style state under SED leadership. Ulbricht and the SED controlled the National Front coalition, a federation of all political parties and mass organisations that technically preserved political pluralism.[36]

The economy of the German Democratic Republic (East Germany) had developed impressively since its founding in 1949.[37] By almost any indicator, it stood at the top of the socialist world in economic development and performance. The country had the highest per capita income, the greatest number of automobiles and hospital beds per 1,000 inhabitants, the highest labour productivity, and the highest yield in the agricultural sector per agricultural worker. It used the most electricity and had the greatest number of television sets and radios among member states of the Council for Mutual Economic Assistance (Comecon), all on a per capita basis. East Germany was a major supplier of advanced technology to the other members. In short, it was the most modern and industrialised socialist state.

By 1950 the results of the state's cautious steps toward the socialising of both industry and agriculture were already discernible. Near the end of 1950, about 66 per cent of all industry, 40 per cent of the construction enterprises, and 30 per cent of the domestic trades were already state owned. In 1952, six years after the land had been distributed to the poorer agricultural population, collectivisation of agriculture began in earnest. By 1960 about 85 per cent of the land had been collectivised.

During the 1950s, East Germany made significant economic progress, at least as indicated by the gross figures. By 1960 investment had grown by a factor of about 4.5, while gross industrial production had increased by a factor of 2.9. Within that broad category of industrial production, the basic sectors, such as machinery and transport equipment, grew especially rapidly, while the consumer sectors such as textiles lagged behind.

In the 1950s, the size, composition, and distribution of the labour force also underwent significant change. Although during that decade the population declined by 1.2 million, the number employed actually increased by about 500,000, a development caused by an increase of over 650,000 in the number of working women. In the same period, the percentage of the total labour force employed in industry increased by about 7 per cent (to 36 per cent of the total), while agricultural labour dropped from 28 to 22 per cent of the labour force. The only other significant shift was in the services area, which increased its share of the labour force from 12.5 to 15 per cent.

Consumption grew significantly in the first years, although from a very low base, and showed respectable growth rates over the entire decade. Fluctuations were considerable from year to year, however. High rates for the years 1954, 1955, and 1958 reflected consumption-oriented policies proclaimed in 1953 (the New Course) and 1958 (the year that witnessed the inauguration of the Seven-Year Plan for 1959-65). In 1955 and again in 1960, downturns were recorded, in the latter year partly because of popular resistance to further steps toward the full collectivisation of agriculture. Disruptions in agriculture and the migration of

East Germans to the West, which reached a high point at the beginning of 1961, helped to produce a general crisis in the economy, as reflected in almost all the economic data for the early 1960s.

The Third Party Congress of July 1950 emphasised industrial progress. The industrial sector, employing 40 per cent of the working population, was subjected to further nationalisation, which resulted in the formation of the Publicly Owned Enterprises (Volkseigene Betriebe—VEBs). These enterprises incorporated 75 per cent of the industrial sector. The First Five-Year Plan (1951-55) introduced centralised state planning; it stressed high production quotas for heavy industry and increased labour productivity.

Stalin died in March 1953. In June the SED, hoping to pacify workers with an improved standard of living, announced the New Course. The New Course in East Germany was based on the economic policy initiated by Georgi Malenkov in the Soviet Union. Malenkov's policy, which aimed at improvement in the standard of living, stressed a shift in investment toward light industry and trade and a greater availability of consumer goods. The SED, in addition to shifting emphasis from heavy industry to consumer goods, initiated a program for alleviating economic hardships. This led to a reduction of delivery quotas and taxes, the availability of state loans to private business, and an increase in the allocation of production material.[38]

Collectivisation and Nationalisation of Agriculture and Industry

In 1956, at the Twentieth Congress of the Communist Party of the Soviet Union, First Secretary Nikita Khrushchev repudiated Stalinism. An SED party plenum in July 1956 confirmed Ulbricht's leadership and presented the Second Five-Year Plan (1956-60). The plan employed the slogan "modernisation, mechanisation, and automation" to emphasise the new focus on technological progress. At the plenum, the regime announced its intention to develop nuclear energy, and the first nuclear reactor in East Germany was activated in 1957. The government increased industrial production quotas by 55 per cent and renewed emphasis on heavy industry.

The Second Five-Year Plan committed East Germany to accelerated efforts toward agricultural collectivisation and completion of the nationalisation of the industrial sector. By 1958 the agricultural sector still consisted primarily of the 750,000 privately owned farms that comprised 70 per cent of all arable land; only 6,000 Agricultural Cooperatives (Landwirtschaftliche Produktionsgenossenschaften–LPGs) had been formed. In 1958-59 the SED subjected private farmers to quota pressures and sent agitation teams to villages in an effort to encourage "voluntary" collectivisation. The teams used threats, and in November and December 1959 resisting farmers were arrested by the SSD. By mid-1960 nearly 85 per cent of all arable land was incorporated in more than 19,000 LPGs; state farms comprised another 6 per cent. By 1961 the socialist sector produced 90 per cent of East Germany's agricultural products. An extensive economic management reform by the SED in February 1958 included the transfer of a large number of industrial ministries to the State Planning Commission. In order to accelerate the nationalisation of industry, the SED offered entrepreneurs 50-per cent partnership incentives for transforming their firms into VEBs. At the close of 1960, private enterprise controlled only 9 per cent of total industrial production. Production Cooperatives (Produktionsgenossenschaften—PGs) incorporated one-third of the artisan sector during 1960-61, a rise from 6 per cent in 1958.

As the 1950s ended, pessimism about the future seemed rather appropriate. Surprisingly, however, after construction of the Berlin Wall and several years of consolidation and realignment, East Germany entered a period of impressive economic growth that produced clear benefits for the people. For the years 1966-70, GDP and national income grew at average annual rates of 6.3 and 5.2 per cent, respectively.

Simultaneously, investment grew at an average annual rate of 10.7 per cent, retail trade at 4.6 per cent, and real per capita income at 4.2 per cent.[39]

During the 1960s, collectivisation of agriculture continued. The number of people employed grew steadily, although marginally, by about 80,000, despite a net population decrease of more than 100,000 and an increase in the percentage of the population either too old or too young to be part of the labour force. By the end of the 1960s, the percentage of women in the work force had reached 48.3 per cent. The most significant shift in the sectoral composition of the labour force was the continued drop in the relative size of the agricultural labour component, which went from 17 per cent of the total in 1960 to about 12 per cent a decade later.

As of 1970, growth rates in the various sectors of the economy did not differ greatly from those of a decade earlier. Production increase continued to be highest in the basic industry areas, while light industry—textile and food-processing branches—still lagged. Production reached about 140 to 150 per cent of the levels of a decade earlier. Agricultural growth was not reported in comparable terms, but it is possible to compare total production of certain key items for the years 1966-70 against those for 1956-60 and thus obtain a rough measure of increase, while minimising the impact of a possible single poor harvest. The growth rates in production resulted in substantial increases in personal consumption.

The Second Five-Year Plan encountered difficulties, and the regime replaced it with the Seven-Year Plan (1959-65). The new plan aimed at achieving West Germany's per capita production by the end of 1961, set higher production quotas, and called for an 85 per cent increase in labour productivity. Emigration again increased, totalling 143,000 in 1959 and 199,000 in 1960. The majority of the emigrants were workers, and 50 per cent were under 25 years of age. The labour drain, which had exceeded a total of 2.5 million citizens between 1949 and 1961, resulted in the August 1961 SED decision to build the Berlin Wall.

In 1963 Ulbricht adapted Liberman's theories and introduced the New Economic System (NES), an economic reform program providing for some decentralisation in decision making and the consideration of market and performance criteria. The NES aimed at creating an efficient economic system and transforming East Germany into a leading industrial nation.

Under the NES, the task of establishing future economic development was assigned to central planning. Decentralisation involved the partial transfer of decision-making authority from the central State Planning Commission and National Economic Council to the Associations of Publicly Owned Enterprises (Vereinigungen Volkseigener Betriebe—VVBs), parent organisations intended to promote specialisation within the same areas of production. The central planning authorities set overall production goals, but each VVB determined its own internal financing, utilisation of technology, and allocation of manpower and resources. As intermediary bodies, the VVBs also functioned to synthesise information and recommendations from the VEBs. The NES stipulated that production decisions be made on the basis of profitability, that salaries reflect performance, and that prices respond to supply and demand.

The NES brought forth a new elite in politics as well as in management of the economy, and in 1963 Ulbricht announced a new policy regarding admission to the leading ranks of the SED. Ulbricht opened the Politburo and the Central Committee to younger members who had more education than their predecessors and who had acquired managerial and technical skills. As a consequence of the new policy, the SED elite became divided into political and economic factions, the latter composed of members of the new technocratic elite. Because of the emphasis on professionalisation in the SED cadre policy after 1963, the composition of the mass membership changed: in 1967 about 250,000 members (14 per cent) of the total 1.8 million SED membership had completed a course of study at a university, technical college, or trade school.

The SED emphasis on managerial and technical competence also enabled members of the technocratic elite to enter the top echelons of the state bureaucracy, formerly reserved for political dogmatists. Managers of the VVBs were chosen on the basis of professional training rather than ideological conformity. Within the individual enterprises, the number of professional positions and jobs for the technically skilled increased. The SED stressed education in managerial and technical sciences as the route to social advancement and material rewards. In addition, it promised to raise the standard of living for all citizens. From 1964 until 1967, real wages increased, and the supply of consumer goods, including luxury items, improved.

Domestically the East German regime replaced the NES with the Economic System of Socialism (ESS), which focused on high technology sectors in order to make self-sufficient growth possible. Overall, centralised planning was reintroduced in the so-called structure-determining areas, which included electronics, chemicals, and plastics. Industrial combines were formed to integrate vertically industries involved in the manufacture of vital final products. Price subsidies were restored to accelerate growth in favoured sectors. The annual plan for 1968 set production quotas in the structure-determining areas 2.6 per cent higher than in the remaining sectors in order to achieve industrial growth in these areas. The state set the 1969-70 goals for high-technology sectors even higher. Failure to meet ESS goals resulted in the conclusive termination of the reform effort in 1970.

This same period also saw the establishment and subsequent dismantling of significant economic reforms. The SED leadership instituted the New Economic System (NES), as the reforms came to be known, at its Sixth Party Congress held in 1963. The theoretical basis of the NES drew upon the ideas of the reform-minded Soviet economist Evsei Liberman. Specifically, East Germans who advocated reform argued that existing procedures placed too much emphasis on numbers (the "tonnage" ideology) at the expense of efficiency, that the distorted pricing system caused excessive waste and improper decision making, and that innovation was being stifled because enterprises had neither the incentive nor the autonomy necessary to introduce progressive changes. The NES substantially decentralised authority, giving a degree of power to production units; central controls were effected essentially through fiscal and monetary instruments. Prices were altered and made more flexible and thus more rational, while enterprises were given much greater control over their investment and other funds.

The reform did not fail in terms of production figures. Yet by the end of the 1960s, its most important features had been rescinded. Apparently the crucial factors prompting its abandonment were both economic and political. Economically, decentralisation had led to unacceptably high investment levels and decisions that were inconsistent with central priorities. Politically, the leadership may have simply been uncomfortable with the trend toward decentralisation. The reform also suffered from its affinity with the liberal economic program of the Alexander Dubcek era in Czechoslovakia.

Most of the reforms of the 1960s having been abandoned, the decade of the 1970s began with a "return to normalcy" in terms of economic organisation. By this time, East German leaders could face the future with a greater measure of confidence than ever before, for both political and economic reasons. The political isolation was ending, as demonstrated by East Germany's conclusion of the Basic Treaty with West Germany in 1972 and its subsequent admission into the United Nations in September 1973. And on the economic side, East Germany's performance was noteworthy.

In the 1970s, with two decades of economic expansion and development behind them, the East German leaders faced a number of new problems. Concern now centred on how East Germany should proceed under conditions of "mature socialism." In the 1970s, in East Germany and in the other member states of Comecon, attention focused on the proper way to respond to the trend toward ever expanding varieties of products needed in an advanced society, many of which were becoming more complex and expensive to produce. Since this trend meant increasing costs for each increment in total product output, prospects for sustained economic growth at previous rates were uncertain.

The Comecon member states agreed that the organisation would move toward greater integration, specialisation, and cooperation of the several economies in what became known as the Comprehensive Program of 1971. The member states would pool their resources for the development of costly and sophisticated projects of organisation wide importance. Members would also specialise in certain areas of production to minimise duplication of effort. For example, no longer would every member manufacture ships or buses; only one or two countries would produce such items, which they would then trade for goods produced elsewhere. All countries would presumably benefit from the greater efficiency of mass production.

This focus inevitably had significant implications for the East German economy, i.e., how it should be structured, what it should produce, and so on. In general, East Germany gradually consolidated production units into larger and larger entities, culminating in the introduction of the *Kombinate* of the late 1970s. Consolidation also occurred in agriculture; by 1980 there were only one-third as many collective farms as there had been in 1960.[40]

Despite these problems, throughout the 1970s the East German economy as a whole enjoyed relatively strong and stable growth. In 1971, first Secretary Honecker declared the "raising of the material and cultural living standard" of the population to be a "principal task" of the economy; and private consumption grew at an average annual rate of 4.8 per cent from 1971 to 1975 and 4 per cent from 1976 to 1980. The economy's sturdy performance was not a result of a growing labour input the size of the work force scarcely increased—but rather of a high level of investment in fixed assets and an increase in materials consumption that actually exceeded the growth of net output. The 1976-80 Five-Year Plan achieved an average annual growth rate of 4.1 per cent.

The Main Task, introduced by Honecker in 1971, formulated domestic policy for the 1970s. The program re-emphasised Marxism-Leninism and the international class struggle. During this period, the SED launched a massive propaganda campaign to win citizens to its Soviet-style socialism and to restore the "worker" to prominence. The Main Task restated the economic goal of industrial progress, but this goal was to be achieved within the context of centralised state planning. Consumer socialism—the new program featured in the Main Task—was an effort to magnify the appeal of socialism by offering special consideration for the material needs of the working class. The state extensively revamped wage policy and gave more attention to increasing the availability of consumer goods. The regime also accelerated the construction of new housing and the renovation of existing apartments; 60 per cent of new and renovated housing was allotted to working-class families. Rents, which were subsidised, remained extremely low. Because women constituted nearly 50 per cent of the labour force, child-care facilities, including nurseries and kindergartens, were provided for the children of working mothers. Women in the labour force received salaried maternity leave which ranged from six months to one year. The state also increased retirement annuities.

In October 1973 at the tenth Plenum of the Central Committee of the SED, the centrepiece of Honecker's economic and social policy was announced: a housing program to run from 1976 through 1990 that would build or modernize between 2.8 and 3 million housing units. Within Honecker's first ten years, more housing units were newly built or rebuilt than during the entire history of the East German economy upto that time. The increased share of national product devoted to the present generation has occurred simultaneously with a shift in the distribution of consumption toward the lower income strata, especially during the earlier Honecker years. In 1971 the minimum monthly salary was raised and the wage rates in the lowest wage groups were increased. In 1974 the minimum vacation was increased by three days and the workweek of workers in shift rotation was shortened.

In February 1974 a new foreign exchange law went into effect that made it legal for East German citizens to receive gifts of hard currency from relatives and friends in the West The Intershops for Western tourists were no longer off limits for East German citizens, and the range of consumer goods dramatically expanded for a considerable portion of the population. These measures promoted the internal circulation of deutsche marks as a parallel and, for many classes of transactions, preferred currency.[41]

Changes in Economic Strategy

The mechanism that serves to coordinate the supplies and demands for individual goods and services in a centrally planned economy is a system of material balances in which the sources and uses of each product are listed opposite each other in separate accounts for each good. The classical model of centrally planned economic growth was based most exclusively upon the extensive mobilisation of labour, capital, and other material inputs. An extensive growth strategy is one where an enterprise is judged by its contribution to its sources side of a material balance. An intensive strategy shifts attention to the uses side of the material balances-conserving a barrel of oil is equal to producing a barrel of oil. During the Honecker years much of the economic policy of the SED was aimed at mobilising the population and decision-makers in government and economy to cut costs. The direct approach to intensive growth was seen in a general tightening of specific energy, material and transport allowances for enterprises and state organisations.

The Honecker era began with criticism of the unbalanced growth strategy implicit in Ulbricht's "structure determining tasks," and, instead, the intention was to pursue a programme of "planned proportional development." Once it became clear that investment resources were inadequate to allocate sufficient investment resources across the board, priorities were established.

1979-80 Kombinate became the Backbone of GDR Industry

As one of several organisational forms in GDR industry, the Kombinate, originally a large, integrated multi-plant enterprise had existed since the 1950's. In 1978 there were 54 centrally directed Kombinate that together accounted for about half of the production of centrally planned industry. IN 1979-80 the Kombinate organisational form became the industry standard, replacing the previous middle level in the administration of East German industry that stood between the ministries and the enterprises.[42]

Miscellaneous Improvements in the System of Planning and Balancing

Two broad classes of improvements took place in the nuts and bolts of planning and material balancing during the Honecker era. Because product cycles and large investment projects invariably cross the temporal bounds of annual plans, much effort was devoted to improving the inter-temporal links between annual plans within the middle-term five-year plans. The SED Politburo commissioned the drafting of a uniform Order Of Planning for both the enterprise and national levels in May 1972. These uniform orders of planning established for each of the last five year planning periods have been subject to significant revision during their nominal lives.

Looking for the Right Prices for Producers, Keeping the Wrong Prices for the Consumers

Planned producer price increases have been regularly introduced in stages. In the first stage of revisions, prices of raw materials and products that were particularly raw material intensive was changed (1976). In the following year, prices were adjusted for semi-finished goods.

Beginning in 1978 and then in 1979, prices for final goods, including consumer goods, were revised. Since 1980, price revisions have been changed simultaneously for successive stages of production.[43]

Price of Labour

On the supply side, wages of production workers were tied more closely to performance. This reform of the wage system was announced at the Eighth FDGB-congress in1972 and began in 1976. by the middle of 1985 almost two-thirds of the employees in the productive sphere had been affected by this reform.

On the demand side, the cost of labour has been significantly increased. After literally no public discussion, a new enterprise tax, "the contribution to social funds," was introduced in 1984. The purpose of the tax was to increase labour costs by 70 per cent to strengthen the financial incentive to economise on labour.

Price of Capital

In order to value structures and equipment built in different years uniformly, a revaluation of the capital stock in 1986 prices was undertaken so that capital consumption allowances would better reflect actual value of capital resources.

Consumer Prices

The shadow cast by the June 17 (1953) uprising is long. The SED leadership appeared to have had a superstitious belief that consumer price stability was necessary for political stability. Nonetheless, the principle of unchanging consumer prices was amended during the course of the Honecker era. In 1979 a signal was given at the Eleventh Plenum of the SED Central Committee. The principle of constant consumer prices was explicitly limited to "basic goods." According to Keren's calculations, between 1973and 1983 there was an average annual inflation of consumer prices of 2.7-2.8 per cent, which is quite modest in any international comparison. Nonetheless, this rate is high enough to be the difference between slow consumption growth and a decline in living standards during the critical period of early 1980's. While the extent of hidden inflation was significant, the stability of certain key prices was quite genuine. However the SED was undoubtedly correct in its assessment that it lacked sufficient popular trusts to warrant attempts at technical corrections in the structure of consumer prices.

Explaining the relatively successful economic record achieved by East Germany after these early troubled years is not as easy as many assert. It is clear, however, that the previous level of German industrialisation and the existence of a trained and diligent labour force have been important factors in the success story. To this, East German leaders themselves would add two other explanations: the socialist character of their system and the help they received from the Soviet Union, particularly after 1953, the year of Joseph Stalin's death.

Like other East European communist states, East Germany had a centrally planned economy (CPE), imposed on it by the Soviet Union in the late 1940s, in contrast to the more familiar market economies or mixed economies of most Western states. The state established production targets and prices and allocates resources, codifying these decisions in a comprehensive plan or set of plans. The means of production are almost entirely state owned. In 1985, for example, state-owned enterprises or collectives earned 96.7 per cent of total net national income.

Advocates of CPEs consider this organisational form to have important advantages. First, the government can harness the economy to serve the political and economic objectives of the leadership. Consumer demand, for example, can be restrained in favour of greater investment in basic industry or channelled into desired patterns, such as reliance on public transportation rather than on private automobiles. Second, CPEs maximise the continuous utilisation of all available resources. Under CPEs, neither unemployment nor idle plants should exist beyond minimal levels, and the economy should develop in a stable manner, unimpeded by inflation or recession. Third, CPEs serve social rather than individual ends; under such a system, the leadership could distribute rewards, whether wages or perquisites, according to the social value of the service performed, not according to the vagaries of supply and demand on an open market.

Critics of CPEs identified several characteristic problems. First, given the complexities of economic processes, the plan must be a simplification of reality. Individuals and producing units could be given directives or targets, but in carrying out the plan they selected courses of action that conflicted with the overall interests of society as determined by the planners. Such courses of action included, for example, ignoring quality standards, producing an improper product mix, or using resources wastefully. Second, critics contend that CPEs had build-in obstacles to innovation and efficiency in production; managers of producing units, frequently having limited discretionary authority, see as their first priority a strict fulfillment of the plan targets rather than, for example, development of new techniques or diversification of products. Third, the system of allocating goods and services in CPEs is thought to be inefficient. Most of the total mix of products was distributed according to the plan, with the aid of a rationing mechanism known as the System of Material Balances. But since no one can predict perfectly the actual needs of each producing unit, some units received too many goods and others too few. The managers with surpluses were hesitant to admit they have them, for CPEs were typically "taut," that is, they carried low inventories and reserves. Managers preferred to hoard whatever they had and then to make informal trades when they were in need and find someone else whose requirements complement their own. Finally, detractors argue that in CPEs prices do not reflect the value of available resources, goods, or services. In market economies, prices, which are based on cost and utility considerations, permit the determination of value, even if imperfectly. In CPEs, prices are determined administratively, and the criteria the state uses to establish them are sometimes unrelated to costs. Prices often vary significantly from the actual social or economic value of the products for which they have been set and are not a valid basis for comparing the relative value of two or more products to society.[44]

The Tenth Party Congress, which took place in April 1981, focused on improving the economy, stabilising the socialist system, achieving success in foreign policy, and strengthening relations with West Germany. Presenting the SED as the leading power in all areas of East German society, General Secretary (the title changed from first secretary in 1976) Honecker emphasised the importance of educating loyal cadres in order to secure the party's position. He announced that more than one-third of all party members and candidates and nearly two-third of the party secretaries had completed a course of study at a university, technical college, or trade school and that four-fifths of the party secretaries had received training in a party school for more than a year. Stating that a relaxation of "democratic centralism" was unacceptable, Honecker emphasised rigid centralism within the party. Outlining the SED's general course, the congress confirmed the unity of East Germany's economic and social policy on the domestic front and its absolute commitment to the Soviet Union in foreign policy. In keeping with the latter pronouncement, the SED approved the Soviet intervention in Afghanistan. The East German stance differed from that taken by the Yugoslav, Romanian, and Italian communists, who criticised the Soviet action.

The SED's Central Committee, which during the 1960s had been an advisory body, was reduced to the function of an acclamation body during the Tenth Party Congress. The Politburo and the Secretariat remained for the most part unchanged. In addition to policy issues, the Congress focused on the new Five-Year Plan (1981-85), calling for higher productivity, more efficient use of material resources, and better quality products. Although the previous five-year plan had not been fulfilled, the Congress again set very high goals. Because it barely went beyond the repetition of previous aims and the continuation of domestic and foreign policies, the Tenth Party Congress had been termed the party congress of continuity.[45]

At the annual meeting of the central committee secretariat with the first secretaries of the SED county organisations in February 1988, Erich Honecker characterised the cumulative changes that had taken place at the GDR economy since he had taken command in 1971 as a Policy of Reform[46]. And so the R-word again became socially acceptable in East Berlin-at least for propaganda purposes. The record showed that some Western analysts had been much earlier in describing the totality of marginal changes in the East German economic system as "reform in small steps."

The bulk of the changes in the East German economy during the Honecker years is better understood as shifts of economic policy of minor significance for the workings of the economic system. Other policy shifts were responses to changing circumstances. Concurrent with these changes in policy, a cautious search for incremental improvement in the methods of management, planning and accounting also took place over much of this period. The economic history of the GDR during the Honecker years was a history of changes. They may be grouped together as changes in policy resulting from (1) changes in the goals of the Party leadership, (2) changes in the SED economic strategy, and (3) changes in international opportunities; institutional changes that had altered the organisational chart without fundamentally changing the logic of economic mechanism; and price changes in relative scarcities and also reflecting modifications in the principles of price-setting. By the end of the Honecker era, the East German economic system had increased its lead over others in its class, but attained just that and no more, the top of its class.

Changing Goals of the SED Leadership

By the early 1980s, establishment of *Kombinate* for both centrally managed and district-managed enterprises was essentially complete. Particularly from 1982 to 1984, the Government established various regulations and laws to define more precisely the parameters of these entities. These provisions tended to reinforce the primacy of central planning and to limit the autonomy of the *Kombinate*, apparently to a greater extent than originally planned. As of early 1986, there were 132 centrally managed *Kombinate*, with an average of 25,000 employees per *Kombinate*. District-managed *Kombinate* numbered 93, with an average of about 2,000 employees each.

An East German journal reported, for example, that during preliminary discussion concerning the 1986 annual plan, 2.2 million employees in various enterprises and work brigades of the country at large contributed 735,377 suggestions and comments. Ultimate decision making, however, comes from above.

The private sector of the economy was small but not entirely insignificant. In 1985 about 2.8 per cent of the net national product came from private enterprises. The private sector included private farmers and gardeners; independent craftsmen, wholesalers, and retailers; and individuals employed in so-called free-lance activities (artist, writers, and others). Although self-employed, such individuals were strictly regulated. In 1985, for the first time in many years, the number of individuals working in the private sector increased slightly. According to German Democratic Republic statistics, in 1985 there were about 176,800 private entrepreneurs, an increase of about 500 over 1984. Certain private sector activities are quite important to the system. The SED leadership, for example, had been encouraging private initiative as part of the effort to upgrade consumer services.

In addition to those East Germans who were self-employed full time, there were others who engaged in private economic activity on the side. The best known and most important examples were families on collective farms who also cultivated private plots (which could be as large as one-half hectare). Their contribution is significant; according to official sources, in 1985 the farmers privately owned about 8.2 per cent of the hogs, 14.7 per cent of the sheep, 32.8 per cent of the horses, and 30 per cent of the laying hens in the country. Professionals such as commercial artists and doctors also worked privately in their free time, subject to separate tax and other regulations. Their impact on the economic system, however, was negligible.

More difficult to assess, because of its covert and informal nature, was the significance of that part of the private sector called the "second economy." As used here, the term included all economic arrangements or activities that, owing to their informality or their illegality, took place beyond state control or surveillance. The subject has received considerable attention from Western economists, most of whom were convinced that it is important in CPEs. In the mid-1980s, however, evidence was difficult to obtain and tended to be anecdotal in nature.[47]

One kind of informal economic activity included private arrangements to provide goods or services in return for payment. An elderly woman could hire a neighbour boy to haul coal up to her apartment, or an employed woman might pay a neighbour to do her washing. Closely related were instances of hiring an acquaintance to repair a clock, tune up an automobile, or repair a toilet. Such arrangements take place in any society, and given the serious deficiencies in the East German service sector, they may be more necessary than in the West. They were doubtless common, and because they were considered harmless, they were not the subject of any significant governmental concern.[48]

Poland

An entirely new stage in Polish national existence began with Soviet success in liberating Poland and the Communist-dominated government being installed in the country in 1945. During the next seven years, Poland became a socialist state modelled on the Soviet Union.

Writings or discussions on Poland during the period 1945 and 1970 are not so commonly found. But if we are to take a look at the East European countries which have introduced economic reforms since 1965, the two countries whose names come immediately to our minds are Poland and Hungary.

From Stalinism to the Polish October

Communist social engineering transformed Poland nearly as much as did the war. In the early years of the new regime, Poland became more urban and industrial as a modern working class came into existence. The Polish People's Republic attained its principal accomplishments in this initial, relatively dynamic phase of its existence. The greatest gains were made in post-war reconstruction and in integration of the territories annexed from Germany. Imposition of the Soviet model on the political, economic, and social aspects of Polish life was generally slower and less traumatic than in the other East European countries following World War II. The PZPR took great care, for example, to limit the pace of agricultural collectivisation lest Soviet-style reform antagonise Polish farmers.

Soviet-style centralised state planning was introduced in the First Six-Year Plan, which began in 1950. The plan called for accelerated development of heavy industry and forced collectivisation of agriculture, abandoning the previous go-slow policy in that area.

A brief liberalising "thaw" in Eastern Europe followed the death of Stalin in early 1953. In Poland this event stirred ferment, calls for systemic reform, and conflict in the ranks of the PZPR. The de-Stalinisation of official Soviet dogma left Poland's Stalinist regime in a difficult position, especially following Nikita S. Khrushchev's 1956 attack on Stalin's cult of personality.

Realising the need for new leadership, the PZPR chose Gomulka as first secretary in October 1956. This decision was made despite Moscow's threats to invade Poland if the PZPR picked Gomulka, a moderate who had been purged after losing his battle with Beirut.

Although Gomulka's accession to power raised great hopes, the 1956 incident proved to be a prelude to further social discontent when those hopes were disappointed.

The elevation of Gomulka to first secretary marked a milestone in the history of communist Poland. Most importantly, it was the first time that popular opinion had influenced a change at the top of any communist government. Gomulka's regime began auspiciously by curbing the secret police, returning most collective farmland to private ownership, loosening censorship, freeing political prisoners, improving relations with the Catholic Church, and pledging democratisation of communist party management. In general, Gomulka's Poland gained a deserved reputation as one of the more open societies in Eastern Europe. Regarding himself as a loyal communist and striving to overcome the traditional Polish-Russian enmity, Gomulka came to favour only those reforms necessary to secure public toleration of the party's dominion. The PZPR was to be both the defender of Polish nationalism and the keeper of communist ideology. By the late 1960s, Gomulka's leadership had grown more orthodox and stagnant as the memory of the Poznan uprising faded[49].

Consolidation of the Opposition in the 1970s

In the wake of the Baltic upheavals, Edward Gierek was selected as party chief. A well-connected party functionary and technocrat, Gierek replaced all of Gomulka's ministers with his own followers and blamed the former regime for all of Poland's troubles. Gierek hoped to pacify public opinion by administering a dose of measured liberalisation coupled with a novel program of economic stimulation. The centre of the program was large-scale borrowing from the West to buy technology that would upgrade Poland's production of export goods. Over the long term, the export goods paid for the loans and improve Poland's world economic position. The program paid immediate dividends by raising living standards and expectations, but it quickly soured because of worldwide recession, increased oil prices, and the inherent weaknesses and corruption of communist planning and administration. By the mid-1970s, Poland had entered a seemingly irreversible economic nosedive compounded by a crushing burden of external debt. Another attempt to raise food prices in 1976 failed after an additional round of worker protests.

The Economic Environment

Polish reforms were introduced in 1973, during the period of the1971-75 Five-Year Plan. Upto 1970, Poland's growth strategy was fairly successful.

National income,(NMP at constant prices)grew at an impressive rate, at least by British standards. In1966-70 the growth rate averaged about 6 per cent per annum, while the outturn for 1971-75 was even better, averaging almost 10 per cent per annum This acceleration in the growth of national income was accompanied in the shift in the basic economic proportions: thus the share of accumulation in national income rose from 27 per centin 1966-70 to around 30 per cent in 1971, reaching a peak of 38 per cent in 1974 before falling back to around 35 per cent. The share of consumption in national income fell correspondingly, though an absolute squeeze on consumption was avoided, as faster growth allowed the total volume of consumption to increase to about 50 per cent between 1970 and 1975.

Living standards apparently continued to rise. In the five years to 1970, real wage rates grew at about 2 per cent per annum, whereas the corresponding figure for 1971-75 rose sharply to a little over 7 per cent, hardly a sustainable rate in the long term. Interestingly, although Poland's meat shortage has attracted Western publicity in recent years, official statistics reveal a sharp rise in per capita consumption: from 56 kilogram per annum in 1071 to 70 kilogram per annum in 1975.

Foreign trade was growing rapidly, even faster than national income. The average rate of foreign trade turnover, in real terms was just over 9 per cent per annum in 1966-70, and this expanded to 13 per cent in 1971-75. The direction of foreign trade also changed, trade with the non socialist countries rising from the one third of the total in 1970 to nearly half in 1975, with a consequent increase in the need to earn convertible currency. Expansion of trade was accompanied by deterioration in the trade balance: from virtual balance in 1970, a widening deficit emerged between 1971 and 1975, amounting to 7.5 billion zlotys in the latter year. The position was worsened by increasing foreign indebtedness, and by the deterioration in Polish terms of trade in 1973 and 1974. However, the deterioration was slight compared with the corresponding Hungarian experience and for most of the 1971-75 period the terms of trade were moving in Poland's favour[50].

The Birth of Solidarity

When the government enacted new food price increases in the summer of 1980, a wave of labour unrest swept the country. Partly moved by local grievances, the workers of the Lenin Shipyard in Gdansk went on strike in mid-August.

Led by electrician and veteran strike leader Lech Walesa, the strikers occupied the shipyard and issued far-reaching demands for labour reform and greater civil rights. The workers' top priority was establishment of a trade union independent of communist party control and possessing the legal right to strike. Solidarity, the free national trade union that arose from the nucleus of the Lenin Shipyard strike was unlike anything in the previous experience of Comecon nations. Although primarily a labour movement led and supported by workers and represented by its charismatic chairman Walesa, Solidarity attracted a diverse membership that quickly swelled to 10 million people, or more than one of every four Poles. Because of its size and massive support, the organisation assumed the stature of a national reform lobby. Although it disavowed overtly political ambitions, the movement became a de facto vehicle of opposition to the communists, who were demoralised but still in power. With the encouragement of Pope John Paul II, the church gave Solidarity vital material and moral support that further legitimised it in the eyes of the Polish population.

In the sixteen months following its initial strike, Solidarity waged a difficult campaign to realise the letter and spirit of the Gdansk Agreement. This struggle fostered an openness unprecedented in a communist East European society. Although the PZPR ousted Gierek as first secretary and proclaimed its willingness to cooperate with the fledgling union, the ruling party still sought to frustrate its rival and curtail its autonomy in every possible way. In 1980-81, repeated showdowns between Solidarity and the party-state usually were decided by Solidarity's effective strikes. The movement spread from industrial to agricultural enterprises with the founding of Rural Solidarity, which pressured the regime to recognise private farmers as the economic foundation of the country's agricultural sector.

In late 1981, the tide began to turn against the union movement. In the midst of the virtual economic collapse of the country, many Poles lost the enthusiasm that had given Solidarity its initial impetus. The extremely heterogeneous movement developed internal splits over personality and policy. Walesa's moderate wing emphasised non-political goals, assuming that Moscow would never permit Poland to be governed by a group not endorsed by the Warsaw Pact. Walesa sought cooperation with the PZPR to prod the regime into reforms and avoid open confrontation with the Soviet Union. By contrast, the militant wing of Solidarity sought to destabilise the regime and force drastic change through wildcat strikes and demonstrations.

Under the pressure of the massive and Solidarity Labour Movement the authorities conceded demands ranging from wage increases through free trade unions to the release of political prisoners and the relaxation of censorship.

Whatever the eventual outcome of the reform movement generated by the strikes, the protest of 1980 will remain remarkable for three firsts in the history of former communist states. The year saw the first mass protest of the age of developed socialism or, more accurately, of socialism with a consumerist face; it demonstrated the hazards of trying to build popular legitimacy on the basis of premature consumerism on the basis of bureaucratic participation and representation. For the first time in a communist state, workers' self assertiveness went beyond violent, fragmented and short-lived protest to emerge as a well-organised, Solidarity labour movement. Instead of pressing for material security and improvement, strikers gave pride of place to institutional change, to the establishment of self-governing trade unions independent of party and government.

Poland's economic growth was favoured by relatively rich natural resources for both agriculture and industry. Eastern Europe's largest producer of food, Poland based its sizeable and varied industrial sector on ample coal supplies that made it the world's fourth largest coal producer in the 1970s. The most productive industries, such as equipment manufacturing and food processing, were built on the country's coal and soil resources, respectively, and energy supply still depended almost entirely on coal in the early 1990s.

Poland's abundant agricultural resources remained largely in private hands during the communist period, but the state strongly influenced that sector through taxes, controls on materials, and limits on the size of private plots. Many small industries and crafts also remained outside direct state control.

The Polish economy also was isolated from the international economy by the post-war nationalisation of foreign trade. Reforms in the 1970s and 1980s gradually gave individual enterprises more direct control over their foreign trade activities, bypassing much of the state planning machinery. The institutional framework of the centrally planned economy was able to insulate it to some extent from the impact of world economic trends. As a result, domestic industry was not exposed to foreign competition that would force improvements in efficiency or to foreign innovations that would make such improvements possible. Above all, the isolation of the system kept domestic prices totally unrelated to world prices[51].

The history of the East European countries like Czechoslovakia, Hungary, East Germany and Poland is of mixed successes. Their aspiration to become a better society everyday was time and again stalled by economic stagnation, social unrest, and various other political factors. Thereby narrating the history of successes only and not looking into the problems they failed to address, the economic stagnation they failed to overcome, the social unrest they failed to redress would be like discussing half of the story. So it would be worthwhile to look into those problems these countries failed along with their successes. But it is also note worthy that there had been a paradigm shift in the political economic and social spheres from what has been discussed here. To give one example, there were discontent within the party in these countries as early as in the 1960's. However, this evolved to become a full blown trade union movement in the 1980's in a country like Poland. This shift, in many other spheres will be noticed in the next chapter.

References

1. Ihor Gawdiak, ed., *Czechoslovakia: A Country Study*; 3rd Ed. Federal Research Division, Library of Congress; Washington D.C. 1989.

2. Edvard Beneš : President of Czechoslovakia from 1945 to 1948. Resigned in protest as the new constitution was based on the Soviet model. Replaced by premier Gottwald.

3. KSC: Communist Party of Czechoslovakia (Komunistická Strana Ceskoslovenska).

4. Antonin Novotný (1904–1975): Czech communist leader of a Stalinist faction who was deposed in the reform movement of 1968. He was admitted to the Politburo in 1951 and became first secretary of the Communist Party in 1953. After the death of Antonín Zápotocký (Nov. 13, 1957), he assumed the presidency and in 1964 was reelected to a five-year term. In January 1968 he was forced to resign the party leadership to Alexander Dubcek, and in late March General Ludvík Svoboda replaced him as President. At the Party Congress of May 1971, with the Stalinists back in power, a compromise was worked out whereby Novotný was reinstated in the party in exchange for leniency toward the ousted Dubcek.

5. *op. cit.*

6. Ihor Gawdiak, ed., *Czechoslovakia: A Country Study*; 3rd Ed. Federal Research Division, Library of Congress, Washington D.C., 1989.

7. Galia Golan, *Reform Rule in Czechoslovakia : The Dubcek Era 1968–1969*, Cambridge University Press, London, 1973, p. 5.

8. *Ibid.*

9. *Ibid.*
10. *Ibid.*
11. *Ibid.*
12. *Ibid.*
13. *Ibid.*
14. *Ibid.*
15. *Ibid.*
16. *Ibid.*
17. *Ibid.*
18. *Ibid.*
19. *Ibid.*
20. Jiri Musil, *Czechoslovakia in the Middle of Transition*, Daedelus Vol. 121, American Academy of Arts and Sciences, Boston, 1992, pp. 175–193.
21. Stephen Burant, ed., Hungary: A Country Study, 2nd Ed. Federal Research Division, Library of Congress, Washington D.C., 1990.
22. *Ibid.*
23. Rudolf L Tõkés, *Hungary's Negotiated Revolution: Economic Reform, Social Change and Political Succession*, Cambrige University Press, Great Britain, 1996, pp. 43-131.
24. *Ibid.*
25. *Ibid.*
26. *Ibid.*
27. *Ibid.*

28. *Ibid.*

29. Council for Mutual Economic Assistance: organisation established in January 1949 to facilitate and coordinate the economic development of the eastern European countries belonging to the Soviet bloc.

30. *op. cit.*

31. *op. cit.*

32. *op. cit.*

33. *op. cit.*

34. Barnabas Racs, The Parliamentary Infrastructure and Political Reforms in Hungary.

35. Yalta Conference: (Feb. 4–11, 1945), major World War II conference of the three chief Allied leaders, President Franklin D. Roosevelt of the United States, Prime Minister Winston Churchill of Great Britain, and Premier Joseph Stalin of the Soviet Union, which met at Yalta in the Crimea to plan the final defeat and occupation of Nazi Germany.

36. Eric Solsten, ed. *Germany: A Country Study*, 2nd ed. Federal Research Division, Library of Congress, Washington D.C.; 1996.

37. *Ibid.*

38. *Ibid.*

39. *Ibid.*

40. *Ibid.*

41. *Ibid.*

42. *Ibid.*

43. *Ibid.*

44. *Ibid.*

45. *Ibid.*

46. Irwin Collier, "GDR: Economic Policy during the Honecker Era", Eastern European Economics, Vol. 21, M.E. Sharpe Inc. New York, 1990-91.

47. *Ibid.*

48. *Ibid.*

49. Glenn E Curtis, ed., *Poland: A Country Study 3rd ed.* Federal Research Division, Library of Congress, Washington DC, 1994.

50. P.G. Hare & P.T. Wanless, *Polish and Hungarian Economic Reforms–A Comparison*; Soviet Studies, Vol. XXXIII, No. 4, Carfax Publishing Co Ltd. Great Britain, October 1981, pp. 491-517.

51. Alex Pravda, *Poland 1980: Premature Consumerism to Labour Solidarity*, Soviet Studies XXXIV, No. 2, Carfax Publishing Co. Ltd. Great Britain, April 1982, pp. 167-199.

3

Critical Issues of East Europe–II

The story of the Communist regimes of East Europe was not exclusively of successes. Besides their stories of triumphs and gains there were also stories of failures and losses. In order to study the critical issues (which includes both successes and failures) of the East European countries it is best to consider them one by one and not by taking into account all of them together. But before that one of the aspects that influenced all the East European countries is that of Stalinism.

Michal Reiman writes: "Observers have always been struck by the cruelty of Stalinism, the monstrous extent and apparent irrationality of its methods of terror and mass extermination, and the absolute character of Stalinist totalitarianism and political dictatorship. This is apparently why one finds so many references in the literature to its arbitrariness or to aspects of Stalinism that cannot be accounted for in any precise way. These aspects include for example, the peculiarities of Stalin's personality, his character, and his personal and political motives; but also certain specific aspects of socialism, of the socialist world outlook, theory, and ideology and their effects on society; and certain features of the Russian national character,

Russian history, the Russian national political tradition and so on.'[1]

Reiman considers Stalinism as an example of ever embracing crisis in every aspect of life. It arose, according to many as a result of the post revolutionary crisis and was reflected in the increasing amount of oppression in the domestic and influenced the international sphere as well. Alec Nove,[2] however considers the cold war as one of the reasons as to why the Stalin phenomena became so big. It was because of the Cold War that Stalin tightened his grasp on the East European countries as well. This was followed by cultural and political repression at home. Theatre critics, scientists were all warned off. After 1946 Nove writes that there was even more stress on Russian nationalism. Stalin died on 5th of March 1953. The Soviets regarded the period of Stalinism from 1934 to 20th Party Congress: the period from the death of Lenin to the Stalin phenomenon as the period marked by factional fights in the central party leadership, process of what Preobrzezinski called socialist primitive accumulation, Stalin's collectivisation and industrialisation and the ascendance of elements of Stalinist terror that were scattered in the political atmosphere in the socialist Russia during the civil war' like the need and creation of an army, primitive communism, emergence of an internal police, the rude behaviour of Stalin and Stalin's contribution subsequently on the national question. An effort to reverse the wrongs of Stalin was made by Khrushchev in the 20th Congress of the CPSU as he called for de-Stalinisation.

Now, let us, first take a look at Czechoslovakia. The history of Czechoslovakia is, like all other East European countries, characterised by the change in the nature of the regime, with a change in the regime in the Soviet Union. The failure of the respective countries was reflected in all the spheres, political, economic as well as social.

Czechoslovakia

Although in social and economic policies, the KSC[3] in Czechoslovakia went slightly further in developing the conceptual basis for a model of socialism quite distinct from that in USSR in 1947,[4] yet, Gottwald[5] could not conceive of a model of socialism with a genuine plurality of parties. The KSC continued to proclaim its "national" and "democratic" orientation. The turning point came in the summer of 1947. In July the Czechoslovak government, with KSC approval, accepted an Anglo-French invitation to attend preliminary discussions of the Marshall Plan. The Soviet Union responded immediately to the Czechoslovak move to continue with the Western alliance. Stalin summoned Gottwald to Moscow; upon his return to Prague, the KSC reversed its decision. In subsequent months, the party demonstrated a significant radicalisation of its tactics.

The KSC raised the spectre of an impending counterrevolutionary coup as a pretext for intensified activity. Originally announced by Gottwald at the KSC Central Committee meeting in November 1947, news of the "reactionary plot" was disseminated throughout the country by communist agents' provocateurs and by the communist press. In January 1948, the communist-controlled Ministry of Interior proceeded to purge the Czechoslovak security forces, substituting communists for non-communists.

Thus it could be apprehended that not only the developments in the Soviet Union, had a considerable effect on the policies and programmes of the East European countries but also Soviet Union made a concerted effort to regulate the matters in any of its Warsaw Pact powers. For instance with the coming of Stalin to power in the Soviet Union and Stalinisation, the nature, and policies of the other East European countries got influenced. Thus, Czechoslovakia too, started showing signs of Stalinisation, in its government, party structure, and almost in every sphere of life during the period of Stalin, but surprisingly even after that, for quite sometime in Czechoslovakia. This inability of the country to keep itself outside the sphere of influence of Soviet Union to this extent cannot be rated as a success of the country.

P.K. Sundaram writes: The political structure in Czechoslovakia, after 1948, had soon assumed the character of a full-fledged Stalinist state[6]. The communist party assumed for itself the role of sole ruling party, despite the formal existence of other parties in the national front, and totalitarian and bureaucratic methods of governance became the norm. Within the communist party itself, the supreme authority became the reigning top leader, whose pleasure went in the name of the will of the party and the people. Police and secret services became the main arms of the state. From 1950 the "purges" started in the party. When Antonin Novotny became first secretary of the party and President of the Republic in 1957, mass trials of citizens including large number of Communists took place. As many as 40 thousand people were executed on trumped up charges. From 1949 to 1962 as many as 616,282 members were expelled from the Communist Party for "anti-party activities". While the Communist Party of Czechoslovakia had two million members in 1948, it was only 1.3 million in 1967–a fall of 35 per cent, and that too in a socialist country.

Under the Stalinist regime, no contact with the outside world was permitted for the people, not to speak of the freedoms within the country even in the fields of art and literature. The terror rule had assumed such ludicrous proportions that even the Warsaw Radio was being jammed to "protect" the people from Gomulka's "national communism."[7] In 1962 the regime set up the world's only known television jamming station to block the television programmes from capitalist Vienna. The de-Stalinisation programme in the Soviet Union and the thaw in all the socialist countries around it did not affect Czechoslovakia in any appreciable manner. There Novotny ruled supreme. As late as June 1961, Rudolph Barak, member of the Politburo of the Communist Party and Vice Premiere and Interior Minister, was thrown in jail for trying to reopen the Slansky Case.[8]

Then came the reforms of 1968 in Czechoslovakia. But before that, disappointment, setbacks, and half fulfilled hopes were the order of the day in Czechoslovakia. It had its root in the movement which began in the mid-50 with the death of Stalin and Khrushchev's secret speech in 1956. It was then that many Czech and Slovak communists began to question some of the methods if not the dubious achievements of their years in power.

Galia Golan writes: "It was perhaps strange that the one country in Eastern Europe with a democratic-humanitarian tradition of several hundred years, the one society which had known a genuine Western-style democracy in this century and a pre-war legal communist party, which itself was notorious in Communist circles for its evolutionary and parliamentary bias, should be one of the most stubborn in throwing off the Stalinist practices condemned even in Russia by 1956. Yet there were a number of circumstances which combined to militate against de-Stalinisation in Czechoslovakia in the 1950's. Among these was the rule of the apparatchiks[9] that is those people such as Party first secretary Antonin Novotny, who had risen to power during the massive purges in the 1949-54 periods. This new leadership was dependent on the old methods because of the basic instability of the regime. The leadership had been so involved in the past excesses that it probably could not survive genuine liberalisation. Novotny himself, as well as most of the others in his regime, had been too directly involved in the preparation of the purge trials–including the trials of the Slovak nationalists which took place after the death of Stalin-to risk a genuine review and rehabilitation which were part of 'de-Stalinisation.'"[10]

Another factor which played a role, albeit a negative one, in the avoidance of liberalisation in the 1950's was Czechoslovakia's geopolitical position and tradition[11]. Of this the most significant element was, perhaps, the feeling of friendship for the Russians. These feelings did account for the absence of a strong anti-Russian sentiment which might have acted as a stimulant for liberalisation, as in the case of Poland and Hungary in 1956. Still another factor which facilitated the regime's efforts to forestall liberalisation was the serious minority problem in Czechoslovakia. The Czech-Slovak conflict often diverted and thereby dissipated what might have been a unified opposition in the Party.

None of these factors were conclusive or static. Given different circumstances or a change in one or another of these factors, some obstacles disappeared or turned into stimulants rather than deterrents for reform. By the end of 1962 the situation was quite different and the factors militating for liberalisation were much stronger or had replaced those which earlier constituted obstacles. The economy was in a clearly unstable situation by 1962, and in August of that year the Third Five-Year Plan had to be scrapped half-way through. The failure of the plan, the continued deterioration of the economy, and the inability for these reasons to promulgate more than ad hoc one-year plans all pointed to the need for reform.

In addition, the chronic weakness of the regime was aggravated by a power struggle–albeit between two conservatives–which impaired the unity of the apparat. Despite Novotny's victory over his Interior minister, Barak, the Party was seriously split over the action against the slightly more popular, yet conservative, competitor for power.

A third factor operating in the direction of de-Stalinisation came from Moscow. The Twenty-Second Congress of the CPSU, with its opening of the second wave of de-Stalinisation, led to pressures on various parties in Eastern Europe, including the Czechoslovak Party, finally to begin to take steps towards de-Stalinisation.

With the accumulation of pressures and objective factors, in 1962, many Slovaks saw that their specifically Slovak interests might be served by de-Stalinisation or even by liberalisation–and that the circumstances were now fortuitous for pressures in this direction together with like-minded Czechs.

But as a positive side that could be derived from the then Czech society was the fact the students, writers and the economic reformers all had revolted in order to show their reservation regarding the ongoing situation in contemporary Czechoslovakia and in 1967 Antonin Novotny was replaced by Alexander Dubcek as first secretary of the party. Dubcek made significant changes in the entire economic, political and social sphere of the country in 1968, which was seen as Prague Spring. But unfortunately, the whole corrective measure that was taken in order to bring about change and reform in the country was reversed only a year later. Czechoslovakia witnessed military intervention in its domestic affair from the Soviet Union and its four allies. The country seemed to be unable to keep its sovereignty intact time and again from the Warsaw Pact powers.

Jiri Musil writes, "In hardly any country of the Soviet bloc was the official doctrine after 1968 more devoid of ideas, more sterile and irrelevant for solving the important issues of society and state than in Czechoslovakia. Hardly any country in the bloc was so resistant to new ideas in the economy, sociology, and political science".

The military intervention in Czechoslovakia by the Soviet Union and its four allies had raised several issues. Sovereignty, independence and equality of socialist countries and their mutual relations; norms of relations between fraternal communist parties and ways of settling disputes among them; right of assessment of the given situation in a country; and, above all whether the Soviet Union and its Communist Party should have the role of arbiter in the theory and practice of socialism-these are some of the questions posed.

Gustav Husak, a centrist was named first secretary (title changed to general secretary in 1971). Only centrists and the conservatives led by Bilak continued in the Presidium. A program of "normalisation"–the restoration of continuity with the pre-reform period–was initiated. Normalisation entailed thoroughgoing political repression and the return to ideological conformity. A new purge cleansed the Czechoslovak leadership of all reformist elements. Of the

115 members of the KSC Central Committee, 54 were replaced.

Reformists were removed from regional, district, and local party branches in the Czech lands and, to a lesser extent, in Slovakia. KSC party membership, which had been close to 1.7 million in January 1968, was reduced by about 500,000. Top levels of government and the leadership of social organisations were purged. Publishing houses and film studios were placed under new direction. Censorship was strictly imposed, and a campaign of militant atheism was organised.

Czechoslovakia had been federalised under the Constitutional Law of Federation of October 27, 1968. The newly created Federal Assembly, which replaced the National Assembly, was to work in close cooperation with the Czech National Council and the Slovak National Council. The Husak regime amended the law in January 1971. Although federalism was retained in form, central authority was effectively restored.

The invasion of Czechoslovakia reaffirmed the tragedy of Eastern Europe-the failure of small countries there to understand their mutual dependence[12]. In 1968, as in 1956, as in 1938-39, as in 1919-20, petty quarrels, divisiveness and territorial ambitions among the East European nations contributed to their national tragedies. The aggressive, short-sighted and brutal actions of the authoritarian regimes in Eastern Europe have been reinforced time and again by the negative attitudes of these people towards their neighbour.

However, in the forty-plus years of communist rule in Czechoslovakia, the country suffered more from the political side, with the continual oppression known as "normalisation" imposed on the Czechs and Slovaks after the 1968 invasion.[13]

The Slovak Question

Czechoslovakia also faced another problem, which involves the question of Slovakia, within the country. Slovakia always claimed to have received a step-motherly attitude by being a part of the country until the Prague Spring of 1968, when a near Unitarian state became a federation of two republics. The tragedy of the Poles and the Czechs and Slovaks over many years of mutual hostility has been the tragedy of all the peoples of the Eastern Europe, which the Soviet Union skilfully exploited to its advantage[14]. The biggest tragedy is the fact that their mutual cooperation and interdependence could have helped them to tide over many problems that the respective nations faced.

The change improved Slovakia's status while at the same time weakening the political standing of the Czechs. An external but not negligible feature of the situation allowed a Slovak–Guatav Husak–to become president of the federal republic, and, more importantly, the leading man in the radically purged Communist Party of Czechoslovakia. An unusual constitutional system of an asymmetric sort was established, with the central federal government on the one hand and the government of the Slovak republic on the other. There was no Czech government; only a not very influential parliament, the Czech National Council. All important institutions were organised in a similarly asymmetric way. Moreover the principle of parity was introduced in all federal institutions, though the Slovaks were only one-third of the federation's population. In the economic sphere, Slovakia's rapid industrialisation continued after the Soviet invasion in 1968; that meant relatively higher investments in the Slovak republic than in the Czech regions. During the whole period between 1945 and the end of the 1980's, Slovakia registered an unusually rapid rate of industrialisation and urbanisation; differences between both parts of Czechoslovakia rapidly disappeared. For Slovakia, this was a period of great social change, with modernisation, high mobility and obviously improved standard of living.

During the socialist period, neither Russia nor the Czech Republic was in fact allotted the same institutional status as the purportedly,"lesser" republics making up their federations[15]. In particular, both of these leading republics were denied their own communist parties, their own academies of sciences, their own media and the like. Instead their only connection was to the all-union or central institutions of the party and the state–a connection open, as well, to all others in the system and, it must be emphasised, defined in terms of socialism, not the nation.

This asymmetric federalism reflected the impact of several considerations–that Russians and Czechs were the numerically dominant group, and not minorities, within their countries; that they had as a result, no special "needs" and, thus, a weak case for institutional "boosting"; and that they were, if anything, the representatives of the centre and socialism. This metaphor applied equally to Czechoslovakia although it was drawn keeping in mind the situation in U.S.S.R.

These worries led Russian leaders to take actions on two fronts. They proposed a series of new, indigenous Russian institutions, and they converted all-union institutions into Russian ones. While the Czechs only did the same, once the state was in the process of formal dissolution, they did share precisely the same burden as that of Russia. There was, in short, a gap between political power and institutional resources-for Russia and the Czech lands. This was a form of nationalism that rejected the regime and socialism but did not require in any way a re-examination of the national question.

Compared to the other aspects, it is even more difficult to address the issues of either the success or the failure of economy of the respective country, because, according to the scholars it is almost impossible to get an authentic and impartial assessment of the countries concerned.

The Czechoslovak economy, too, had serious problems. Investments made in industry during the late 1970s and early 1980s had not yielded the results expected. Consumption of energy and raw materials was excessive. Czechoslovak leaders themselves decried the economy's failure to modernise with sufficient speed. According to many Western analysts, other constraints were inherent in the communist system imposed in the late 1940s; yet the cautious Czechoslovak leadership of the 1980s appeared reluctant to make major changes.

The Czechoslovak economy emerged from World War II relatively undamaged. Industry, which was the largest sector of the economy, included large firms in light and heavy industry. During the war, the German occupation authorities had taken over all major industrial plants. After the war, the reconstituted Czechoslovak government took control of these plants. Foreign trade was still in private hands, however, and remained important in the economy. Exports of machinery and consumer goods paid for imports of materials for processing. The quality of Czechoslovak export products was comparable to that of products produced in other industrialised countries. Agriculture also remained in private hands, and farming was still largely a family affair. The labour force as a whole was skilled and productive, and management was competent. This mixed system, containing elements of socialism and private enterprise, operated efficiently in 1947 and 1948 under a two-year plan in which goals were general and indicative rather than mandatory. The country received considerable assistance from the West through the United Nations, and most of its trade was with the West. Until prohibited by Stalin in 1947, Czechoslovakia intended to participate in the United States Marshall Plan to rebuild Europe. By 1948 Czechoslovak production approximated pre-war levels, agricultural output being somewhat lower and industrial output somewhat higher than earlier levels. When the KSC assumed complete political and economic control in February 1948, it began immediately to transform the Czechoslovak economy into a miniature version of that of the Soviet Union. By 1952 the government had nationalised nearly all sectors; many experienced managers had been replaced by politically reliable individuals, some of them with few technical qualifications. Central planning provided a mandatory guide for institutions and managers to follow in nearly all economic activity.

During the early 1960s, industrial production stagnated. The agricultural sector also registered a relatively poor performance. Agriculture had been a weak part of the economy throughout the 1950s, consistently failing to reach planned output targets, and the minimal reforms of 1958-59 had done little to alter the situation. Targets set for the national economy in the Third Five-Year Plan (1961-65) quickly proved to be overly ambitious, particularly with regard to foreign trade. The plan was dropped after a recession in 1962, and annual plans covered the remainder of the period. National income actually declined in 1963. By 1965 it was only 1.9 per cent higher than in 1960, in comparison with a 6.9 per cent growth rate in the 1956-60 periods. Many factors contributed to the economy's poor performance, including adverse weather for agriculture, cancellation of orders by China resulting from the Sino-Soviet dispute, and unrealistic plan goals. By this time, however, reform-minded economists had reached the conclusion that much of the blame lay in deficiencies of the Soviet model. They began to prepare additional reform measures to improve the economy's efficiency.

Serious defects in the Soviet model for economic development had long been recognised by some Czechoslovak economists, and calls for decentralisation had occurred as early as 1954. Economists and others had argued that it was inappropriate to apply the Soviet model to Czechoslovakia in a dogmatic manner. The country was already industrialised, had few natural resources and a small internal market, and remained dependent on foreign trade in significant ways. The model emphasised extensive development, such as building new factories, rather than intensive investment in which production processes were modernised and efficiency improved. The pressure for greater investment and defence production during the 1950s had caused private consumption to grow more slowly than net material product. The result had been a chronic inflationary bias, reflected in shortages of consumer goods and forced savings by the population. Plants and construction firms held large inventories of materials to compensate for irregular deliveries from suppliers. Completion of most investment projects required an inordinate amount of time, freezing funds in unproductive uses. Inadequate investment in agriculture had contributed to the latter's chronically poor performance. Prices were also a problem, based as they were on often conflicting policies; prices reflected neither scarcity nor cost, bore little rational relationship to one another in the domestic market, and had become increasingly divorced from world prices. The system appeared to stifle innovation and to offer no basis for selecting between investment and production alternatives or for judging efficiency.

By the early 1960s, several Czechoslovak economists had analysed these problems and had remedies to offer. One spokesman for the reformers was the economist Ota Sik, a member of the KSC Central Committee and its Economic Commission.

The energy and trade problems Czechoslovakia faced in the late 1970s were also major factors in the slowdown in industrial growth. The terms on which Czechoslovakia conducted foreign trade had begun to deteriorate sharply by the mid-1970s. After 1974 the rapid rise of world oil prices was partially reflected in the price of oil from the Soviet Union, Czechoslovakia's principal source of fuel and raw materials. Prices of other materials on which the country's economy depended also increased faster than the prices of its exports, which consisted primarily of manufactured goods (especially machinery). Party and government leaders were cautious about increasing foreign indebtedness and attempted to maintain a high level of exports. Increasingly in the 1970s, a substantial portion of the country's production of consumer goods and machinery was diverted to export markets to meet the rising import bill. Restraints on imports from non-communist countries reduced inputs for domestic industries.

At the beginning of the 1980s, the economy had substantial limitations, which were recognised by economists, political leaders, and even the public at large. The country had perhaps the oldest stock of plant and equipment in Eastern Europe, a stagnant resource base, and growing dependence on energy and material imports. To reduce requirements for energy and raw materials and to increase the competitiveness of Czechoslovak exports, domestic production needed to become more efficient. Furthermore, consumption standards continued to be well below those found in Western Europe.

Economic planners set relatively modest growth targets for the Seventh Five-Year Plan, revising their goals downward two years into the plan. "Intensification" of the economy-focusing on efficient use of resources rather than simply quantitative growth–was the keynote of government policy. The revised goals called for a growth rate in net material product of 10.5 to 13.5 per cent. Gross industrial output was to increase by 14 to 18 per cent, and gross agricultural output by 7 to 10 per cent. Personal consumption was to rise by less than 3 per cent.

The early years of the Seventh Five-Year Plan saw a serious slump in the economy. During 1981 and 1982, personal consumption actually declined. The cost of living rose more rapidly than wages. During the final three years, however, an economic recovery made up for the earlier poor performances; according to official calculations, the country succeeded in either meeting or surpassing domestic goals during the plan period as a whole. Official reports listed the growth rate of net material product at 11 per cent, growth of gross industrial output at 14.5 per cent, growth of gross agricultural output at 9.8 per cent, and increase in personal consumption at 5.5 per cent. Results of the "intensification" effort were disappointing, however, as leaders acknowledged. During the plan, consumption of energy decreased by only 1.7 per cent per annum, less than the 2 per cent goal of the plan.

Despite its favoured position within the economy, the industrial sector had serious weaknesses in the mid-1980s. The country declined as an industrial power from tenth to fortieth in the world during the 1980's. A particularly significant problem was the high energy and material inputs required for a unit of industrial output[16]. Czechoslovak machinery was often heavier than comparable West European equipment and was usually less productive. The slow rate of technological innovation had caused a decline in the country's share of machinery markets in developing nations, non-communist industrialised countries, and Comecon countries in comparison with the 1950s. Related problems were design limitations and lengthy project completion times, which frequently caused investments to be less productive than hoped. In addition, old equipment was retired slowly. In 1986 the average age of industrial machinery and equipment was 12 years; 10 per cent of the machinery was more than 25 years old, and the percentage was reportedly increasing. These circumstances contributed to the low productivity of Czechoslovak workers compared with their counterparts in Western Europe. Moreover, the overall quality of Czechoslovak exports was frequently below world standards; official government pronouncements emphasised the inadequate technological level of activities in the economy as a whole. Imbalances persisted between supply and demand, both at home and on foreign markets. In 1986 a prominent Czechoslovak economist argued that industry's problems stemmed in part from inadequate specialisation, insufficient use of foreign licenses, and cumbersome restraints on research projects.

Most of these problems had already existed in some form during the 1970s, and the government had introduced several measures intended to correct the deficiencies. Laws introduced in 1971 (which went into effect in 1975) had granted limited powers and a degree of decentralisation to the intermediate level of administration, positioned between ministries and production enterprises. The intermediate level consisted of associations of industrial enterprises in the same or closely related branches, resembling trusts. The intent was to reduce overhead expenditures, such as planning and research, while promoting innovation and technological development. Changes also were introduced in the wage and price systems in an attempt to improve efficiency. Despite these measures, there was reason for continuing dissatisfaction in the 1980s.

In the mid-1970s, the terms of trade for Czechoslovakia began to deteriorate rapidly. In 1975 the pricing system used to set values on imports and exports in trade between communist countries was adjusted to make them more current and closer to world prices. The adjustment raised the price of fuels and raw materials (primarily Czechoslovak imports) much more than it did manufactured goods (the country's main export). The same trend manifested itself in trade with Western industrialised countries. During the late 1970s, the terms of trade continued to worsen; greater and greater quantities of exports were required to purchase the same volume of imports. The combination of worsening terms of trade and the difficulty of expanding exports caused Czechoslovakia's trade imbalance to grow in almost every area. Between 1975 and 1979, the country's excess of imports over exports was nearly $1.2 billion with the Soviet Union, $690 million with Eastern Europe, and $3.3 billion with non-communist developed countries. These imbalances emerged despite efforts to conserve fuel and raw material use, to slow the volume of other imports, and to increase exports.

During the 1970s, Czechoslovakia, like other countries of Eastern Europe, turned to West European credit sources to obtain financial help for imports as well as longer term investments in modern technology. Czechoslovakia did not publish information on these credits. However, one Western estimate placed Czechoslovakia's hard currency debt to the West at the end of 1979 at $4 billion gross and about $3.1 billion net. Czechoslovak officials had been much more prudent in building up a foreign currency debt than had several other East European nations, however, and the country's credit standing remained good.

Beginning in 1980, Czechoslovakia was able to achieve a trade surplus with non-communist countries, but only by drastically curtailing imports. When Western banks tightened credit to Eastern Europe in 1982 (largely in reaction to Polish insolvency), Czechoslovakia redoubled its efforts to curb imports and pay off its debt. This cautious attitude continued to prevail even after the creditors' policy eased.

Undue restrictions in the social and cultural sphere were also noticed in Czechoslovakia. Restrictions in the writings of authors, in the works of art etc were noticed in the country every now and then. The years preceding the Prague Spring of 1968 saw historical misinterpretation of T.G. Masaryk as well as Kafka were withheld. Even during the1970's and 80's in the country not a single book by a Western non-Marxist author dealing with serious contemporary political or economic issues was published.[17] While Polish, Hungarian and even Soviet intellectuals were allowed to become acquainted with some of the main tendencies of thought in the outside world, their Czech and Slovak colleagues were deliberately barred from the international intellectual community. The results: ignorance and lack of information; more seriously, a gradual decay of analytical and theoretical thought and language.

Ultimately, massive strikes and demonstrations in Czechoslovakia in late 1989 were the only means by which the Czech and Slovaks achieved the overthrow of the Husak-Jakes regime so quickly.[18] Without the support of the workers the Czechs and Slovak intellectuals and writers, who had dissented quietly but with tremendous resolution against overwhelming odds since they signed the Charter in 1977 demanding human rights guaranteed in the 1975 Helsinki Agreement and international covenants, including the United Nations Declaration on Human Rights, could not have sustained the freedom movement in that country, which was a loose melange of intellectuals, students, environmental activists and religious Catholics who had been engaged in significant pilgrimages in 1980's.

Hungary

Let us now consider the case of Hungary. In Hungary also it is alleged that the Communist Government in the country followed the path of industrial development the way it was done in the Soviet Union without taking into consideration the fact that Hungary should not follow the U.S.S.R. blindly and should also take into consideration its indigenous problems as well. Thus, after 1949 Hungary's communist government under Matyas Rakosi[19] applied the Soviet model for economic development. According to some the government used coercion and brutality to collectivise agriculture, and it squeezed profits from the country's farms to finance rapid expansion of heavy industry, which attracted more than 90 per cent of total industrial investment.[20] At first Hungary concentrated on producing primarily the same assortment of goods it had produced before the war, including locomotives and railroad cars. Despite its poor resource base and its favourable opportunities to specialise in other forms of production, Hungary developed new heavy industry in order to bolster further domestic growth and produce exports to pay for raw-material imports. The Soviet Union became Hungary's principal trade partner, supplying crude oil, iron ore, and much of the capital for Hungary's iron and steel industry. Heavy Soviet demand also led Hungary to develop shipbuilding and textile industries. Trade with the West declined considerably. Soviet pressure, a Western trade embargo, and Hungarian policies favouring domestic and regional autarky combined to reduce the flow of goods between Hungary and the West to a trickle during the Cold War period.

Rakosi's regime also established wage controls and a two-tier price system made up of producer and consumer prices, which the government controlled separately. In the early 1950s, the authorities used these new controls to limit domestic demand and cut relative labour costs by tripling consumer prices and holding back wages. Popular dissatisfaction mounted as the economy suffered from material shortages, export difficulties, and mounting foreign debt.

The Hungarian government went for collectivisation of agriculture. But according to Dr. Bela Balassa the attempt failed.[21] The extent of the failure of collectivisation in agriculture can best be shown by an examination of relevant production figures. According to the data of the Hungarian Ministry of Agriculture, published during the revolution, the productivity (crop/ acre) of communist-run state farms was some 20 per cent and that of individual privately owned farms some 50 per cent above the productivity of the kolkhozes.[22]

Dr. Bela Balassa concluded that the economic system in Communist Hungary was a failure and from there on he went on to say that the inherent deficiencies of the collectivist economic planning and the catastrophic economic policy had caused the national standard of living to fall below the pre-war level. But Hungarian agriculture also had its shadowy side.[23] The distribution of land holdings was exceedingly unequal; a semblance of feudalism was still evident. As a result, cultivation was extensive. The land reform of 1945 at first gave some hope for further development. Yet instead of development, the last decade had displayed the steady deterioration of Hungarian agriculture. Hungary was no longer able to export products of land in considerable quantity. In fact, Hungary had been compelled to import food. The deterioration of agriculture was due directly to communist policy. Balassa discusses Lenin, who urged the fight against the Kulak[24] (an independent farmer who owns more than twenty-five acres land) and who declared the necessity of agricultural collectivisation as a support for socialist industry. The Hungarian communist leaders did their best to fulfil these goals.

In the Soviet Union the Kulak held important political and economic power before his decline. Soviet leaders endeavoured to destroy the leading elements of the peasantry, therein strengthening communist rule in the villages. In Hungary, kulaks held neither strong economic nor political power. After the land reform of 1945 there were no differences in wealth in Hungary as was the case in Russian villages. Yet the enterprising, individualistic Hungarian kulak was the most industrious element of the Hungarian peasantry, which had reached a somewhat better economic position in life largely through its own personal efforts. Hungarian communists caused a serious setback in agriculture by separating the kulaks from their property. Marketable production had come primarily from the kulak surpluses. Furthermore, crops were usually of better quality on kulak lands. Lenin's dictum prescribed the collectivisation of agriculture. The author mentioned that there were a number of differences between the Soviet and the Hungarian agricultural reality and experience. "Firstly, the density of population is approximately indexed at four per square mile in the USSR and thirty-nine in Hungary. These figures alone indicate that the problems of Hungarian agriculture differ considerably from those of Soviet agriculture.

"The methods of extensive cultivation of land operate with relatively low unit costs and yield per acre based on mechanisation and low labour costs. In the Soviet Union extensive cultivation in large units is feasible. But it was wrong to apply the production organisation and methods employed in the Soviet Union to Hungarian agriculture. Yet political considerations induced the Hungarian communist government to imitate the Soviet example: to enforce collectivisation, thereby creating large units under inefficient cultivation. Thus the trend of earlier Hungarian agricultural policy dating to the twenties was reversed, bringing about a general decline in Hungarian agriculture."

> "One of the fundamental causes of failure of the communist economic system in Hungary, a consequence of collective economic planning itself, was the lack of initiative. Bela Balassa writes that collectivist planning neither is nor can be an equivalent substitute for private initiative."[25]

He writes that another important factor which contributed to the failure of communist economic policy in Hungary was the catastrophic agricultural policy of the regime. Instead of intensifying the development of agriculture, the Government embarked upon collectivisation which according to him was enforced on the people by the regime.

The Hungarian experience has shown that there was no such drive in a collectivist economy, which would impel one to reduce costs. Due to extreme specialisation of manufacturing there was a tendency to allot the production of one type of goods to one factory only. The consumer has no choice whatsoever and he was forced either to buy the product desired, regardless of quality, or refrain from purchasing altogether. This deterioration of quality was felt most heavily in the fields of consumer investment goods. This fact was even acknowledged by the government.

Modernisation of plant and industrial techniques were still other aspects of initiative. In a free enterprise system the entrepreneur was compelled to modernise in order to keep up with the forces of competition. In a collectivist system such compulsion does not exist. For example, in case of Hungarian light industry, political and military considerations favouring heavy industry led to the neglect of even the proper maintenance of machines in the light industrial areas.

Apart from the alleged imitation of the Soviet Union by Hungary, the country had to also face various humiliations from the side of the U.S.S.R. Soviet Union continued to manipulate Hungary's foreign trade; it also manipulated the country to cut down upon its volume of trade with the other Western powers. Hungary too cannot be considered as one of the East European countries which might have escaped the evil effects of Stalinism. Many a heads rolled a number of times in Hungary during Stalin's rule in the USSR. Nigel Swain writes that Hungary was not in a position to adopt the nature of the Plan that was taken up in the Soviet Union. Thus, right from the beginning the whole idea of Plan in Hungary ran into rough weather and by 1953 the country was in a crisis leading to a revolution and then a reform.[26]

National Income and Standard of Living

In connection with consumption and standard of living figures, one can usually usefully check the number of dwellings constructed as an indicator of living standard.[27] According to official Hungarian data, in 1955, some 32,000 apartments were built, in 1956, about 12,000 and plans involved approximately an additional 40,000 for 1957. In 1955, the number of apartments constructed was only 0.32 per cent of the population, in 1956, 0.1 per cent and the planned figure for 1957 approached 0.4 per cent. Considering the housing shortage and the yearly 0.7-0.8 per cent increase of the population, the number of the new dwellings constructed is not nearly sufficient.

There are, however, no reliable Hungarian figures comparing standards of living under communism with the standard of the pre-war period. According to different estimates, agreement on the decrease in the standard of living generally amounts to 10 or 15 per cent.

Revolution of 1956

On October 23, a Budapest student rally in support of Polish efforts to win autonomy from the Soviet Union sparked mass demonstrations. The police attacked, and the demonstrators fought back, tearing down symbols of Soviet domination and HWP rule, sacking the party newspaper's offices and shouting in favour of free elections, national independence, and the return of Imre Nagy[28] to power. Gero called out the army, but many soldiers handed their weapons to the demonstrators and joined the uprising.[29] Soviet officials in Budapest summoned Nagy to speak to the crowd, but the violence continued. At Gero's request, Soviet troops entered Budapest on October 24. The presence of these troops further enraged the Hungarians, who battled the troops and state security police. Crowds emptied the prisons, freed Cardinal Mindszenty, sacked police stations, and summarily hanged some member of the secret police. The Central Committee named Nagy prime minister on October 25 and selected a new Politburo and Secretariat; one day later, Kádár replaced Gero as party first secretary.

Nagy enjoyed vast support. He formed a new government consisting of both communists and non-communists, dissolved the state security police, abolished the one-party system, and promised free elections and an end to collectivisation, all with Kádár's support. But Nagy failed to harness the popular revolt. Workers' councils threatened a general strike to back demands for removal of Soviet troops, elimination of party interference in economic affairs, and renegotiation of economic treaties with the Soviet Union. On October 30, Nagy called for the formation of a new democratic, multiparty system. Non-communist parties that had been suppressed almost a decade before began to reorganise. A coalition government emerged that included members of the Independent Smallholders' Party, Social Democratic Party, National Peasant Party, and other parties, as well as the HWP. After negotiations, Soviet officials agreed to remove their troops at the discretion of the Hungarian government, and Soviet troops began to leave Budapest. Nagy soon learned, however, that new Soviet armoured divisions had crossed into Hungary.

In response, on November 1 Nagy announced Hungary's decision to withdraw from the Warsaw Pact and to declare Hungary neutral. He then appealed to the United Nations and Western governments for protection of Hungary's neutrality. The Western powers, which were involved in the Suez crisis and were without contingency plans to deal with a revolution in Eastern Europe, did not respond.

The Soviet military responded to Hungarian events with a quick strike. With Soviet support, Kádár struck almost immediately against participants in the revolution. Over the next five years, about 2,000 individuals were executed and about 25,000 imprisoned. Kádár also reneged on a guarantee of safe conduct granted to Nagy, who was arrested on November 23 and deported to Romania. In June 1958, the Hungarian government announced that Nagy and other government officials who had played key roles in the revolution had been secretly tried and executed.

Kádár's Reforms

The Revolution of 1956 discredited Hungary's Stalinist political and economic system and sent a clear warning to the leadership that popular tolerance for its policies had limits. In response, regime leaders decided to formulate economic policies leading to an improvement of the population's standard of living. Pragmatism and reform gradually became the watchwords in economic policy-making, especially after 1960, and policymakers began relying on economists and other specialists rather than ideologists in the formation of economic policies. The result was a series of reforms that modified Hungary's rigid, centrally planned economy and eventually introduced elements of a free market, creating a concoction sometimes called "goulash communism".

In late 1956, the party named a committee of mostly reform-minded experts to examine Hungary's economic system and make proposals for its revision.

By the early 1960s, Hungary was ripe for a political shake up. Khrushchev had consolidated his position in the Kremlin and had begun a second wave of de-Stalinisation, thus leading Kádár to believe that the Soviet leadership would support political changes in Hungary. Kádár replaced Ferenc Munnich as Prime Minister (who had served in that position since January 28, 1958), and thus assumed the top government post, as well as the leadership of the HSWP. He then dismissed other hard-line officials. Kádár's consolidation of power led to a more flexible, pragmatic atmosphere in which persuasion took on greater importance than coercion. Kádár relaxed government oppression and released most of those imprisoned for participating in the revolution. Soon Hungary became the leader of the reform movement within the Soviet alliance system. Kádár intended to provide the regime with some legitimacy and political stability based on solid economic performance. The Soviet Union demonstrated its support with its decision to withdraw its advisers to the Hungarian government.

Plans for reforming the centrally planned economy steadily took shape after the Eighth Party Congress. Central Committee secretary Rezso Nyers, who supported a comprehensive reform rather than continued piecemeal adjustments to the economic system, took charge of economic affairs. The regime also appointed committees to prepare reform proposals.

New Economic Mechanism

The Kádár regime gave serious attention to implementing the NEM[30] from 1968 to 1972. The bureaucrats perceived the NEM as a threat to their privileged positions. In November 1972, the Central Committee introduced a package of extraordinary measures to recentralise part of the economy, but the regime did not formally abandon the NEM.

By 1978 Hungary's dismal economic performance made it clear even to the counter reformers in the leadership that a "reform of the reform" was necessary. Return to central control had only rewarded inefficiency and stifled innovation and initiative. Enterprises ignored market signals, and shortages plagued producers. Large amounts were invested in poorly conceived projects, and a trade deficit accumulated. Hungary's hard-currency debt reached $7.5 billion by 1978 and had jumped to $9.1 billion by 1980.

There was a mounting debt crisis in Hungary at the end of the 1970s and in the first years of 1980s.[31] As a result of this the government initiated two changes of direction: in 1978 it began a policy of reducing domestic consumption to try and contain the debt, while restructuring was supposed to take place; and in the 1980's it initiated a degree of institutional reform by reducing the number of ministries and promoting new forms of small cooperatives.

In 1978 the government admitted that its attempt to shield Hungary from world economic conditions could not be continued. Hoping to improve its trade balance with the West and avoid forced rescheduling of its debt, the government announced its intention to boost exports. This policy change marked the beginning of a new wave of reforms. First, the price system was restructured to bring consumer prices gradually in line with world market prices and to ease the burden of subsidies on the state budget. Next, producer prices were reformed to bring about more rational use of energy and raw materials. Finally, the government overhauled exchange-rate and foreign-trade regulations.

All averred that Hungary's economic future lay in a 'mixed economy', with a large private sector, in which competing insurance companies would play a significant role, in which there would be extensive.[32]

However, big may be the problem that the country faced right from its birth, yet, Nigel Swain traces the crisis in the Hungarian economy and says that it started with the 13th Congress of the HSWP in 1985 and the acceptance of the 7th five-year plan beginning in 1986.

Although, the mid-80's, were characterised by successive technical reforms, but continued resistance to change in the area of 'restructuring' did take place. This resistance suggested that institutional reform was not enough, that a socio-economic interest was at stake, and that action in the political sphere would be necessary to defeat it. Developments were superficially contradictory. Hungary joined the IMF and the World Bank on successive days in June 1982, and a string of reforms followed.

Even in the field of agriculture, it is undeniable that the structure of subsidies that existed in Hungary was distorted.[33] 'Throughout the eighties the biggest share of subsidies has been used as a special stimulation to exports, and as a compensation for the paradoxical accounting system in socialist trade, while the general public was largely unaware of this fact'.

Katalin Botos argues that "while producers totally dependent on socialist markets treat external sales as a form of domestic delivery, the responsibility is not shared by the other socialist countries, but is borne solely by the supplying country". This situation was again aggravated by Hungary's debt crisis.

Agricultural subsidies declined radically from 1975-85 as a percentage of net production volume (from 56.7 per cent to 28.4 per cent) and even in absolute terms (from Ft 26,122 million to Ft 23,479 million). Excessive taxation of agriculture has been coupled with excessive subsidisation of the food industry, at least since 1986. Taxes exceeded subsidies in agriculture after 1982, while the food industry was a net tax payer from 1979 to 1985.

The taxation campaign and the pressure to increase exports were responsible for narrowing the horizons of economic management many units had to struggle for day to day existence. The situation in agriculture is more dangerous, for here we can witness an erosion of irreplaceable resources in addition to the exhaustion of replaceable fixed assets. Farms are not only unable to replace deteriorating machinery with up-to-date equipment, but there is also the danger of ruining the quality of land. The 1981-85 land preservation programmes was completed financially, but in real terms this was only an 80 per cent fulfilment-owing to the effects of inflation.

Dr. Bela Balassa gives a detailed analysis of the causes of failure of the Communist government in the country. Balassa again writes that "the individual is not at all interested in the welfare of the state; he is interested in his own welfare. Workers in communist Hungary felt that they were not in fact the owners of the factories. The workers felt that a small group held both economic and political power and the worker was literally compelled to labour for this class. These political and psychological factors frequently led workers in Hungary from acts of simple negligence to conscious sabotage."[34]

Economic Exploitation

Soviet style rule in Hungary had its impact on politics and ideology as well as on economic matters. Moscow dictatorship of economic life consisted not only in servile imitation of Soviet methods and policy, but also in the deliberate and planned exploitation of Hungarian resources for the overall advantage of the USSR. Exploitation of the Hungarian economy and more generally the economies of the satellite countries assumed various forms.

Besides the unsatisfactory planning of investments in a wider sense, there were considerable deficiencies in planning of investments in a narrow sense, that is, actual planning and organisational work for individual enterprises. Frequently coordination and cooperation between different projects was completely lacking.[35]

Finally there was extreme dissatisfaction in all levels around 1982 to 84. There was a demand that reforms from below will have to be carried out. The years 1988–89, marked the re-emergence of political pluralism in Hungary. The starting point was at Lakitelek, in September '87. There at a meeting of the populist writers and intellectuals, was founded the first big opposition movement called Hungarian Democratic Forum (FORUM). The FORUM tried to keep an intermediate position very consciously between the regime and the Democratic opposition, and enjoyed some support form the reform wing of the Communist party. What pushed events forward was Poszgay's[36] action at the end of January 1989. Poszgay recognised that there would be no consensus without the revaluation of the events of 1956. Poszgay declared that what happened in Hungary in 1956 was not a counter-revolution, as the official communist histriography considered the events, but a 'national uprising.' Grósz[37] called together an extraordinary session of the Central Committee of the HSWP in two weeks time. The crucial event that caused the psychological breakdown of the communist regime was the Imre Nagy question: The reburial and rehabilitation of the PM of the 1956 revolution. The coming anniversary of his execution, kept the regime under intense pressure. The Communists and Janos Kádár himself were blamed for the executions, and for the suppression of the revolution. The HSWP[38] was not allowed to take part in the reburial ceremony. The HSWP never recovered from this humiliation, and psychological collapse took place then.

East Germany

It is generally considered that German reconstruction was complicated by the massive effort to introduce socialism that began almost immediately after the Second World War. Immediately after that in 1946 agrarian reforms began in Germany, which involved redistribution of all land holdings over 100 hectares. Before that, in October 1945, the Soviet Military Administration in Germany ordered the confiscation of all properties belonging to former Nazis and their sympathisers. Agricultural labourers, poor farmers, and Germans who had re-settled from the "lost territories" in Eastern Europe received about two-thirds of this confiscated land, and the remainder was converted into state farms.[39]

The public reaction to reparations and land reform, though muted, was mixed. Reparations costs could hardly be well received by the impoverished population, whatever their political views. Dispossession of the ex-Nazis and large landowners may have been popular with many, including those who received parcels of land; but many individuals who were dispossessed fled to the West with their much needed expertise, if not their movable resources. In addition, dividing the land into small units (the plots averaged about eight hectares) was unlikely to lead to the institution of efficient farming methods, although initially the level of mechanisation in agriculture was so low that the matter was of little significance.

The post-war years and the early 1950s were very difficult ones for the East Germans. About two million more people lived in East Germany during the immediate post-war years than in the 1930s, straining the country's limited resources. Nevertheless, official statistics suggest that by 1950 the extent of economic recovery was already impressive.[40]

By 1950 the results of the state's cautious steps toward the socialising of both industry and agriculture were already discernible. Near the end of 1950, about 66 per cent of all industry, 40 per cent of the construction enterprises, and 30 per cent of the domestic trades were already state owned. In 1952, six years after the land had been distributed to the poorer agricultural population, collectivisation of agriculture began in earnest. Discontent with the economy openly surfaced for the first time in 1953. Building workers in Berlin went on strike against the new norms imposed upon them. The exodus Westward as well as the continuing economic sabotage led to a crisis. By 1960 about 85 per cent of the land had been collectivised.[41]

In 1955 and again in 1960, downturns were recorded, in the latter year partly because of popular resistance to further steps toward the full collectivisation of agriculture. Disruptions in agriculture and the migration of East Germans to the West, which reached a high point at the beginning of 1961, helped to produce a general crisis in the economy, as reflected in almost all the economic data for the early 1960s.

As the 1950s ended, pessimism about the future seemed rather appropriate. Surprisingly, however, after construction of the Berlin Wall and several years of consolidation and realignment, East Germany entered a period of impressive economic growth that produced clear benefits for the people. For the years 1966-70, GDP and national income grew at average annual rates of 6.3 and 5.2 per cent, respectively. Simultaneously, investment grew at an average annual rate of 10.7 per cent, retail trade at 4.6 per cent, and real per capita income at 4.2 per cent.

Berlin became a flashpoint from which one dangerous situation led to another. In 1961 Nato troops were put on alert and the GDR built the wall.[42] The emotional impact of this was enormous. Families were divided. The historical entity of a once unified capital city had been brutally torn as under. This means of defence required tough measures to prevent illegal crossings, resulting in some shootings and killings. The building of the Wall deepened the already simmering discontent and created bitter feelings. Nevertheless a minor economic miracle occurred under the protection afforded by the Wall.

The reforms that took place in East Germany as in other East European countries failed to produce either a consistent or a positive growth during the time of the communist rule. The NES as it was known, at its Sixth Party Congress held in 1963. The theoretical basis of the NES drew upon the ideas of the reform-minded Soviet economist Evsei Liberman. Specifically, East Germans who advocated reform argued that existing procedures placed too much emphasis on numbers (the "tonnage" ideology) at the expense of efficiency, that the distorted pricing system caused excessive waste and improper decision making, and that innovation was being stifled because enterprises had neither the incentive nor the autonomy necessary to introduce progressive changes. The NES substantially decentralised authority, giving a degree of power to production units; central controls were affected essentially through fiscal and monetary instruments. Prices were altered and made more flexible and thus more rational, while enterprises were given much greater control over their investment and other funds.

The reform did not, however, fail in terms of production figures. Yet by the end of the 1960s, its most important features had been rescinded. Apparently the crucial factors prompting its abandonment were both economic and political. Economically, decentralisation had led to unacceptably high investment levels and decisions that were inconsistent with central priorities. Politically, the leadership may have simply been uncomfortable with the trend toward decentralisation.

Thus quite naturally most of the reforms of the 1960s having been abandoned and the decade of the 1970s began with a "return to normalcy" in terms of economic organisation. By this time, East German leaders could face the future with a greater measure of confidence than ever before, for both political and economic reasons. The political isolation was ending, as demonstrated by East Germany's conclusion of the Basic Treaty with West Germany in 1972 and its subsequent admission into the United Nations in September 1973. And on the economic side, East Germany's performance was noteworthy.

In the 1970s[43] , unforeseen international developments forced East German leaders to modify their strategy in some areas. First, came the 1973 price explosion for petroleum, accompanied by a more general inflationary spiral on the world market. A slowdown in the rate of growth in Soviet petroleum export capabilities clouded the future, as did the fact that prices for raw materials rose much more steeply on the world market than did prices for the kinds of products East Germany exported. In the late 1970s, a worldwide recession also had a negative impact on the performance of the East German economy. Because much of its trade was with the Soviet Union and the other European members of Comecon, the East German economy was somewhat insulated from the immediate effects of changes on the world market. Nevertheless, over the long run these interrelated developments affected East Germany, and in each case the impact was decidedly negative. As early as 1970, East Germany began to show a deficit in trade with the West and after 1975 with the Soviet Union.

Despite these problems, throughout the 1970s the East German economy as a whole enjoyed relatively strong and stable growth. In 1971, first Secretary Honecker declared the "raising of the material and cultural living standard" of the population to be a "principal task" of the economy; and private consumption grew at an average annual rate of 4.8 per cent from 1971 to 1975 and 4 per cent from 1976 to 1980. The economy's sturdy performance was not a result of a growing labour input since the size of the work force scarcely increased—but rather of a high level of investment in fixed assets and an increase in materials consumption that actually exceeded the growth of net output. The 1976-80 Five-Year Plan achieved an average annual growth rate of 4.1 per cent. Labour productivity was 40 per cent higher in the Federal Republic than in the GDR. Restrictions on investments resulted in a backward infrastructure, especially in water, sewage, electricity, gas, heating, road, and highway construction, and transportation in general, and in the telephone system. The purchasing power of the GDR mark fell further in the economy. Since 1975, prices in industry, construction, and agriculture increased by 56 per cent[44]. Despite large expenditures for housing construction, the city centres deteriorated. An especially sad manifestation of the resolute exploitation of all production factors was not only the neglect of workers' safety, but also the incredible environmental devastation. Social frustration and depression were reflected in an abrupt increase in the number of travel applications, which reached hundreds of thousands.

By the end of the 1970s, the country's growing indebtedness both to the West and to the Soviet Union was becoming a serious problem. A major priority of the East German economic strategy for the 1980s, therefore, was holding down imports and accelerating the growth of exports. The new economic strategy called for speeding up scientific-technological advances; reducing specific production consumption (primary materials consumed per unit of national income), particularly with regard to energy use; making limited, carefully targeted investments geared toward modernisation rather than new projects; and improving labour productivity (especially important because little expansion of the labour force could be expected). The stated goals were an overall "intensification" of economic processes and elimination of "reserves," or excess capacity in the system. In the 1970s, with two decades of economic expansion and development behind them, the East German leaders faced a number of new problems. Concern now centred on how East Germany should proceed under conditions of "mature socialism." In the 1970s, in East

Germany and in the other member states of Comecon, attention focused on the proper way to respond to the trend toward ever expanding varieties of products needed in an advanced society, many of which were becoming more complex and expensive to produce. Since this trend meant increasing costs for each increment in total product output, prospects for sustained economic growth at previous rates were uncertain.

The Comecon member states agreed that the organisation would move toward greater integration, specialisation, and cooperation of the several economies in what became known as the Comprehensive Program of 1971. The member states would pool their resources for the development of costly and sophisticated projects of organisation wide importance. Members would also specialise in certain areas of production to minimise duplication of effort. For example, no longer would every member manufacture ships or buses; only one or two countries would produce such items, which they would then trade for goods produced elsewhere. All countries would presumably benefit from the greater efficiency of mass production.

This focus inevitably had significant implications for the East German economy, i.e., how it should be structured, what it should produce, and so on. In general, East Germany gradually consolidated production units into larger and larger entities, culminating in the introduction of the *Kombinate*[45] of the late 1970s. Consolidation also occurred in agriculture; by 1980 there were only one-third as many collective farms as there had been in 1960.

The Five Year Plan of 1981-85 called for maintenance of previous growth rates, both in the basic producing spheres and in the consumer sector, while at the same time mandating a reduction of 6.1 per cent per annum in specific consumption of "nationally important" energy supplies, raw materials, and other materials. To reduce dependence on imported fuels, East Germany sought to develop the capability of mining 285 to 290 million tons of lignite annually by 1985, a substantial increase over the 1980 production level of just less than 260 million tons. On the consumer side, the government sought to hold prices for the basic necessities at existing levels, necessitating increasing subsidies from the state over time. The plan projected an expansion in supplies of consumer goods retail trade by 20 to 23 per cent and net personal income by about the same amount. Housing construction was to continue to receive special attention, and more than 900,000 units were to be completed by 1985.

The 1981-85 plan period proved to be a difficult time for the East German economy. The first serious problem was the decision by Western banks in 1981 and 1982 to clamp down on credit for East Germany and the concurrent decision of the Soviet Union to reduce oil deliveries by 10 per cent. The immediate East German response—retrenchment on Western imports and stepped up exports—resulted in domestic bottlenecks and a growth rate of less than 3 per cent. However, by the end of the period the economy had chalked up a respectable overall performance, with an annual average growth rate of 4.5 per cent (the plan target had been 5.1 per cent).

Industrial production proved especially disappointing; affected as it was by scarcity of resources, it grew at an annual rate of about 4 per cent instead of the targeted 5.1 per cent. In the limited investment program, which amounted to roughly the same amount as in the previous plan period (264 billion GDR marks at 1980 prices), metallurgy, the chemical industry, and microelectronics received high priority, necessarily at the expense of other areas. During the 1981-85 periods, however, specific energy consumption (primary energy consumption per unit of national income) was reduced by 3.5 per cent per year, an impressive record. The savings were largely in the production sector; household consumption increased markedly (energy prices for consumers remained stable, and acquisition of energy-using consumer durables continued apace). Oil consumption dropped sufficiently to more than compensate for the cutback in Soviet oil exports that occurred in 1982-83; by the end of the plan period, East Germany was able to make available for export (as crude oil and various oil products) about 40 per cent of its oil imports from the Soviet Union. At 312 million tons, lignite production exceeded plan targets in 1985 by 22 to 27 million tons. In the 1984-85 periods, the agricultural sector registered a particularly good performance, and record harvests were reported. During the plan period, the state raised crop and livestock prices, and it eliminated subsidies to the input sector (for example, fuels, foodstuffs, and construction materials) to promote greater efficiency. The situation of the individual consumer deteriorated somewhat during the early years of the plan because of shortages and supply bottlenecks. In 1984 the growth rates in private consumption customary in earlier years resumed.

During the 1981-85 plan periods, East Germany also managed to reduce substantially its debt both to the West and to the Soviet Union. Lower oil prices were helpful in some respects, and East Germany would benefit increasingly as the Comecon price was adjusted to the new world prices during the 1986-90 Five-Year Plan period. It was true that lower prices also made East Germany's re-export of oil products to the West less profitable. In general, however, by 1985 East Germany was again considered to be a "good debtor," so that the foreign trade balance was a less sensitive issue, at least for the time being.

In 1985, productive investments fell to below the 1977 level. The totally obsolete and worn out equipment could not be sufficiently discarded because there were no replacements.[46] This resulted in an increased need for maintenance and repairs, which tied down labour. The forward looking use of research in science and technology was also totally deficient, so that the GDR economy always limped along behind the developed Western industrial countries. Ecological challenges were simply disregarded or suppressed. The performance principle was neglected. Performance in general did not pay in the GDR. The negative social policy had the effect that in the past year alone, i.e.

mainly in the last eight weeks after the opening of the Wall, 343,000 persons left the GDR for the Federal Republic. In January 1990, another 58 thousand left. This meant a decrease in manpower of 220,000 or 3.1 per cent of the employed.

Along with these factors, there was frustration with the unwillingness of the GDR leadership to reform. The people supported the reformist programme of Gorbachev and wished for similar changes in the GDR. This desire for change was strongly felt even among members of the Socialist Unity Party. There was also increasing frustration at the failure of the GDR press to report on the dramatic events in nearby Poland and Hungary. Secondly, the economy showed signs of worsening in the 80's. This too was ignored in the media. Thirdly, the continuing restrictions on travel were an additional source of frustration.[47]

More immediately, the results of the local election of May 1989 triggered a wave of anger.[48] The figures of 95 per cent in support of the existing regime were treated with deep sense of suspicion by the people. Then, came the mass exodus to West Germany via Hungary, which again was not initially reported in the East German press. Gorbachev's visit in the autumn of 1989 was further catalyst for change. However, his warning not to leave reforms too late went unheeded by the leadership. Actually, at the end of 1989, the foreign debt was $18.5 billion.[49]

The failure of the leadership to address many of these problems in the 40th anniversary celebrations further fuelled the mounting discontent. This was quickly followed by large-scale demonstrations in Leipzig, demanding change in the GDR. At this point, the division within the Socialist United Party and even within the leadership began to surface openly. Honecker was ousted and was quickly followed by Krenz. The exposure of corruption in early December led to the resignation of the entire party leadership. The end of January saw the formation of a national unity coalition government. The party had already changed its name to Socialist Unity

Party-Party of Democratic Socialism (SED-PDS). New Forum had by then split on the reunification issue and the 'social market economy', with the majority being in favour of both.

Although the demonstrations still continued, the issues discussed had changed. In an opinion poll 70 per cent of the GDR citizens opposed to re-unification, later estimates showed the majority in favour.

Party members were either confused or angry at being 'betrayed' or have left and gone over to other groups. They felt bitter because they devoted their lives in building 'socialism' but were then reviled for their party membership. Moreover they felt let down by their leaders. Non-party members fond surprisingly little to gloat over. They were angry with developments that they had always criticised. Some no doubt looked forward to the prospect of sharing West Germany's prosperity. Some were primarily interested in visiting their relatives.

The Church too was crucial in exposing the moral and intellectual poverty of the SED and in bringing about its downfall. It had as a result earned a great deal of respect from both believers and non-believers".[50]

The Party (SED)

The essence of socialism in the GDR before the "turn" was the ideologically based power of the political bureaucracy, sustained by an over-proportioned security apparatus, and the network of the apparatus and transmission belts, which it orchestrated in the state and society, in a unified trade union, a unified youth, and the broken bourgeois parties. The economic core was of course, hardly anything else than the appropriation of the ruling class of the surplus value created by the workers.[51]

Since the founding of the GDR, the power of the SED had rested on its rights of command vis-à-vis society and the state. All important areas of society were brought under the control of party socialists by means of a refined nomenclature system. Critical positions could be held only if the person was a member of the SED, was obedient and submissive, and was compliant and agreeable. All state organs, all parties, and all asŝociations submited to the SED's claims of leadership, which were also anchored in the Constitution. The GDR was largely identical with the Socialist Unity Party. Since the population never identified with the German Democratic Republic, when the state party collapsed the state collapsed with it; it imploded as it were.

The SED was far and away the strongest political force, with 2.3 million members and candidates. The financial accounts presented for 1989 included proceeds of 1.5 billion marks and expenditures of 1.6 billion marks. A large portion came from the profits of the party's enterprises. The SED also had 101.5 million marks in Western currency in its disposal: 75.6 per cent of these were spent for "solidarity support for progressive political movements," i.e., for the West German Communists and the "liberation movements" in the Third World.

The SED socialists effectively had a monopoly over the media, which of course, was nullified by the effects of the Western radio and television programmes. Supposedly, 20.2 per cent of expenditures went to support the party press in the past year. Still the SED possessed sixteen newspaper publishers, twenty-six printing offices, and 90 per cent of the editions of all newspapers, effectively controlled the monopoly of paper manufacture and the sale of paper, and controlled over 70 per cent of the fine literature book publishers. But there was more. The West-East gift service "Genex" was the party's property. The former party leadership received 20 per cent of every DM taken in the sole GDR advertising firm, BEWAG. Thirty-seven holiday and rest homes, with 1,914 beds, were administered by the former central committee. SED foreign exchange procurers, who at the same time were for the Ministry of State Security, provided the rulers with the necessary Western currency. Much of its appropriated property was relinquished again in accordance with the decision of its presidium on January 15, 1990.

Poland

Like all other East European countries, in the post-war years, Poland too adopted a fundamentally similar inward-looking development strategy following the Soviet model of accelerated industrialisation and collectivisation of agriculture. Planners attempted to enforce excessively high rates of growth and to achieve a relatively high degree of self-sufficiency.

The initial central planning organisation that began work in Poland in late 1945 to steer the country out of its extremely disorganised pre-war industrial base, stressed socialist rather than communist economic goals: relative decentralisation, increased consumer goods production to raise the standard of living, and moderate investment in production facilities. In 1949[52], however, that approach was scrapped in favour of the completely centralised Soviet planning model. During the 1950s, planners followed Stalin's requirements for a higher growth rate in heavy industry than the overall industrial rate and a higher growth rate in the steel industry than that of heavy industry as a whole. This approach neglected the other economic sectors: agriculture, infrastructure, housing, services, and consumer goods. The sectors that were emphasised were all capital, fuel, and material-intensive.

Stalinist planning also forcibly redirected foreign economic relations. Poland's extensive interwar commercial links with Western Europe were reduced, and some important pre-war markets were lost as trade with the Soviet Union expanded rapidly. For Poland this trade was based mainly on export of coal and manufactured goods primarily from the rapidly growing heavy industries. In return, Poland became dependent on the supply of Soviet oil, natural gas, iron ore, and some other raw materials. This arrangement meant that Poland's industrial structure adjusted to Soviet needs and specifications, yielding many products that could be sold only to the Soviet Union or its allies. Thus exports became heavily dependent on markets in Comecon. But Poland started to witness a fall in their standard of living compared to the other Western countries. The awareness of this fact in the post-war period led to social unrest, a situation which became a tradition during the next thirty-five years.

The basic planning unit for the transformation of the country was the five-year plans which started in 1956. These plans were in most cases inconsistent and needed revision. The Soviet system already started showing problems almost right from the beginning.

Maladjustments, shortages, and bottlenecks appeared in the implementation of that plan, which was intended to create the infrastructure for the industrial future: heavy industry, mining, and power generation. In 1956, after workers' riots in Poznan, a general uprising was averted only by a change in the leadership of the communist party, the Polish United Workers' Party (Polska Zjednoczona Partia Robotnicza—PZPR). The new government of Wladyslaw Gomulka promised modification of the system and changes in the development strategy. Consumer goods received a larger share of the national product, and some quantities of grain and food were imported from the West. State control was mitigated by giving limited policy input to enterprises, and the rate of investment was reduced. Although a lively debate occurred on so-called "market socialism," actual systemic reforms were limited and short-lived. Among the reform measures of 1956, the only significant lasting change was the decollectivisation of agriculture.

Development of the Centrally Planned Economy

This development strategy brought about a specific pattern of economic growth in Poland. As in the other centrally planned economies, rates of growth depended on increases in the quantity of inputs rather than on improvements in productivity. Material production remained high as long as greater quantities of inputs were available. This pattern of growth priorities and the emerging industrial structure left no possibility of raising wages significantly. Wages had been reduced during the first industrialisation drive of the early 1950s. For this reason, the Polish standard of living lagged behind that of Western Europe as the continent recovered from World War II. Already in the first post-war decade, awareness of this disparity began to cause social unrest, a situation that became a tradition during the next thirty-five years.

Establishing the Planning Formula

Centralised planning ranged from broad, long-range statements of fundamental future development to guidance on the operation of specific enterprises. The basic planning unit for transformation of the Polish economy was the five-year plan, the first of which began in 1956. Within that framework, current production goals were established in an annual operational plan, called the National Economic Plan. As the years passed, these plans contained more and more specific detail; because requirements and supplies could not be forecast in advance, plans were inconsistent and constantly needed revision.

According to Andrzej Korbonski[53], unlike Hungary, in Poland October 1956 was remembered for some time by many Poles as an all too brief period of national glory. After then things simply went downhill, from bad to worse. The inability of the Gomulka as well as the Gierek regime to keep political as well as economic promises affected the attitudes and perceptions of the Polish people. The people lost their faith in the ability of the ruling elite to deliver on its promises.[54] This, in combination of the traditional dislike and distrust of authority, meant that the masses approached all reforms imposed 'from above' with considerable suspicion. The successive failures of the reforms simply reinforced that feeling, with the result that by 1980 the Polish regime had practically lost all credibility, making the acceptance and implementation of the new ideas next to impossible. The defeat of 'Solidarity' and the imposition of martial law in December 1981 destroyed not only whatever remained of the Polish regime's legitimacy and credibility but all chances of meaningful reforms. The lack of progress of economic reforms in the past few years is a good testimony to popular contempt for the ruling oligarchy.

The next systemic component to be discussed in structures-parties, legislatures, executives and bureaucracies. The chief characteristic of the Polish party has been for many years the lack of basic unity. This was certainly true during the Gomulka period (1956-70) which witnessed, first, the three way struggle between the liberal wing, the Stalinist faction and the centrist group around Gomulka himself. Once this conflict was won in the early 1960's by the centrist faction, the latter was challenged in turn by the so-called 'Partisans' who forced a showdown in March 1968 which eventually led to Gomulka's ouster some two years later. It took the new leader, Edward Gierek, a few years to neutralise the remnants of the 'Partisans' but just when it appeared that he had the situation under control, Gierek himself was challenged once again from two sides: the conservative Central Committee secretaries representing mostly the apparatus, which favoured maintenance of the status quo, and a 'reformist' wing eager to initiate another round of economic reforms.

By the early 1960s, economic directives again came only from the centre, and heavy industry once more received disproportionate investment.[55] At that point, the government began a new industrialisation drive, which was again far too ambitious. Rates of investment were excessive, the number of unfinished industrial projects increased, and the time required for project completion was considerably extended. Structural distortions increased, and the rates of growth in high-priority sectors were adversely affected by the slower than expected growth in low priority sectors. Bottlenecks and shortages increased inefficiency. By the late 1960s, the economy was clearly stagnant, consumer goods were extremely scarce, and planners sought new approaches to avoid repetition of the social upheavals of 1956. At this point, depression of consumption to its previous levels had become politically dangerous, making a high rate of accumulation problematic at a time when demand for investment funds was growing rapidly. Because of these factors, additional investment funds were allocated to the neglected infrastructure and to the production of consumer goods.

There was a switch from an "extensive" growth pattern (unlimited inputs) to an "intensive" pattern of growth that would ensure high rates of growth through improvements in productivity rather than in the amount of inputs. The new emphasis helped drive another reorganisation of industry in the early 1970s. State enterprises were combined into a number of huge conglomerates called Big Economic Organisations. They were expected to increase efficiency by economies of scale. Wage increases were tied to net increases in the value of outputs as an incentive to labour productivity. In practice, however, central planners could now control a smaller number of industrial units and regulate their activities more intensely. The system was never implemented fully, and no improvement in efficiency resulted. The failure of the 1973 reform demonstrated that the technological level of industrial products was still too low to permit significant increases in efficiency.

The Polish reforms were introduced in 1973, during the period of the 1971-75 five year plan.[56] However, on unchanged policies, a decline in the growth rate threatened, as a result of demographic trends which presaged a slowdown in the growth of the labour force, and a general lack of modern technology. The 1971-75 five-year plans envisaged a shift towards more capital-intensive growth, achieved through higher productivity and a rate of accumulation, initially financed by increasingly foreign debt. This shift, however, led to a deterioration of Poland's economic position after 1973, particularly her external position and the degree of domestic inflationary pressure.

There was economic disturbance in the 1970s, when major shifts in economic policy were being introduced, accompanied by a deterioration in the balance of payments and disequilibrium on the home market. Apprehensions about social and political unrest in Poland, weakening the authority of the party and government, merely exacerbated the difficulties of reform. Moreover, a previous attempt at reform had been announced in 1970. Some of the proposals put forward then were highly unpopular, combining as they did increases in many consumer prices (including foodstuffs) with restraint on wages. The ensuing wave of popular protest, strikes and riots caused the party's First Secretary, Gomulka, to resign. His replacement, Gierek, restored order by, among other things, cancelling the reform announced by Gomulka.

The episode served to weaken the position of the authorities and made them extremely cautious about any reform programme, especially proposals for price increases. Nevertheless, a special Part—State Commission was set up to consider proposals for fresh reforms; this reported back in mid 1972 and reforms were introduced from the beginning of 1973. As is clear from the above, these reforms were intended to sustain, and improve on, Poland's previously rather successful economic performance, but coincided with a rapid worsening of the country's economic equilibrium and a period of serious political weakness.

The Fate of the Reforms

The Polish reforms of 1973-75 were beset with difficulties, largely of their own making, though exacerbated by external problems. First necessary price reforms were never undertaken and other reforms were only partly implemented. Second, no decisive break was ever made with the 'old' system of management; because the new system was introduced piecemeal, the 'old' and the new systems had to coexist, and the habits of the old system, notably the extent of bureaucratic interference in production decision continued. Third, this new management system was never fully integrated with the rest of the economy. No changes were made in the statutes dealing with the legal status of enterprises or associations nor in the method of central planning, and no formal changes were made in the supervisory role of the economic ministries. In these important respects, the existence of the new system went virtually unrecognised. Fourth, no effort was made to increase competition in the domestic economy and producers were given increased powers to set prices for goods. Fifth, the parameter governing the growth of wage funds proved difficult to set correctly, with the result that wage funds grew unacceptably fast. Finally, the reforms were introduced at a time when the economy was already under strain, due to increased economic growth, balance of payments problems and excess demand leading to inflationary pressure.

Poland was also hesitant in cashing on the opportunities when in the 1970s, recession in the West created an opportunity for the East European countries to import technology and capital from the West to restructure and modernise their industrial base. The share of trade with Comecon declined, and trade with other countries increased quite dramatically during the first half of the 1970s.

The technology import strategy was based on the assumption that, with the help of Western loans, a large-scale influx of advanced equipment, licenses, and other forms of technology transfer would automatically result in efficient production of modern, high-quality manufactured goods suitable for export to the West. Under those conditions, repayment of debts would not be difficult. Expansion of exports encountered considerable difficulties, however, partly because of the oil crisis and stagflation in the West, but mainly because the central planners remained unable to effect the required changes in the structure of production. The investment drive, financed by foreign borrowing, exceeded the possibilities of the economy. Removed from direct contact with the foreign markets, centralised selection of exportable was ineffective in expanding the markets for Polish goods. At the same time, the dependence of the economy on imported

Western materials, components, and machines inevitably increased. By the middle of the 1970s, large trade deficits had been incurred with the Western countries. The negative balance of payments in convertible currencies increased from $100 million in 1970 to $3 billion in 1975. During the same period, the gross convertible currency debt increased from $1.2 billion to $8.4 billion. Unable to expand exports to the West at the necessary pace, Polish planners began centralised restriction of imports. This policy in turn had an adverse effect on domestic production, including the production of exportable goods.

Reform Failure in the 1980s and the Solidarity Movement

Meanwhile, the enormous investment drive of the early 1970s had destabilised the economy and developed strong inflationary pressure.[57] Rates of NMP growth dropped throughout the second half of the decade, and the first absolute decline took place in 1979. Although planners should have been adjusting the level of aggregate demand to the declining aggregate supply, they found this task politically and administratively difficult. The authorities also feared major price revisions, especially after workers' riots forced withdrawal of a revision introduced in 1976. In the late 1970s, some prices were increased gradually whereas other increases were concealed by designating them for new, higher quality, or luxury items. The rest of the inflationary gap was suppressed by fixing prices administratively.

By 1980 it had become clear that the large-scale import of capital and technology from the West could not substitute for economic reform.[58] On the contrary, systemic reforms were needed to ensure satisfactory absorption and diffusion of imported technology. Significant expansion of profitable exports to the world markets was impossible for an inflexible and overly centralised economic system. On the other hand, without an increase in exports, reducing or even servicing Poland's rapidly increasing international debt was extremely difficult.

A look at the private sector in Poland that it had a considerable share in the national income produced in Poland.. According to official figures this was 18.2 per cent in 1986 with 10.2 per cent contributed by agriculture and 8 per cent by the registered non-agricultural activity. However, the author states that these figures are understated as they did not include activity by unregistered private entrepreneurs, illegal work by Polish residents in the West. Again, the contribution of the socialised sector to national income produced is exaggerated as a tendency of the enterprises to overstate production so as to be able to claim fulfillment of plans. However, it should be remembered that private economic activity in Poland cannot be traced by looking into its contribution to national income or by assessing personal incomes. But the fact remains that private economic activity in Poland in 1980s could not be considered as a marginal phenomenon as, despite efforts being taken to cut down on private agricultural activity, almost 80 per cent of national income generated in agriculture came from the private sector, and as big as almost 32 per cent of personal services were provided by the registered private sector by 1986[59]. But until 1989 only socialised sector could enter into joint venture agreements and there were administrative controls over material supplies on the private sector. But despite every thing the private sector in Poland continued to grow.

By the late 1970s, the shortage of consumer goods was acute. Nominal income increases continued as a "money illusion" to minimise social discontent and provide a work incentive. This strategy increased the "inflationary overhang," the accumulated and unusable purchasing power in the hands of the population. At the same time, suppressed inflation spurred maladjustments and inequities in the production processes, further reducing the supply of goods. The deteriorating situation in the consumer goods market resulted in a series of watershed events: a wave of strikes that led to the formation of the Solidarity Union in August 1980, a third enforced change in the communist leadership in September 1980, and the imposition of martial law in December 1981. In the summer of 1980 Poland experienced a worker's movement more extensive, better organised and more successful than any of the major outbursts of popular protest that had punctuated its political development over the previous quarter century.[60] Although in the 1970's there was liberalisation of the economy or of the society with the nation opening up to the West gradually, yet, the level of social frustration was also equally high among the people. It was reflected in the high rate of suicide among the people of the country.

Between 1978 and 1982, the NMP of Poland declined by 24 per cent, and industrial production declined by 13.4 per cent. The decline in production was followed by prolonged stagnation. Recognising a strong grass-roots resistance to the existing system, the new government of Stanislaw Kania, who had replaced Edward Gierek, established the Commission for Economic Reform in late 1980. This body presented a weakened version of drastic reforms recommended by the independent Polish Economic Society, an advisory board of economists formed earlier in 1980. Implemented hastily in mid-1981, the reforms nominally removed the PZPR from day-to-day economic management and gave the enterprises responsibility for their own financial condition and for planning. These decentralising reforms were distorted by the constraints of martial law that had been imposed nationally in December 1981, however, and they failed to improve the economic situation. Internally inconsistent and insufficiently far-reaching, the reforms reduced central administrative control without establishing any of the fundamentals of an alternative market system. Thus, in effect, the economy operated from 1981 to 1989 in a systemic vacuum.

After 1985 the foreign trade situation further complicated Poland's economic crisis. The relative importance of Comecon trade declined yearly, necessitating expanded trade with the West, particularly the European Community. This shift was a policy change for which neither the communist regime nor the economic system was prepared in the late 1980s.

Political demands did not stop at representation and participation. For the first time in Eastern Europe, workers were in the forefront of the struggle for civil liberties, a cause which is commonly, and perhaps mistakenly, regarded as being of greater concern to intellectuals.

The Roots of 1980 Turmoil

Much of the workers' discontent stemmed from economic performance and the way material wealth was distributed. Their readiness to protest was conditioned by a decline in the legitimacy of a leadership incapable either of managing the economy or of controlling powerful corporate interests. Willingness openly to challenge the regime was increased by mounting frustration with a bureaucratised system of representation and participation.

Factors Leading to Solidarity

Economic factors were uppermost in precipitating the events of 1980. Increases in the price of meat triggered the first wave of strikes; economic issues quantitatively dominated striker's demands and, in retrospect, most Poles attributed the crisis to government mishandling of the economy. To a great extent, the discontent fuelling blue-collar protest in 1980 was the result of the boom strategy launched by Gierek in 1971 in a bid to make consumption the engine of growth and political support. Such consumption and consumerism, promoted as part of the strategy, were doubly premature. Funded largely by western credits, boom development proved imbalanced, generating high income growth without providing a commensurate rise in the availability of goods and services. More importantly having set consumer expectations on a high spiral, boom turned into recession, thus opening up a large gap between popular demand and economic performance. To this extent, 1980 was a classic case of protest produced by disappointed rising expectations.

During the first half of the 1970's Gierek's[61] strategy seemed successful. In 1975 three out of four poles thought that their material conditions had improved over recent years. Workers' response to the price increases announced in June1976 revealed the fragility of public confidence in the economy. A majority of the Poles thought that 1970-78 had seen a slight rather than a substantial rise in living standards; the one in ten reporting a marked improvement were balanced by those whose situation had deteriorated; members of the intelligentsia emerge as the clearest beneficiaries of the boom strategy; workers come out as the least advantaged. And within these groups it is those in the highest income brackets who have best and those in the lowest who have been hardest hit. True, living standards had apparently improved overall, but to many it seemed that the rich had become richer and the poor poorer. This mixed verdict in part reflected the premature-ness and imbalance of Gierek's consumerism, which generated economic discontent on two scores. Disproportionate investment in capital projects meant that the development of light industry, agriculture, health and housing was relatively neglected. Though food consumption grew, supplies remained erratic and were rated as poor by a majority of Poles in the late 1970's. Housing was given high official priority yet its share of investments dwindled and construction plans were unfulfilled, thus lengthening waiting lists for accommodation.

The flawed nature of public economic confidence made it all the more vulnerable to the recession of the late 1970's. Growth rates slowed sharply after 1975 and foreign indebtedness mounted. Of greater relevance to workers was the concomitant slowdown in pay growth and the burgeoning of inflation which resulted in a fall in real wages in 1978 and 1979.

Exactly how the Poles viewed this reversal in economic development is critical to any assessment of the economic roots of the 1980 events. However, actual downturns took some time to register in public consciousness.

Triggered in part by a relatively sudden realisation that the country was in the throes of a deep economic crisis, the protest of 1980 was generated not by material pauperisation but by a widening gap between rising expectations and falling performance.

Coming after a long period of relative price stability, the 30 per cent jump in prices between 1975 and 1979 must have severely shaken worker's confidence in such control. Amid reports of failing exports and mounting indebtedness, growing public and semi-public criticism of government economic mismanagement furthered the image of a leadership which had lost control over its strategy.

Economic changes in the 1970's broadened the scope of conflict between labour and management. With the growth of material incentives, workers' earnings became more dependent on management discretion and performance. Differences over pay and the distribution bonuses emerged as the most common cause of contention. Industrial relations were also affected by the changing complexion of both labour and management. Better educated were more critical of conditions.

Considerations such as consumer demand and worker job satisfaction, familiar in Western capitalist systems, were ignored. Isolated from the processes of the marketplace, pricing and production levels were set to advance the master plans of the ruling party. The socioeconomic disproportions that resulted from this isolation were a burdensome legacy to the reform governments in the early post-communist era.

It is not as if that the party in Poland did not suffer any crisis within itself. It too did.

The Crisis of the Party

First of all it is important to recall that however, great may be the gulf between the party and the Polish society, the party nonetheless is not immune from the sentiments of the people. Secondly, although it is prepared to mediate within its Soviet protector and its own working class, it does not relish its state of dependence. The PZPR[62] had emerged from the conflict considerably shaken and increasingly aware and self critical of its own weaknesses. While a power struggle simmered at the summit of the party, the base was in complete turbulence. The party leadership must more than ever feel like generals without an army when they see even the most faithful rank-and file communists enrolling en masse in the new unions: by some estimates as many as a third of the Party's three million members may have joined the Solidarity. This coalescence of the Party grassroots and the workers' opposition is the spectre which haunts the Politburo, since the party must rely upon the commitment of its membership if it is to restore its leading role in society, its ability to plan the economy and its capacity to absorb the ideological shocks which it has received.[63]

Following Gierek's ouster in September 1980 the new party leadership under Stanislaw Kanioa[64] appeared once again sharply divided on a variety of political and economic issues. After the 'Solidarity crises of 1980-81 the Polish party for all practical purposes, lost its leading role and relinquished its hegemony to the military.

Ultimately in 1981, Jaruzelski, the Polish general proclaimed Martial Law, which did disrupt the Solidarity movement but could not kill it. In the meantime, however, economic malaise and runaway inflation had depressed Polish living standards and deepened the anger and frustration of society. In early 1988, strikes again were called in Gdansk and elsewhere, and a new generation of alienated workers called for representation by Solidarity and Walesa. Amid widespread predictions of a social explosion, Jaruzelski took the momentous step of beginning round table talks with the banned trade union and other opposition groups. This measure was taken over the objections of the still-formidable hard-line faction of the PZPR. Solidarity used its newly superior position to broker a coalition with various small parties that until then had been silent satellites of the PZPR.

The coalition produced a noncommunist majority that formed a cabinet dominated by Solidarity. Totally demoralised and advised by Gorbachev to accept defeat, the PZPR held its final congress in January 1990. In August 1989, the Catholic intellectual Tadeusz Mazowiecki became Prime Minister of a government committed to dismantling the communist system and replacing it with a Western-style democracy and a free-market economy. By the end of 1989, the Soviet alliance had been swept away by a stunning succession of revolutions partly inspired by the Polish example. Suddenly, the history of Poland, and of its entire region, had entered the post-communist era.

The tragedy is that the main failure in the East European countries under socialist rule did not lie in economic stagnation or the socio-political failures per se. Every country, socialist or otherwise, goes through periods of economic slumps or stagnation. Every country, at some stage, enacts laws which are not suitable for the well being of the nation. However, the failures of the countries under discussion lay in their abandoning their indigenous inherent strengths and their blind, or forced, emphasis on following the economic and political system of the Soviet Union. But the chief failure lay in their inability, due to external coercion from the Soviet Union, or due to their inability to group together against external aggression, in reforming their system and replace policies and programmes which were detrimental to the economy and social well-being, while still remaining within the boundaries of the socialist system. In every case, the failure of the reforms led to intensifying of the national crisis to the point, so that when the external environment changed with the advent of Gorbachev's Perestroika and Glasnost, the political system of these countries imploded on itself and it was no longer possible for any reform to remain within the socialist framework.

In the 1980s, the intensifying crisis in these countries meant that, led by the Soviet Union, the East European countries attempted a transition to a more suitable socio-economic and political system. Unfortunately, no model other than the Western liberal system was available and repeated crushing of reform movements in the Socialist countries had weakened the ability of political theorists to create any viable alternative models and guide the transition from one model to the other. Nor were there any historical analogy for a smooth transition for the leaders of the reform to follow. Thus, in conclusion, when the socialist system in the East European countries collapsed, the lack of alternate models to chose from led to a Western socio-economic and political system filling the vacuum and the lack of any suitable theory of transition made the change traumatic, to say the least.

References

1. Michal Reiman, *The Birth of Stalinism—The USSR on the eve of the Second Revolution*, I.B. Tauris and Company Ltd, London, 1987.

2. Alec Nove, *Stalinism and After*, George Allen and Urwin, Boston, 1984.

3. KSC, Communist Party of Czechoslovakia (Komunistická Strana Ceskoslovenska).

4. M.R.Myrant, *Socialism and Democracy in Czechoslovakia 1945-48*, Western Printing Services Limited, Cambridge University Press, Great Britain, 1981, pp. 85-155.

5. Gottwald, Klement: Czechoslovak Communist politician and journalist, successively Deputy Premier (1945–46), Premier (1946–48), and President (1948–53) of Czechoslovakia.

6. P.K. Sundaram ed: *Wither Czechoslovakia: Essays and Documents on Czechoslovak Crisis*, Dawn Publishers, New Delhi, January 1969, pp. 16-21.

7. Gomulka's "national communism": policies based on the principle that in each country the means of attaining ultimate communist goals must be

dictated by national conditions rather than by a pattern set in another country. The term, popular from the late 1940s to the 1980s, was particularly identified with assertions by Eastern European communists regarding independence from Soviet leadership or example.

8. Slansky case: Rudolf Slánský, joined the Communist Party in 1921, editor of the party organ, *Rudé Právo,* in 1924. He became regional party secretary in Ostrava in 1927 and a member of the Central Committee of the party in 1929. In 1935 elected to the Czechoslovak National Assembly. Prominent in the Czechoslovak Communist leadership in Moscow during World War II. After the war named secretary-general of the party, second only to the leader, Klement Gottwald, becoming a vice premier. In September 1951 he was removed from his secretariat, and in November he was arrested. Under strong psychological and physical pressure, he confessed to the charges that had been prepared against him, among others that he had been a Zionist agent and had engaged in espionage for the West. In November 1952 he and 13 others were tried; 11 of them, including Slánský, were sentenced to death. The Slánský trial was marked by strongly anti-Semitic overtones (most of the condemned were Jews), and the falseness of the charges proved an embarrassment to the party leadership in later years. The Slánský case was later reviewed, and in 1963 he was posthumously absolved of the criminal charges of treason and espionage for which he had been condemned. He was restored to party membership in 1968.

9. Apparatchiks: A person who is a member of the Party apparatus.

10. Galia Golan; *Reform Rule in Czechoslovakia, The Dubcek Era 1968-69*, Cambridge University Press, London; 1973.

11. *ibid.*

12. Stephen E. Medvec; *Poland and Czechoslovakia: Can they find that they need each other?*; The Polish Review, Vol. XXXVI, No. 4, New York, 1991, pp. 451-469.

13. *Ibid.*

14. *Ibid.*

15. Valerie Bunce; *Peaceful versus Violent State Dismemberment: A Comparison of the Soviet Union, Yugoslavia, and Czechoslovakia, Politics and Society*; Vol. 27, No.2, Sage Publications, New Delhi; June 1999, pp. 217-237.

16. Stephen E. Medvec, *Poland and Czechoslovakia: Can They Find That They Need Each Other?* The Polish Review, Vol. XXXVI, No.4, 1991, The Polish Institute of Arts and Sciences of America; New York; pp. 451-469.

17. Jiri Musil; *Czechoslovakia in the middle of Transition*, Daedalus, Vol. 121, American Academy of Arts and Sciences, Boston, 1992, pp. 175-193.

18. Stephen E. Medvec, art: *Poland and Czechoslovakia: Can they find that they need each other?* The Polish Review, Vol. XXXVI, No.4, The Polish Institute of Arts and Sciences of America, New York, 1991, pp. 451-469.

19. Matyas Rakosi, Hungarian Communist ruler of Hungary from 1945 to 1956.

20. Stephen R Burant ed. *Hungary: A Country Study*, Defence Deptt. Library of Congress Country Studies 1989.

21. *op. cit.* pp. 219-254.

22. Kolkhozes: Collective Farms.

23. *op. cit.*

24. Kulak: (Russian: "fist"), in Russian and Soviet history, a wealthy or prosperous peasant, generally characterised as one who owned a relatively large farm and several head of cattle and horses and who was financially capable of employing hired labour and leasing land.

25. *op. cit.*

26. Nigel Swain art: *Hungary's Socialist Project in Crisis*, New Left Review; The New Left Review Ltd. London 1989, No: 173-178.

27. *op. cit.*

28. Imre Nagy: Hungarian statesman, independent Communist, and premier of the 1956 revolutionary government whose attempt to establish Hungary's independence from the Soviet Union cost him his life.

29. Gero: Deputy to Rakosi and succeeded him after Rakosi was removed from office. Ruled Hungary at the time of the 1956 revolution. Eventually replaced by Kádár.

30. NEM: New Economic Mechanism : Introduced the profit motive into State directed enterprises. Initiated in 1968.

31. Nigel Swain, *Hungary's Socialist Project in Crisis*; New Left Review, No. 173-178; New Left Review Ltd; London;1989.

32. *Ibid.*

33. Katalin Botos; *Financial aspects of agricultural Policies in Hungary*, Soviet Studies, Vol. 42, No. 1, January, Carfax Publishing Company, United Kingdom, 1990, pp. 82-87.

34. *op. cit.*

35. *Ibid.*

36. Imre Pozsgay: Member of a quadrimvirate who took charge of a deeply split party in 1989

37. Károly Grósz: Prime Minister from 1987, replaced Kádár in 1988, part of the ruling quadrimvirate of Pozsgay, Grósz, Németh and Nyers in 1989. Initiated economic reforms that led to the collapse of the HSWP

38. HSWP: Hungarian Socialist Worker's Party.

39. Eric Solsten ed., *Germany: A Country Study*, Defence Dept, Library of Congress Country Studies, 1996.

40. What is life like in the GDR: Living standards and the way of life under Socialism, Panorama DDR, Grafischer Grossbetreib Volkerfreundschaft, Dresden November 1977.

41. Len Goldman; *Commentary on the recent events in the German Democratic Republic, Capital and Class, No.1940-42*; Conference of Socialist Economists, London, 1990, pp. 7-14.

42. *Ibid.*

43. Eric Solsten (Ed.), *Germany: A Country Study*; Defence Dept, Library of Congress Country Studies; 1996.

44. Fred S. Oldenburg; *The October Revolution in the GDR-System, History, and Causes*, Eastern European Economics, Vol. 21, M.E. Sharp, Inc, 80 Business Park Drive, New York, 1990-91.

45. Kombinate: large nationally owned combines formed around a core provided by the leading firm

in the branch of industry concerned, with perhaps 25,000 workers under a single managing director.

46. *op. cit.*

47. *op. cit.*

48. *Ibid.*

49. *op. cit.*

50. Karl Cordell; *Political Change In The GDR: The Role Of The Evangelical Church, International Relations, Vol. 10*, David Davies Memorial Institute of International Studies, England, 1990-91.

51. Fred S. Oldenburg, *op. cit.*

52. Curtis, Glenn E ed., *Poland: A Country Study* Defence Dept. Library of Congress–Country Studies, 1994.

53. Andrzej Korbonski, *The Politics of Reform of Eastern Europe: The Last Thirty Years, Soviet Studies, Vol. XLI, No. 1*; Carfax Publishing Company; United Kingdom; 1989.

54. *Ibid.*

55. Curtis, Glenn E ed., *Poland: A Country Study*; Defence Dept. Library of Congress–Country Studies; Washington DC; 1994.

56. P. G. Hare and P.T. Wanless, art: *Polish and Hungarian Economic Reforms-A Comparison*, Soviet Studies, Vol. XXXIII, No.4; Carfax Publishers; United Kingdom; 1981; pp. 491-517.

57. Curtis, Glenn E, *op. cit.*

58. *Ibid.*

59. Bogdan Mroz; *Poland's Economy in Transition to Private Ownership*; Soviet Studies, Vol. 43; Carfax Publishers, United Kingdom, pp. 677-688, 1991.

60. Alex Pravda; *Poland 1980: From Premature Consumerism to Labour Solidarity*; Soviet Studies, Vol. XXXIV, No. 2; Carfax Publishers, United Kingdom, 1982, pp. 167-199.

61. Edward Gierek: Communist Party organiser and leader in Poland, who served as first secretary from 1970 to 1980.

62. PZPR: Polish United Workers' Party (Polska Zjednoczona Partia Robotnicza).

63. Tamara Deutscher, art: *Poland-Hopes and Fears*, New Left Review, No: 125, The New Left Review Ltd, London, 1980-81.

64. Stanislaw Kanioa: replaced Gierek and was later replaced by Polish General Wojchiech Jaruzelski as head of Poland.

4

Soviet Union–Critical Issues and the Gorbachev Years

The last two chapters have tried to look into the political-economic-social conditions in the existing socialist countries of Czechoslovakia, East Germany, Hungary, and Poland between 1945-89/90. It has been seen that the socio-economic political conditions in most of these countries were influenced by the type of regime and situation in the USSR. However, it has become important now to see what the political situation was like in the USSR, after the Bolshevik Revolution of 1917 and how did it handle the crisis that arose especially after the 1980s. This chapter has two parts- (i) the first section deals with the critical issues in the USSR, (ii) the next section deals with Gorbachev and his *Perestroika*, the measure he took up to traverse the crisis.

Since the 1917 the USSR had grown to become the second largest industrial power of the world from being a largely underdeveloped country. The country's share in the world industrial production grew from four per cent to twenty per cent from 1913 to 1980. Although many Western scholars consider those figures to have been inflated, but there is no denial of the fact that the Soviet Union did make a considerable improvement in the economic sphere after the

World War II, at least so that it could become one of the most powerful nations of the world. Living standards, compared to any other Western country of the world, had improved, and Soviet citizens of the late 1980s had a measure of economic security. However, the country's growth in the economic, social and political sphere was not always smooth and steady.[1]

In tune with the nature of any nascent government at the beginning of 1918, the communist government in USSR made vigorous but somewhat haphazard efforts to shape and control the country's economy under the policy of war communism[2] during the civil war. But in 1920, agricultural output had attained only half its pre-war level, foreign trade had virtually ceased, and industrial production had fallen to a small fraction of its pre-war quantity. Factors, such as the disastrous harvest of 1920, major military actions and expenditures by the Red Army, and general wartime destruction and upheaval exacerbated the economy's problems. Lenin decided to adopt New Economic Policy (NEP),[3] "thereby conciliating the peasant majority and making it possible to restore quickly the ruined economy."[4] Alec Nove considers NEP as a compromise. There was very little central planning effective in the country. Lenin's policy of NEP gave permission to some private enterprise, in agriculture and light industry, services and internal trade, to restore pre-war economic strength. The nationalisation of heavy industry, transportation, foreign trade, and banking that had occurred under war communism remained in effect.

Joseph Stalin came to power in the mid 1920s by literally sidelining all the other members of the Party after Lenin. In the late 1920s, Stalin abandoned NEP in favour of centralised planning, which was modelled on a project sponsored by Lenin in the early 1920s that had greatly increased the generation of electricity. Stalin sought to rapidly transform the Soviet Union from a predominantly agricultural country into a modern industrial power. He and other leaders argued that by becoming a strong centrally planned industrial power, the country could protect itself militarily from hostile outside intervention and economically from the booms and slumps characteristic of capitalism and that is how the Five Year Plans started in the year of 1928.

The First Five-Year Plan (1928-32) during Stalin's regime, focused rather narrowly upon expansion of heavy industry and collectivisation of agriculture. Stalin's decision to carry out rapid industrialisation made capital-intensive techniques necessary. International loans to build the economy were unavailable, both because the new government had repudiated the international debts of the tsarist regime and because industrialised countries, the potential lenders, were themselves coping with the onset of the Great Depression in the early 1930s. Stalin chose to fund the industrialisation effort through internal savings and investment. He singled out the agricultural sector in particular as a source of socialist capital accumulation.

The First Five-Year Plan called for collectivisation of agriculture to ensure the adequacy and dependability of food supplies for the growing industrial sector and the efficient use of agricultural labour to free labour power for the industrialisation effort. The regime also expected collectivisation to lead to an overall increase in agricultural production. In fact, forced collectivisation resulted in much hardship for the rural population and lower productivity. By 1932 about 60 per cent of peasant households had joined state farms or collective farms. During the same period, however, total agricultural output declined by 23 per cent, according to official statistics. Heavy industry exceeded its targets in many areas during the plan period. But other industries, such as chemicals, textiles, and housing and consumer goods and services, performed poorly. Consumption per person dropped, contrary to the planned rates of consumption. Stalin, however, continued with his primary emphasis on heavy industry, also during the Second Five Plan (1933-37) which carried on even in the successive Five Year Plans. Agriculture had always been neglected in the next few plan periods along with the social sectors, viz., housing and community services. By the late 1930s, however, collectivised farms were performing somewhat better (after reaching a nadir during the period 1931-34). In 1935 a new law permitted individual peasants to have private plots, the produce of which they could sell on the open market. According to official statistics, during the Second Five-Year Plan gross agricultural production increased by just fewer than 54 per cent. In contrast, gross industrial production more than doubled.

Stalin initiated the "Stalin Plan for the transformation of Nature" which refers to building canals and hydroelectric plants and establishing tree plantations in the Armenian, Azerbaydzhan, Georgian, and Ukrainian republics and in the Volga River area of the Russian Republic to shield land from drying winds.

Throughout the Stalin era, it is said that the pace of industrial growth was "forced". On those occasions when shortages developed in heavy industry and endangered plan fulfillment, the government simply shifted resources from agriculture, light industry, and other sectors. The situation of the consumer improved little during the Stalin years as a whole. Major declines in real household consumption occurred during the early 1930s and in the war years. Although living standards had rebounded after reaching a low point at the end of World War II, by 1950 real household consumption had climbed to a level only one-tenth higher than that of 1928. Judged by modern West European standards, the clothing, housing, social services, and diet of the people left much to be desired. It is said that Stalin paid little attention to the needs of the general people.

Industrial planning showed signs of over-centralisation. It became really difficult to organise industries by orders issued from Moscow. Nove calls the planning system as conservative[5]. There was lack of new and modern machine despite the fact that the country had laid more emphasis on heavy industries. The wage system was in jeopardy as well as there were serious problems of coordination between plans made by different ministries. In the field of agriculture the problem as cited by Nove was poor and lopsided mechanisation, very low harvests, gross misuse of labour, appallingly low incomes for collective works, farms very short of money, because of low prices paid for produce, very inadequate supplies of fertiliser, and finally heavy tax and delivery burdens on private allotments and animals which formed the basis of the collectivised peasants livelihood, all these cried out for remedy. It was not only true that the Stalin phenomenon had affected industry or agriculture in USSR. It had adversely affected almost every sphere of human lives in the USSR. Stalinism does not have any fixed connotation and it had never been used by the official Soviet ideologists. Stalinism was considered to be an international phenomenon. This period was characterised by the use of terror against political opponents, the increased severity and intimidation within the party, the suppression of independence and enforcement of servility in philosophy, art, literature and science too.

Although Stalin died in 1953, the Fifth Five-Year Plan (1951-55) as a whole reflected his preoccupation with heavy industry and transportation, the more so because no single leader firmly controlled policy after Stalin's death. The tremors resulting out of Stalin's death was felt in almost all walks of life in USSR. It would have been really intriguing if Stalinism and eventually de-Stalinisation, which had so very much affected the lives of the people and their socio-economic conditions in the East European countries, would not have any impact on the lives of the people in the Soviet Union.[6]

After Stalin's death there was quite naturally a change of guard in the helms of affairs in the Soviet Union. Khrushchev took over power. "Khrushchev inherited Soviet power in an era ... when it was no longer certain who is encircling whom. For a price he broke with Stalin's isolationist traditions; for a price he transformed the dictatorship of the proletariat from a national into an international force again. The era in which Soviet will might be surrogate for world communism had ended with the irresistible pressure to accommodate heterogeneous demands by undigested, nationally conscious elements of Stalin's unexpected empire."[7]

An ambitious Sixth Five-Year Plan was launched in 1956. After initial revision, prompted at least in part by political considerations, the regime abandoned the plan in 1957 to make way for a seven-year plan (subsequently reduced to a five-year plan) that focused particularly on coal and oil production and the chemical industry. Khrushchev, who became principal leader after 1956, took particular interest in these areas of production. The seven-year plan provided substantial investment funds-over 40 per cent of the total-for the eastern areas of the country. Khrushchev also sponsored reforms to encourage production on the private plots of collective farmers. Although most of the reforms that took place before the 1980's were half-hearted, yet, some efforts towards radical reforms were made during the period of Nikita Khrushchev. Between 1957 and 1965, however, a radical change was made, when Khrushchev sponsored a shift from the pre-dominantly sectoral approach to a regional approach.

The reform abolished most industrial ministries and transferred planning and administrative authority to about 100 newly created regional economic councils. The regime hoped to end unsatisfactory coordination among the industrial ministries and ineffective regional planning. Khrushchev apparently hoped to end the traditional concentration of administrative power in Moscow, reduce departmentalism, and make more efficient use of specific economic resources of the various regions. Other changes under Khrushchev included extension of the usual five-year cycle to seven years, from 1959 to 1965, which was subsequently reduced to five years. When the regional system proved to be even less effective than the organisational structure it had replaced and the weaknesses of the ministerial system reappeared in a regional context, Khrushchev sponsored an additional series of minor changes. But in 1965, after when Leonid I. Brezhnev and Aleksei N. Kosygin[8] had replaced Khrushchev as head of party and head of government, respectively, the regime abolished the regional economic councils and reinstituted the industrial ministerial system, although with greater participation of regional bodies in the planning process, at least in theory.

Several reforms of the mid-and late 1960s represented efforts to decentralise decision-making processes, transferring some authority from central planning authorities and ministries to lower-level entities and enterprises. A series of minor reforms in 1965 modified the incentive system by shifting emphasis from gross output to sales and profits, a reform associated with the name of the eminent economist Evsei Liebermann. The reforms attempted to provide a more precise measure of labour and materials productivity. They also granted enterprise managers slightly greater latitude in making operating decisions by reducing the number of plan indicators assigned by higher authorities. In addition, the reforms introduced charges for interest and rent. Attention focused particularly on experiments with khozraschet[9], which, the late 1980s, required enterprises to cover many expenses from their own revenues, thereby encouraging efficient use of resources. In the agricultural sector, state farms and collective farms received greater latitude in organising their work activities and in establishing subsidiary industrial enterprises such as canning and food processing, timber and textile production, production of building materials, and actual construction projects.

During the seven-year plan, industrial progress was substantial, and production of consumer durables also grew. The national income increased 58 per cent, according to official statistics. Gross industrial production rose by 84 per cent, with producer goods up 96 per cent and consumer goods up 60 per cent. Growth rates slowed noticeably during the final years of the plan, however. Party leaders blamed Khrushchev's bungling efforts to reform the centralised planning system and his tendency to overemphasise programs in one economic sector (such as his favourite, the chemical industry) at the expense of other sectors. Agriculture's performance proved disappointing in the 1960s;

adverse weather in 1963 and 1965, as well as Khrushchev's interference and policy reversals, which confused and discouraged the peasants' work on their private plots, were contributing factors. Khrushchev's economic policies were a significant, although not sole, reason for his dismissal in October 1964.

After removing Khrushchev there developed a contest for power between Aleksei N. Kosygin, Nikolai V. Podgornyi[10], and Leonid I. Brezhnev and ultimately Brezhnev became the President[11] of Soviet Union in 1966.

The Eighth Five-Year Plan (1966-70), under the leadership of Khrushchev's successor as party head, Brezhnev, chalked up respectable growth statistics: national income increased 41 per cent and industrial production 50 per cent, according to government statistics. Growth in producer goods (51 per cent) outpaced that in consumer goods (49 per cent) only slightly, reflecting planners' growing concern about the plight of consumers. During the late 1960s, Brezhnev raised procurement prices for agricultural products, while holding constant retail prices for consumers. Agriculture thus became a net burden on the rest of the economy. Although production increased, the sector's performance remained unsatisfactory. The country had to import increasing amounts of grain from the West. But this growth was recorded in the Eighth Five-Year Plan was followed by two successive plan periods of negative growth in almost every sphere-a near complete situation of stagnation. The growth rate of labour force even, had declined during the Plan Period in the 1970s and 1980s. Although by the 1960s, the Soviet Union had shown the fastest growth in employment of all major industrial countries, yet, the Soviet growth rates in productivity of both labour and capital had been the lowest. In the 1970's, the labour force grew more slowly.

By the 1970s, however, prospects for extensive growth were limited. During the 1960s, the Soviet Union had shown the fastest growth in employment of all major industrial countries, and the Soviet Union together with Japan had boasted the most rapid growth of fixed capital stock. Yet Soviet growth rates in productivity of both labour and capital had been the lowest. In the 1970s, the labour force grew more slowly. Drawing on surplus rural labour was no longer possible, and the participation of women in the work force was already extensive. Furthermore, the natural resources required for extensive growth lay in areas increasingly difficult, and expensive, to reach. In the less-developed eastern regions of the country, development costs exceeded those in the European parts by 30 per cent to 100 per cent. In the more developed areas of the country, the slow rate at which fixed assets were retired was becoming a major problem; fixed assets remained in service on average twice as long as in Western economies, reducing overall productivity. Nevertheless, in the late 1970s some Western analysts estimated that the Soviet Union had the world's second largest economy, and its GNP continued to grow in the 1980s.

Serious imbalances characterised the economy, however, and the Soviet Union lagged behind most Western industrialised nations in the production of consumer goods and services. A stated goal of Soviet policy had always been to raise the material living standards of the people. Considerable progress had been made; according to Western estimates (less flattering than Soviet), from 1950 and 1980 real per capita consumption increased 300 per cent. The country's leaders had devoted the bulk of the available resources to heavy industry, however, particularly to "production of the means of production." Levels of consumption remained below those of major capitalist countries and most of the socialist countries of Eastern Europe. By the late 1970s, policy makers had recognised the need to improve productivity by emphasising quality factors, efficiency, and advanced technology and tapping "hidden production reserves" in the economy.

Although these past achievements were impressive, in the mid1980s Soviet leaders faced many problems. Since the 1970s, the growth rate had slowed substantially. Extensive economic development, based on vast inputs of materials and labour, was no longer possible; yet the productivity of Soviet assets remained low compared with other major industrialised countries. Product quality needed improvement. Soviet leaders faced a fundamental dilemma: the strong central controls that had traditionally guided economic development had failed to promote the creativity and productivity urgently needed in a highly developed, modern economy.

During the last years of Brezhnev's rule, the leadership remained relatively complacent about the system despite the economy's slowing growth rates. Increases in world oil and gold prices contributed to this attitude because they enhanced hard-currency purchasing power in the early 1970s and made it possible to import increasing amounts of Western technology.

In response to the stagnation of the late Brezhnev era, a new reform attempt began under Iurii V. Andropov, who succeeded Brezhnev as general secretary in 1982. On an experimental basis, the government gave a number of enterprises greater flexibility in the use of their profits either for investment purposes or for worker incentives. The experiment was formally expanded to include the entire industrial sector on January 1, 1987, although by that time its limited nature and modest prospects for success had been widely recognised. Concern about productivity characterised the Eleventh Five-Year Plan (1981-85). The targets were rather modest, and planners reduced even those after the first year of the period. Achievements remained below target. The plan period as a whole produced a modest growth rate of 3 to 4 per cent per year, according to official statistics. National income increased only 17 per cent. Total industrial output grew by 20 per cent, with the production of consumer goods increasing at a marginally higher rate than producer goods. Agricultural output registered a meagre 11.6 per cent gain.

In the meantime, however, Gorbachev, a leading proponent of both these reforms and more extensive changes, was making his influence felt, first as adviser on economic policy under Andropov and his successor, Konstantin U. Chernenko, and then as general secretary beginning in 1985. Some of Gorbachev's early initiatives involved mere reorganisation, similar to previous reform efforts. For example, from 1985 to 1987 seven industrial complexes-organs that were responsible directly to the Council of Ministers and that monitored groups of related activities-were established: agro-industrial, chemicals and timber, construction, fuel and energy, machine building, light industry, and metallurgy. The ministries remained reluctant to undertake more extensive reforms that would reduce their centralised power and give greater initiative to lower-level economic units. But the conviction was growing that the centralised planning mechanism needed major changes and that simply fine-tuning the economy with minor reforms would not be sufficient.

At Gorbachev's urging, on June 30, 1987, the Supreme Soviet approved a set of measures contained in the Basic Provisions for Fundamentally Reorganising Economic Management. The Supreme Soviet subsequently adopted an additional ten decrees, as well as the Law on State Enterprises (Associations). Taken as a whole, the actions of the Supreme Soviet signalled a substantial change in the system of centralised planning, with significant amounts of authority devolving upon middle and lower levels of the administrative hierarchy. Gorbachev named the economic restructuring programme *Perestroika.*

Perestroika, was the tool, which Gorbachev used to overcome the crisis that came about in the Soviet State. *Perestroika* he thought would serve the purpose of traversing the period of transition that was needed in all spheres of Soviet life. In order to come out of the stagnation that had taken place in the Soviet economy, what was required, Gorbachev thought was restructuring. Restructuring would have to take place in all spheres of life in the country. The country's economy, polity, military policy, foreign policy, science and technology everything needed restructuring, because according to him all these would have a tremendous effect on the country's internal policies as well. Gorbachev thought that a serious restructuring might show the way out of the crisis that the country was then facing.

Gorbachev considered *Perestroika* as a necessity arising from the conditions that prevailed in the USSR in the 1980s.[12] He wrote that the USSR had lost its momentum, which was reflected in economic failure, and economic stagnation. There was a slowing down of economic growth and the national income growth rates had also registered a considerable fall. As time went on material resources became difficult to gain and more expensive. On the other hand the extensive methods of fixed capital expansion resulted in an artificial shortage of manpower. So the inertia of extensive economic development was leading to an economic deadlock and inertia.'[13] All these had resulted in the degradation of ideological and moral values of the people of the Soviet Union. 'Decay began in public morals: the great feeling of solidarity with each other that has forged during the heroic times of the Revolution, the first five-year plans, the Great Patriotic War and post-war rehabilitation was weakening; alcoholism, drug addiction and crime were growing; and the penetration of mass culture alien to us...'[14]. *Perestroika*, however, meant a whole lot of things and it covered almost every part of the lives of the Soviet people. It meant overcoming the stagnation process, mass initiative, all-round intensification of the Soviet economy, a resolute shift to scientific methods, priority development of the social sphere aimed at ever better satisfaction, and finally elimination from the society of the distortion of socialist ethics. In a meeting with the media executives and the heads of ideological institutions and professionals at the Central Committee of the Communist party Of the Soviet Union in Moscow (May 7th) Gorbachev stated that the Party needed to consult these people if a policy having a scientific basis was to be formed[15]. Here in this meeting with the above members he emphasised on pluralism and said that such meetings were important to make *Perestroika* a success. This meeting was devoted to the forthcoming Nineteenth Party Conference and committed stalwarts of *Perestroika* were to be elected delegates to the Conference. Gorbachev once again reiterated his faith in the decisions taken in the 27th Party Congress. In 1988 he says that the coming years would be difficult for the country as this would be the boost period for *Perestroika*. Strategies that had been formulated so far had been transformed into real policies. Gorbachev wanted to realise the ideals of Lenin and restore his image through *Perestroika*. The humanist potential of *Perestroika* was to be brought out and the state and society would enjoy a healthy relationship. He writes: 'we cannot pursue *Perestroika*, which aims to upgrade socialism to meet to the parameters of Lenin's thinking in the interest of the people, by practicing a free-for-all. We aren't after all destroying the social system or changing the forms of ownership. The Soviets (elected governing councils) will stay. Listen to Lenin: Socialism should be built with the human material inherited from capitalism. We are affecting *Perestroika* with people born under socialism.'

Looking back into history Gorbachev writes that when the Soviet Union started building a new society, it was all alone in the capitalist world. Thus it needed quickly to overcome economic and technological backwardness. To do that the country had to drastically increase the proportion of savings in national income. The bulk of the money was allocated to the development of heavy industry, and defence industry. Gorbachev went back to Lenin when he wrote that Lenin had the rare ability to change his strategy as is suited to the condition prevalent at the period without wasting time.

For Gorbachev *Perestroika* was a revolution. It was an instrument of transition. It was a decisive acceleration of the socio-economic condition of the country at that moment. Gorbachev considered Perestroika as a sequel to the October Revolution of Lenin of 1917s–an extension and a development. Any revolution needs many other revolutions to carry its work ahead, thus in the same manner *Perestroika*, he thought would help in carrying forward the work of the October Revolution of 1917.

Two and a half years after the policy of Perestroika began; the problems and the course of *Perestroika* were being enthusiastically discussed by all sectors of Soviet society. The programme of *Perestroika* had already found expression in a series of state legislative acts approved by Parliament–the Supreme Soviet of the USSR. The 27th Congress adopted major resolutions, which were of tremendous influence for the future of USSR. According to Gorbachev it was a courageous Congress where shortcomings, errors and difficulties were openly talked about. All the Soviet people, the entire party, including the Central Committee and its Politburo, and the government were in the process of restructuring.

The new atmosphere that had been brought about as a result was called Glasnost. Democratisation of the atmosphere had taken place because of glasnost. The mass media had played a very important role in the process. Glasnost was aimed at strengthening the society. The intelligentsia had also supported the restructuring. Congresses of creative unions of film-makers, writers, artists, composers, architects, theatrical figures and journalists had been held and all the Congresses sincerely supported *Perestroika*.

But the question still arises as to where from Gorbachev got the idea of *Perestroika*. Many scholars say that the concept had a western origin. The discussions in the American Congress on Peace, SIPRI Report* and West European and Canadian Studies of Soviet Academy influenced him. However, in the 26th Party Congress of the CPSU, the Party criticised the fact that it was unable to transit from extensive to intensive economy. Ten years later in the Tula Speech, Brezhnev said that there should be defensive defence in terms of Soviet military strategy. The Novosibirsk Report suggested that there should be an economic reform in the agricultural sector. Balekov, who was the head of the Soviet Space Centre, suggested that Space science needed to be reoriented. It is said that nobody in the Western world, as late as 1989, expected that the Soviet Union would collapse. Brzezinski, in an interview, said that perestroika had nothing to do with America's War on Independence, and he least expected that the Soviet Union would become a democratic country.

The Economic Policy

The reforms attempted to decentralise distribution. The law enabled enterprises to deal with the suppliers of their choice, either producers or wholesale outlets. Rationing would continue for only the scarcest producer goods, less than 4 per cent of total industrial output in 1988. For the remainder, producers would be free to sell directly to users. Finally, the law permitted some enterprises to engage in foreign trade directly, on their own account, and to retain some of the foreign currency gains.

According to official Soviet sources, primary expenditures in the 1985 budget were grants for economic purposes (56 per cent of the budget); funds for social and cultural services (32.5 per cent); defence spending (4.9 per cent); and administrative costs (0.8 per cent). A small surplus remained (typical of Soviet budgets, according to published data). Western analysts considered these statistics unreliable; most Western observers believed the defence budget's share was far greater than official figures suggested. Furthermore, Soviet definitions of various economic measurements differed markedly from Western concepts (for example, the use of net material product to measure output).

Over the years, this centralised system had produced prices with little relationship either to the real costs of the products or to their price on the world market. For several decades, the government kept the price of basic goods, such as essential foods, housing, and transportation, low, which many consider to have been artificially kept so, regardless of actual production costs. As agricultural costs had increased, for example, subsidies to the agricultural sector had grown, but retail prices remained stable. Only prices for luxury goods had risen, particularly during the price overhauls of 1965 and 1982.

The Twelfth Five-Year Plan, 1986-90

When Gorbachev attained power in 1985, most Western analysts were convinced that Soviet economic performance would not improve significantly during the remainder of the 1980s. "Intensification" alone seemed unlikely to yield important immediate results. Gorbachev tackled the country's economic problems energetically, however, declaring that the economy had entered a "pre-crisis" stage. The leadership and the press acknowledged shortcomings in the economy with a new frankness.

Restating the aims of earlier intensification efforts, the Basic Directions for the Economic and Social Development of the USSR for 1986-1990 and for the Period to the Year 2000 declared the principal tasks of the five-year plan period to be "to enhance the pace and efficiency of economic development by accelerating scientific and technical progress, retooling and adapting production, intensively using existing production potential, and improving the managerial system and accounting mechanism, and, on this basis, to further raise the standard of living of the Soviet people." A major part of the planned increase in output for the 1986-90 periods was to result from the introduction of new machinery to replace unskilled labour. New, advanced technologies, such as microprocessors, robots, and various computers, would automate and mechanise production. Obsolete equipment was to be retired at an accelerated rate. Industrial operations requiring high energy inputs would be located close to energy sources, and increasing numbers of workplaces would be in regions with the requisite manpower resources. Economic development of Siberia and the Soviet Far East would continue to receive special attention.

Gorbachev tackled the problem of laxness in the workplace and low worker productivity (or, as he phrased it, the "human factor") with great vigour. This attention to individual productivity and discipline resulted in the demotion or dismissal of influential older officials who had proved to be corrupt or inefficient. Gorbachev called for improved motivation among rank-and-file workers and launched a vigorous antialcohol campaign (also a priority under Andropov).

At the Central Committee plenum in January 1987, Gorbachev demanded a fundamental reassessment of the role of the government in Soviet society. His economic reform program was sweeping, encompassing an array of changes. For example, it created a new finance system through which factories would obtain loans at interest, and it provided for the competitive election of managers. These changes proceeded from Gorbachev's conviction that a major weakness in the economy was the extreme centralisation of economic decision making, inappropriate under modern conditions. According to Abel Aganbegian[16], an eminent Soviet economist and the principal scholarly spokesman for many of Gorbachev's policies, the Soviet Union was facing a critical decision: "Either we implement radical reform in management and free driving forces, or we follow an evolutionary line of slow evolution and gradual improvement. If we follow the second direction, we will not achieve our goals." The country was entering "a truly new period of restructuring, a period of cardinal breakthroughs,"[17] he said, at the same time stressing the leadership's continuing commitment to socialism.

In one of his most controversial policy decisions, Gorbachev moved to encourage private economic activities and cooperative ventures. The action had clear limits, however. It established a progressive tax on profits, and regulations limited participation mainly to students, retired persons, and housewives. Full-time workers could devote only their leisure hours to private activities. Cooperatives that involved at least three people could engage in a broad range of consumer-oriented activities: using private automobiles as taxis, opening private restaurants, offering private medical care, repairing automobiles or appliances, binding books, and tailoring. In addition, the reform encouraged state enterprises to contract with private individuals for certain services. Other regulations gave official approval to the activities of profit-oriented contract brigades. These brigades consisted of groups of workers in an enterprise or collective farm who joined together to make an internal contract with management for performance of specific tasks, receiving compensation in a lump sum that the brigade itself distributed as it saw fit. Additional decrees specified types of activities that remained illegal (those involving "unearned income") and established strict penalties for violators. The new regulations legitimised major portions of the second economy and permitted their expansion. No doubt authorities hoped that the consuming public would reap immediate, tangible benefits from the changes. Authorities also expected these policies to encourage individuals who were still operating illegally to abide by the new, more lenient regulations.

In keeping with Gorbachev's ambitious reform policies, the specific targets of the Twelfth Five-Year Plan (1986-90) were challenging. The targets posited an average growth rate in national income of about 4 per cent yearly. To reach this goal, increases in labour productivity were to average 4 per cent annually, a rate that had not been sustained on a regular basis since the early 1970s. The ratio of expenditure on material inputs and energy to national income was to decrease by 4 to 5 per cent in the plan period. Similar savings were projected for other aspects of the economy.

The plan stressed technical progress. Machine-building output was to increase by 40 to 45 per cent during the five-year period. Those sectors involved in high technology were to grow faster than industry as a whole. The production of computers, for example, was to increase 2.4 times during the plan period. Growth in production of primary energy would accelerate during the period, averaging 3.6 per cent per year, compared with 2.6 per cent actual growth per year for 1981-85. The plan called for major growth in nuclear power capacity. (The Chernobyl accident[18] of 1986 did not alter these plans.)

Capital investment was to grow by 23.6 per cent, whereas under the Eleventh Five-Year Plan the growth rate had been only 15.4 per cent. Roughly half of the funds would be used for the retooling necessary for intensification. The previous plan had earmarked 38 per cent for this purpose. Agriculture would receive large investments as well.

The plan called for a relatively modest improvement in the standard of living. The share of total investment in services was to rise only slightly, although the proportion of the labour force employed in services would continue to grow.

The regime also outlined very ambitious guidelines for the fifteen-year period beginning in 1986. The guidelines called for a 5 per cent yearly growth in national income; national income was projected to double by the year 2000. Labour productivity would grow by 6.5 to 7.4 per cent per year during the 1990s. Projected modernisation of the workplace would release 20 million people from unskilled work by the year 2000. Plans called for increasingly efficient use of fuels, energy, raw materials, metal, and other materials. The guidelines singled out the provision of "practically every Soviet family" with separate housing by the beginning of the twenty-first century as a special, high-priority task.

Results of the first year of the Twelfth Five-Year Plan, 1986, were encouraging in many respects. The industrial growth rate was below targeting but still respectable at just above 3 per cent. Agriculture made a good showing. During 1987, however, GNP grew by less than 1 per cent, according to Western calculations, and industrial production grew a mere 1.5 per cent. Some problems were the result of harsh weather and traditional supply bottlenecks. In addition, improvements in quality called for by Gorbachev proved difficult to realise; in 1987, when the government introduced a new inspection system for output at a number of industrial enterprises, rejection rates were high, especially for machinery.

Many of Gorbachev's reforms that immediately affected the ordinary working person-such as demands for harder work, more rigid quality controls, better discipline. As the Nineteenth Party Conference of 1988 demonstrated, party leaders continued to debate the pace and the degree of change. Uncertainty about the extent and permanence of reform was bound to create some disarray within the economy, at least for the short term. Western analysts did not expect Gorbachev's entire program to succeed, particularly given the lacklustre performance of the economy during the second year of the Twelfth Five-Year Plan. The meagre results of past reform attempts offered few grounds for optimism. But most observers believed that at least a portion of the reforms would be effective. The result was almost certain to benefit the economy.

When Gorbachev delivered his report on the CPSU's economic policy on June 12, 1985, he noted that growth in exports, particularly machinery and equipment, was slow because the poor quality of Soviet goods prohibited them from being competitive on the world market. In the next three years, Gorbachev introduced many changes that would enable the foreign trade complex to better support his economic policy of acceleration. By May 1988, the structure of the Soviet foreign trade complex had been changed, and operations had been dramatically overhauled.

The price reform called for by the Twenty-Seventh Party Congress was an important step in improving Soviet international economic involvement. Soviet officials admitted that pricing was "economically unsubstantiated" and "unrealistic." They understood that although fully convertible rouble would not be possible for some time, prices that more accurately reflected production costs, supply and demand, and world market prices were essential for developing a convertible currency. The nonconvertible rouble and the Soviet pricing system discouraged Western businessmen who could not accurately project production costs nor easily convert their rouble profits.

The new joint venture law, passed on January 13, 1987, opened up the Soviet economy to foreign participation, particularly in manufacturing. It was believed that the experience gained in such ventures would facilitate integration into the world economy. Specifically, through upgraded production processes, the Soviet Union could export more competitive manufactured goods and decrease its dependency on energy and raw materials to earn hard currency.

In August 1987, the Soviet Union formally requested observer status in the General Agreement on Tariffs and Trade[19]. The Soviet Union also expressed its desire to join other international economic organisations and establish contacts with other regional groups. A major step in this direction occurred in 1988 when the Soviet Union signed a normalisation agreement with the EEC. The Soviet government, however, professed no interest in joining the World Bank or the International Monetary Fund. Although Soviet officials claimed that the international monetary system “”was not managed properly,”” it is more likely that IMF and World Bank regulations were the obstacles: both institutions required that members’ currencies be freely convertible and that members provide accurate information concerning gold sales and economic performance.

Gorbachev transformed the role of foreign trade in the Soviet economy. Whereas imports previously were regarded exclusively as a vehicle to compensate for difficulties in the short term, Soviet economists under Gorbachev declared that imports should be regarded as alternatives to domestic investment and that exports should serve to gauge the technical level of domestic production. Foreign economic ties were to support growth in production beyond the capacities of the domestic economy. The Soviet Union could thus take a place in the world market that was commensurate with its scientific and technical progress and political weight.

Gorbachev writes: 'I would say that the concept of economic reform, which we submitted to the June Plenary Meeting, is of an all-embracing, comprehensive character. It provides for fundamental changes in every area, including the transfer of enterprises to complete cost accounting, a radical transformation of the centralised management of the economy, fundamental changes in the economy, fundamental changes in planning, a reform of the price formation system and of financial and crediting mechanism, and the restructuring of foreign economic ties'[20].

The immediate concern of *Perestroika* was the structural reorganisation of the economy, in reconstruction of its material base, in new technologies, in investment policy changes, and in high standards in management. Along with all these the primary concern remained the economy, to tightening up and disciplining and also to raise the level of organisation and responsibility. And certainly it was not by chance that after the April Plenary Meeting the first move that the new leadership of the Soviet Union made was to discuss these matters at an important conference of the CPSU Central Committee in June 1985. During this year substantial comprehensive programmes were worked out in the sphere of science and technology and engineering.

Gorbachev thought that restructuring should start with enterprises and amalgamations–the main link in the economic system. Reforming the upper management without reforming the lower had not yielded any results whatsoever. 'We are contemplating democratising planning. This means that plan making–not formal but actual–will begin within enterprises and work collectives. We envisage broadening openness at all stages of planning, and introducing wide discussion of state and regional, social, economic, scientific, technological and ecological problems.' As distinct from the previous practice, the central bodies decided to control the enterprises in a limited number of areas–in the fulfilment of state orders, profits, labour productivity and general indicators of scientific and technological progress and the social sphere. The fulfilment by enterprises of contract obligations and state orders for the more important products, types of work and services became a major criterion of the activities of enterprises. The composition and volume of state orders would gradually be reduced with the saturation of the market in favour of the growing direct ties between the manufacturers and consumers. Perestroika, Gorbachev thought would diminish party control on the economy. In a June 1987 address, Gorbachev called for the dismantling of the state planning commission (Gosplan), central ministries, thus freeing factory managers from the old restrictions and encouraging and challenging local initiative. Each enterprise would develop its own five-year plan would negotiate the best prices for its raw materials and seek the most profitable markets for its finished products[21].

The system of material and technical supplies would undergo radical changes. The emphasis would be on transition from forming funds to centralised distribution of resources, to wholesale trade.

By looking at the equipments the country had, it was found that they fell short of the world standard and Gorbachev thought that the country would do better' to pass through the pains of developing new equipment now and then, through advances in machine building, make a breakthrough to the newest technology.

Science and Technology

Gorbachev, however, mentioned that this period was not all of darkness with considerable highs being made in the field of science, and technology.

Soviet scholars identified the causes of the lag to the global factors and internal factors. Among the global factors, Trapeznikov said that in the development of science, there were many years of the systemic destruction of minds and the lack of comprehension of the importance of intellectual labour and the role of science, which led to the decrease of the overall intellectual potential of the country. Naturally, this had led to a drain in significant areas of solid state physics and nuclear physics, applied mathematics, biotechnology and molecular biology, and chemistry, a shortage of which, according to A.Karavayev, a specialist in Science and Technical Progress Department of the Administration of Affairs of the USSR Council of Ministers, adversely affected capabilities in the long run. The Soviet scientists had not done well as there was potential partly because of the non-availability of a free atmosphere to interact with people across cultures and frontiers.

The internal situation in the Soviet Union prior to *Perestroika* showed the negative impact of Stalinism and stagnation which denigrated participation of the scientists in decision making on directions of science and policy, and wrong priorities were determined, which caused accumulation of social problems to such an extent that the Director of the Academy of Sciences of the USSR, G.I.Marchuk, said in an interview: "The average level of the remuneration of the labour of scientists during the 20 years prior to the start of the radical economic reform slipped from first place among the sectors of the national economy to sixth or seventh place."

The impact of Stalinism was all pervading. Since the response of Stalin to containment was authoritarian, its impact on science and technology led to stifling of openness and determination of wrong priorities.

Stalin himself was responsible for quasi-science in linguistics. The command-administrative system in the Academy of Sciences of the USSR resulted in the false honorific titles at the top of the ladder and putting the lid on the talent of the young in the pyramid. The USSR had a very large corps of scientific personnel. There was a scientific bureaucracy that developed which was self-perpetuating and failed to decide on the direction of scientific strategy. According to 1986 statistical data, the total number of people working at scientific organisations of the country was 4,546,000. Among them there were 803, 000 scientific personnel i.e. 17 per cent. The actual number of scientists and specialists, who were real creators of something new, was significantly less than the impression one gets from statistics. Of the 83 per cent of the personnel Shulgina has examined, 57 per cent were poorly qualified in science, while the remainder were of low skill. Some 2.7 million people were engaged in bureaucratic management work in science. This was indicated by the fact that the Soviet science developed the most in the military related areas. The scientific wonders, owing to secrecy, could not be utilised sector. Stalin, who was suspicious of scientists who had their own opinions, employed scientists during the Great Patriotic War for the satisfaction of the need to develop nuclear weapons.

The net result of Stalinism and stagnation was to play the game of arms race which turned out to be a zero-sum game. Under *Perestroika*, reform of Soviet science and technology was emphasised. The areas identified for concentration were micro-electronics, bio-technology and non-ferrous metallurgy. At the April meeting of the Central Committee that decided on acceleration, the machine-tool industry as an input into acceleration was identified. In this area, according to the 27th Congress programme the fundamental scientific and technical ideas were materialised, where new implements of labour and machine systems that determine progress in other branches of the national economy were developed. The technical modernisation that has to take place in this was related to computers. In this area the following have been identified.

In order to bring about the change, the Soviets have provided for laws to establish international contacts; intellectual property rights to check piracy have been emphasised along with a democratised USSR Academy of Sciences, and they have introduced cost accounting, increased resources and reform management of science and technology. New economic organisations were set up to integrate science and production, which aimed at the acceleration of the development and introduction of fundamentally new types of equipment and technology.

The problems connected with restructuring of science and technology during the 1980s are three-fold. The literature showed the lack of environment of innovation, obstruction by bureaucracy and operational difficulties in the civilian sectors, and foreign-exchange shortage. In the 1980s, the decline of raw materials like oil halved "our foreign exchange revenues".

The above phenomena affected security in complex ways and in many aspects. Science and technology was closely related to the problem of restructuring of the economy from the security angle. In the forty-second session of the U.N. Gorbachev had also mentioned the establishment of a world space organisation, which would work closely as an autonomous part of its system and was also in favour of increasing the role of the International Atomic Energy Agency. Gorbachev had in the same report, spoken of the militarisation of the Soviet economy. It is well known that the military sector of science and technology worked efficiently in the Soviet Union and that this aspect of the Soviet economy was relatively crisis free.

Social Policy

In the social sphere too, Gorbachev and his Perestroika had many things to offer, which he believed would lead to the betterment for the people of USSR. He writes, 'We proceed from the assumption that only the strong social policy proclaimed by the 27th Congress of the CPSU can ensure success for *Perestroika*. The standard of living should be raised and the housing situation eased; more foodstuffs should be produced and the quality of commodities improved; public health services should be accomplished, and many other social problems should be resolved'[22]. According to Gorbachev the country has achieved a lot in the sphere of education and now it wanted to adopt programmes that would lead to radical transformation of higher and secondary schools. Measures to improve the country's public health were also under consideration. The 27th Congress of the

CPSU had actually adopted measures to address the problem arising due to the lack of social justice.

Consolidating in the Soviet people a sense of responsibility for the country's destiny was considered as one of the main tasks of restructuring, by Gorbachev. There was certain alienation, caused by weakened ties between state and economic bodies, work collectives and rank and file workers, and by the underestimation of their role in the development of socialist society, which had a disturbing effect.

The human factor remained, in the broadest sense, the main priority. The country, through *Perestroika*, had been working for a balance between two aspects–the economy and the social sphere. The social sphere, he realised, must not be built in such a way that the base is eroded, since then the very possibility for dynamic social development is undermined. Gorbachev admitted that the moral aspect is the most important, as people wanted to see changes in attitudes on the part of the plant manager, shop superintendent and foreman, i.e. practically in all spheres of life.

It was realised that a major psychological change had to be brought about in the country. So a primary task of *Perestroika* was to be the awakening of the masses. 'Today our main job is to lift the individual spiritually, respecting his inner world and giving him moral strength.'Gorbachev wrote that he needed broad democratisation of all aspects of society and admit that many of the country's problems could be dealt away with had the country had the democratic processes evolved normally in the country. It was through *Perestroika* that democracy and also socialism could come about in the country. Gorbachev followed Lenin when he wrote that there was essentially no contradiction between the terms socialism and democracy as through democratic freedoms the working masses come to power. Fundamentals of Radical Restructuring of Economic Management which was adopted in the June 1987 Plenary Meeting of the CPSU

Central Committee was perhaps the most radical of the reforms after the New Economic Policy of 1921 started by Lenin. This restructuring would help in bringing about consciousness and disciplined citizens.

Laws on the school reform, individual labour, on combating illicit incomes, alcoholism and drug addiction; laws to improve public health and environmental protection and to enhance care for mothers and children were issued.

Gorbachev paid special attention to consolidating the guarantees of the rights and freedoms of the Soviet people. Decrees of the Presidium of the USSR Supreme Soviet making suppression of criticism punishable by law, and establish a procedure for compensation for damage caused to citizens by unlawful actions by government and public bodies and officials.

Political and Administrative Policy and Trade Union

Political alienation became one of the most important characteristic features in the Soviet Union during the pre-Gorbachev period. When the first socialist state was formed in 1917 in U.S.S.R, Lenin, it is said, had given up the participatory model of democracy. Neil Harding writes that 'the emphasis in Lenin's New Economic Policy (NEP) on the importance of the Party, the blurring of the distinction between worker and citizen, and the principle of from each according to his capacity and to each according to his work, formulated during 1918-20 undermined the participatory model of State and Government.'[23] Lenin became extremely conscious of the increase of power of the bureaucracy. He realised that in order to bring about democracy it was important to fight the bureaucracy and this would finally enable the Soviet Union to transit from the dictatorship of the proletariat to self-rule. Lenin was apprehensive that if the bureaucracy affected the Soviet institutions it was bound to have an effect on the Party as well, as the upper ranks of the Party and the Soviet institutions were the same. Thus Lenin felt that it was absolutely necessary to not only fight the bureaucracy, but also to try and incorporate as many new and young people in the system as was possible. This same stand was reiterated by Gorbachev so many years later in his 27th Congress of the CPSU. Milovan Djilas wrote that everything happened in a different way in the Soviet Union as against what was expected, by the people like Marx, Engels, Lenin or Trotsky and others. In 1936 Stalin had declared that a classless society was already in place in the Soviet Union, and that the exploiting class no longer existed. But unfortunately, Djilas wrote that the bureaucracy, particularly, the political bureaucracy had become the 'new class' by then, playing the role of a new exploiting class.[24] Djilas goes on to write that Stalin was the future creator of the ruling class, and that 'the new ruling class had been gradually developing from this narrow stratum of revolutionaries."[25] The new class had its origin in the proletariat and as it grew the Party became weaker. Trotsky too considered the bureaucracy as the new privileged strata who continued to deprive the working class from its rights. Stalinism according to him was the ideology of the new privileged class. Trotsky believed that only a revolution that can overthrow the dictatorship of the bureaucracy and establish democracy would be in a position to salvage the Soviet Union from the low it had reached.[26]

After Stalin's death at the Twentieth Congress of the CPSU, Khrushchev made his famous speech on the cult of personality, giving a detailed account of Stalin's crimes. As a result of this Congress various attempts were made towards decentralisation. There were also attempts to take up economic reforms. The Brezhnev interlude was described by Gorbachev as bureaucratism when the word stagnation was used.

Gorbachev's glasnost had come into being as an attempt to surmount the political crisis. Burlatsky shows that because of Glasnost a group of writers could actually reverse the plan of the Party's Central Committee to divert rivers in Siberia.[27] During the 1970s there was a constant pessimism all over the country and unfortunately no respite from it was imminent[28]. It was taken for granted that the country would pass into gradual decay. Mikhail Gorbachev was to a great extent able to change the mood of the population. During Brezhnev's period the reformist faction of the ruling circles had practically no serious backing. The rehabilitation of the victims of terror in 1954-56, the debunking of Stalin's cult of personality, the loosening of state control over cultural life and the vital extension of individual rights in that period were a very great historical achievement, but it should be remembered that all of these radical measures also played a major role in the struggle between factions of apparatus interests by weakening the position of one faction and structure and promoting the role of the others. Khrushchev's early success was connected with the unanimous desire of the ruling circles to put an end to the omnipotence and irresponsibility of the repressive organs at that time, and to place the reorganised state security service under party control.

The most important peculiarity of the Brezhnev period consisted in the ability of the leadership of that time to maintain a stable compromise between factions in the apparatus while simultaneously raising people's standard of living.

If Khrushchev attempted to blend political reforms with the maintenance of the traditional principles of economic management then, Brezhnev, at first chose to do directly the opposite. Political stability had to be combined with economic reform, the intension of which was to broaden the rights of the intermediate link of the economic apparatus and to form layer of Soviet managers. By the beginning of the 1980s opinion had formed among the most varied strata of the Soviet society that Brezhnevism had exhausted itself. The new generation, which had grown up during the years of 'stability', was more educated and demanding. An inconsistent modernisation of the way of life had generated new demands and, in the end, a new dissatisfaction. People felt themselves more independent and demanded respect for their civil and human dignity.

A paradoxical situation had arisen. On the one hand, society was fully ripe for change, but on the other hand, there was no serious movement of any kind of reform. Compared with the 1960s, when the human rights movement was born, a significant evolution had taken place by the end of the Brezhnev period. After the defeat of the 'Prague Spring', a general move to the right could be discerned in this milieu. By the end of the 1970s the dissident movement was in serious crisis. A significant section of activists had left the country, many had been arrested, and some had dropped out of public activity. The most important cause of the crisis, however, was not repression but the absence of a political perspective. The characteristic features of the 1979-82 periods were, on the one hand, a strengthening of reformist tendencies within the establishment and, on the other, the emergence of a new socialist opposition. Unofficial left groups existed among the youth back in the 1950s, but under 'mature Brezhnevism', their number was insignificant. People who had suffered for such activity during the 1950's and 1960's have either given up their political struggle or joined the dissidents, losing their socialist ideology in the process. Because of the crisis in the dissident movement and the weakness of the Left, official reformism remained the only real alternative to Brezhnevism.

Bureaucracy, to many have remained one of the sore points with that of socialism in any country[29], Moreover, the Gorbachev leadership had no models or blueprints to follow. Students of democracy from its genesis to its being hijacked into devolution of participation in Western capitalist countries know that pluralist institutionalism has not resolved the problem of alienation in that society. In the USSR social alienation could only be removed through reformation of the economic as well as the political sphere. Reformation according to him could only be brought about through participation, which in turn could be brought about by Perestroika and Glasnost. The Soviet political system would have to combine the skills of all strata of people for fighting bureacratism in the party and the Soviets.

Both Robert Rozhdestvensky[30] and Vladimir Mytarev[31] had mentioned in an interview that the situation in USSR was actually that bad that it ultimately led to the decision to take up *Perestroika.* However, none of them elaborated on as to how bad the situation really was that prompted *Perestroika* to be taken up.

A whole series of important legislative acts had already been adopted in the course of *Perestroika.* They included the law on the State enterprise Association, laws on changing the system of running the agro-industrial complex.

Gorbachev considered it to be especially important to enhance the role of the courts as an elective body very close to the population, to guarantee the independence of the judges, and to observe most strictly democratic principles in legal proceedings, objectiveness, contested election and openness. He also realised that another task of the soviets would be restoring their lost prestige. The Soviets had been formed just after the October Revolution of 1917 and he admitted that without the Soviets it would not have been possible for Lenin and his people to win the Civil war.

In case of the trade unions Gorbachev wrote that in conditions of *Perestroika* the trade unions should give 'stronger social orientation to economic decisions, offsetting technocratic encroachments which had become widespread in the economy in the last few years.'[32] Gorbachev had also paid attention to the conditions of the youth and women of the society. The January Plenary Meeting addressed the issue of raising women to important administrative posts and to put an end to any form of discrimination.

Media

Gorbachev had time and again reiterated his faith in carrying out *Perestroika* and Glasnost in the USSR. The media too, he remarked had a role to play in the process. It could itself reform and also help in propagating the principles of *Perestroika.*[33] *Perestroika* was to be conducted in society in the form of debates, comprehension and realisation of this process. It would also in the process, enable to overcome alienation 'which deplorably takes place under socialism when it is deformed by authoritative bureaucratic deformations'. Glasnost had led to unprecedented outpouring of information in the country. People at home and abroad heard about 'alcoholism, absenteeism in the workplace, juvenile delinquency, corruption within party and government ranks, and unrest among the country's many nationalities.'[34] The media had become 'an instrument of change and a prime political battleground'[35] with Gorbachev's Perestroika and Glasnost. After 1985 the press started enjoying certain amount of liberty, and it was allowed to discuss a whole range of issues and thereby form a strong public opinion. However, the old apparatchik kept on strangulating the press and threatening it with dire consequences whenever any form of press release did not suit their convenience. In the summer of 1988, the author writes, nationalist movements in the Baltic Republics of Lithuania, Estonia, and Latvia were practically born in the local television discussion shows. So was the case also in Georgia, Armenia, Azerbaijan, and elsewhere. There were certain nationalities in the Soviet Union which had grown more than the others, resulting in rising demand for cultural identity, and turning more and more people against the Party. The Moscow Media Vremya had given tendentious widespread coverage of how violently the nationalist movements were put down by the Soviet military in Georgia, Azerbaijan, Latvia or Lithuania.

Vzglyad, a weekly magazine show, portrayed in the eve of the March 1990 elections as to why one liked the Communist Party and why one did not. They used hard-hitting reporting on problems that Soviet propaganda used to relegate to the capitalist West. It was the first to report on AIDS in the Soviet Union revealing that there were eighty-one cases of children with the virus in the provincial cities of Elista and Volgograd. It also pointed its figures at the hospitals. Even when the Soviet troops were in Afghanistan,

Vzglyad, showed a powerful footage on the carnage being carried out in the country. It continued to attack the military on its various policies. It also was the first to broadcast the proposal that Lenin's mausoleum is removed from the Red Square and he is given a normal burial beside his mother. Although Gorbachev had reservations regarding many of the steps being taken by the Soviet media, yet, he did not show any interest in strangulating the media because of the role it was playing to the extent that it also allowed the *Fifth Wheel* editor, Bella Kurkova to stand for elections.

Gorbachev actually wanted to bring in more democracy in the all levels of government in the country. In the 27th CPSU of the Party he called for Democratisation of the society and promotion of the 'peoples socialist self-government'. He took up steps to heighten the activities of the Soviets, the trade unions, the komsomol, the work collectives, and the peoples control bodies. Gorbachev argued that the Soviets of the Peoples Deputies had stood the test of time, displaying their viability and vast potentialities in securing full power for the people in uniting and mobilising the masses. Gorbachev appealed to the Congress delegates of the local soviets that they can serve as the most effective means of mobilising the masses for the effort to accelerate the country's socio-economic development. The autonomy and activity of these local government bodies was worked out in the CPSU Central Committee. 'Their goal is to make each Soviet a complete and responsible master in all things concerning the satisfaction of people's everyday needs and requirements; in using the allocated funds, the local potentialities and reserves; in co-ordinating and supervising the work of all organisations involved in servicing the population'[36]. He felt that the government should involve all forms of direct democracy by the masses in the 'elaboration, adoption, and execution of governmental and other decisions'. The Soviet Constitution had given considerable importance to nation-wide discussions and referendums and Gorbachev expressed that channels for the development of direct democracy would be enhanced in the country through 'citizen' meetings, constituent mandates, letters from the people, the press, radio, TV, and all other meetings through which public opinion could be formed. Moreover new institutions like Congress of People's Deputies were formed. This period saw the formation of directly elected Presidency, new electoral laws were passed, and a Party conference on nationalities was formed. The Constitution too was amended to end the CPSU's monopoly of power.

Foreign and Military Policy

Gorbachev believed in the dictionary meaning of the word interdependence as to mutual dependence. Engels had in a number of occasions mentioned that we are in some way or the other dependent on every other in the Universe

Any discussion on the military policy of any country undoubtedly brings into its fold discussions on a number of other factors, especially foreign policy. Mertes, the State Minister at Bonn Foreign Office, once said that the Soviet Union wanted to achieve super-security through spreading insecurity among its neighbours. Thus Mertes writes that the Soviet Union's policy in Europe was to achieve Euro-strategic superiority through the hegemonial weapon, SS20.[37] Mertes's point had been supported by the Pentagon Study of the Soviet military power and also by the Rand Commission Report published thereafter. They even went a step further in assessing that the aim of the Soviet Union would be to see that the NATO countries are occupied and that the European countries could be used by Soviet Union in order to enable itself to come out of the its economic problems, if any. The Soviet Union would in this way, according to them, be able to spread its superiority over the other nations in Europe and also in a way neutralise the power of United States and to spread socialism in other parts of the world. Curtis Keeble, the British Diplomat to the Soviet Union had considered the designs of Soviet Union as imperial. But Gorbachev in his Speech at the French National Assembly in 1985 said that the world was heading towards a situation where it could not do away with the fact that all the countries of the world are mutually dependent on one another. He said "this is an indispensable precondition for world economic development, of scientific and technological progress, of accelerating information exchange, conveyance of passengers and commodities overland and via outer space."[38] The Soviet Union had proposed a reduction in the arms forces and armaments of both sides in Central Europe. The Soviet Union, Gorbachev said was ready to agree on a total ban on strike space weapons by both sides and 50 per cent reduction in nuclear weapons which had each others territories within their striking range. Gorbachev felt that this is a positive addition to the outcome of the Geneva Talks where both parties had decided to stop arms race.

About the intermediate-range nuclear weapons in Europe, Gorbachev promised to come to a positive conclusion regarding that. But at the same time he said that the Soviet Union was aware of the nuclear capabilities of the various European nations and that it cannot let it take its own path also. Although the Soviet Union would like to discuss the nuclear capabilities of countries like France, Britain, yet, it would not hesitate to take into account its security dimensions also. Not only this, the Soviet Union had also deployed 243 combat-ready SS20 missiles in Europe, however, any further deployment made after June 1984 had been removed by the country. The Soviet Union had also dismantled the powerful SS-5 missiles and was in the process of dismantling SS-4 missiles as well from the scene. The above steps taken by the Soviet Union reiterated the country's position in the mid-1985 that there cannot be any victor in a nuclear war. Gorbachev requested the European countries to pool in their efforts so that steps towards dismantling chemical weapons could also be made and then dependable security on the basis of Helsinki could be made. Soviet Union at that point of time also looked up at establishing economic and business ties with the COMECON and the EEC.

Gorbachev supported the proposal put forward by the East German and The Czechoslovak Governments to form a nuclear weapons free corridor in Central Europe but maintained that this effort put forward by these two countries should also be reiterated by the NATO side of the corridor[39]. Regarding the question of the German unification, Gorbachev said that the principles of the Helsinki Accord would be respected and the Soviet Union would stand by whatever had been discussed in the Accord.

The Soviet Union has a long history of association with the Asian countries as well. The Soviet Union had entered the political scenario of Asia as early as the 1937. It helped China in its war against Japan. The Soviet Union, according to Gorbachev would move towards complete normalisation of relations with China. The victory of the Soviet Union against the Japanese was recognised by countries like Mongolia and North Korea. The Soviet Union also showed its concern over the growing militarisation of the southern part of the Korean peninsula. He said that "the Soviet Union had voiced resolute support for the efforts of the Democratic People's Republic Of Korea towards peaceful reunification of the country and its proposal for the establishment of a nuclear-free zone in the whole of the Korean peninsula.[40] The contemporary period was also characterised by the emergence of a number of newly independent countries in Asia as well as in Africa. U.S.S.R. did recognise the fact that these countries which emerged from colonial rule were heterogeneous by nature. The 27th Congress of the CPSU mentioned that in the political sphere the Soviet Union would pursue a policy of political cooperation, non-interference and political solutions. The Congress also wanted to eliminate military solution to any problem in the Asian countries. Gorbachev had opposed nuclear and chemical weapons proliferation in the region and considered it to be vital for the Soviet Union also.

In a joint News conference held in New Delhi with the Indian Prime Minister Rajiv Gandhi, Gorbachev explained that proposal that would solve the problems in Afghanistan and bring about enduring peace in the continent would be given much importance. The Soviet Union according to President Gorbachev would take an active stand in pursuing a political settlement and called on everyone who really had anything to do with Afghanistan to take part in it and find out a political solution to it. The Soviet Union had already ordered six regiments of its troops to pull out from Afghanistan and it did not show any intention in carrying out its military offensive against the country for long. This was a change in the country's position regarding its relationship with Afghanistan. Soviet Union showed its desire to form a security zone in the Indian Ocean that would also include Pakistan, as the President considered it to be feasible to have a security zone in the Indian Ocean with Pakistan in it.

In the 27th Party Congress of the CPSU, Gorbachev also mentioned his desire to show its solidarity with all the newly liberated nations of the world, the non-aligned nations, non-communist movements and even religious organisation who were against war.

The military policy of the Soviet Union also saw a remarkable change during the time of Gorbachev. But some changes were being made in the military policy of the Soviet Union right from the days of Khrushchev. The Soviet Union did not seriously contemplate nuclear disarmament or arms reduction in the 1940s, 1950s, and most of the 1960s. During the early to mid-1960s, however, the United States and the Soviet Union agreed to ban nuclear and other weapons from Antarctica and nuclear weapons tests in the atmosphere, outer space, and under water. Except for these tentative measures, during the 1960s the Soviet Union built up its strategic nuclear armaments. By the late 1960s, the Soviet Union under Khrushchev, had reached a rough parity with the United States in some categories of strategic weaponry and at that time offered to negotiate limits on strategic nuclear weapons deployments. Also, the Soviet Union wished to constrain American deployment of an antiballistic missile (ABM) system and retain the ability to place multiple independently-targetable re-entry vehicles (MIRVs) on missiles.

The Soviet-American Strategic Arms Limitation Talks (SALT), initially delayed by the United States in protest of the August 1968 Warsaw Pact invasion of Czechoslovakia, began in November 1969 in Helsinki. The Interim Agreement on the Limitation of Strategic Offensive Arms, signed in Moscow in May 1972, froze existing levels of deployment of intercontinental ballistic missiles (ICBMs) and regulated the growth of submarine-launched ballistic missiles (SLBMs). As part of the SALT process, the Anti-Ballistic Missile Treaty was also signed, allowing two ABM deployment areas in each country (a protocol to the treaty later reduced the number of deployment areas to one).

The SALT agreements were generally considered in the West as having codified the concept of mutual assured destruction, or deterrence. Both the United States and the Soviet Union recognised their mutual vulnerability to massive destruction, no matter which state launched nuclear weapons first. A second SALT agreement was signed in June 1979 in Vienna. Among other provisions, it placed an aggregate ceiling on ICBM and SLBM launchers. The second SALT agreement was never ratified by the United States Senate, however, in large part because of the Soviet invasion of Afghanistan in December 1979. Both the Soviet Union and the United States nonetheless pledged to abide by the provisions of the agreement.

The 27th Party Congress starting off from here renounced any attempt at military superiority. The country realised that in the present scenario there cannot be any military superiority, or that there could not be any victors in the present world. The joint statement issued by Gorbachev and Ronald Reagan at the Geneva Summit in 1985 reiterated that position. Not only this, the 27th Congress of the CPSU writes:[41] "The Soviet state and its allies do not seek military superiority and will not, "allow the military strategic parity existing on the world scene to be changed."[42]

Gorbachev stated that since the interconnection between the people and the society was increasing, a host of social changes had prompted him to go about with a change in the military policy of the country as well. So it was very important to have a world without weapons[43]. Gorbachev extended the logic of mutual security to the US, where once again the Soviet State had been seeking the path of restructuring of international relations to a situation where all the nations of the world could live in harmony.

The concept of peaceful co-existence, had led Lenin too, to propose General and Complete Disarmament. However, the Disarmament Conference failed after the First World War. Lenin wrote," to propose a general reduction of armaments and to support all proposals tending to lighten the burden of militarism, on condition that reduction is applied to the armies of all countries, and the rules of war are complimented by the absolute prohibition of its most barbarous forms, such as poison gas, aerial warfare and, in particular, means of destruction against the civilian population"[44]. At Geneva Gorbachev had proposed fifty per cent arms reduction as well as ban on some nuclear space programmes. Gorbachev's U.N. speech too dealt with the issue of disarmament. However, there were a number of Soviet leaders who felt that it was absolutely impractical to go for a completely nuclear weapons free world.

Another issue which remains intimately linked to the question of military policy and disarmament is the question of security, and the issue with which the security concerns of a nation are intimately linked are the geo-politics and military doctrine of other powers and Soviet responses to the same. After the withdrawal of troops from Afghanistan a few things had taken place. Unification of Germany had already taken place, and the Warsaw Pact Powers have moved towards the West. These two had led to the strengthening of the NATO alliance and the rumblings of the CSCE process for peace and security.

Apart from discussing the anniversary of the signing of the INF[45] treaty, reduction of troops in Asia in cooperation with Mongolia, submission to U.N. plans of conversion of armament industry, Gorbachev also emphasised on 'reasonable sufficiency for defence'[46]. Gorbachev argued during the forty-second session of the United Nations that it was possible to arrive at "the unanimous conclusion that 95 per cent of all nuclear arms of the USA and the USSR can be eliminated without stability being disrupted."[47] He argued that the division of the world's countries into possessing nuclear weapons and not possessing it is also detrimental to the concept of security as the definition of this term also gets split. Incidents like Chernobyl had led him to expand the concept of security and impart new features and specificities to it. It is argued by some scholars that the "external strategic context of the Soviet security is setting for the quest for economic, political and security community inside the Soviet Union. This community is necessary for external security and internal stability."[48] At Madrid, Lobov[49] was questioned on this. He said "I am convinced that the Soviet political and military leadership has real levers capable of preventing the disintegration of a single defence space and the collapse of the armed forces'. The criterion for these opportunities has been and remains control of nuclear weapons.

Gorbachev could also be credited for signing a treaty with the U.S.A., called START that would ultimately lead to a reduction of nuclear warheads, missiles and bombers that could carry those. The START was considered to be a successor of SALT of the 1970's. President Bush and Mikhail Gorbachev decided for 15 per cent and 25 per cent reduction in their nuclear weapons respectively.

That the role of nuclear weapons has declined in the military doctrine is evident since the writings of Nikolai Ogarkov[50] and particularly, after Gorbachev enunciated his 1986 vision of ridding the world of nuclear weapons. To General Moiseyev[51], in line with the changed military doctrine of the Soviet Union, the reasonable defence sufficiency principle"signifies approximate equality in such armaments between the USSR and the USA. Their structures may differ but their potential combat capabilities must be comparable at any level of arms reduction". After the August coup, Lobov said: "I think the nucleus should consist of the principles of prevention of both means of mass destruction and conventional means. It should deal with the prevention of both external (inter-state) and internal (inter-ethnic, civil) wars involving the use of both means of mass destruction and conventional means. It should deal with the prevention of not only large-scale wars and conflicts, but also their localisation and the resolution of conflicts that it has proved impossible to prevent; finally, pre-emptive actions in latent phases of seats of tensions."

There was a myth in the Soviet Union the country was no match for the US, because of Stalinism, force of tradition, and the inertia of the established institutions. This had given birth to an idea that the country's strategic thought was not up to the mark.[52]

In laying down the military doctrine and military science the Party leadership paid heed to the strategic doctrines that shaped the strategies of the west, apart from Marxism-Leninism, the scientific-technological revolution and the accompanying economic strength. The break in Soviet thinking provided both by Lenin's emphasis on peaceful co-existence and scientific development of space flights and nuclear weapons made Khrushchev, Mikoyan[53] and Malenkov think of the danger of nuclear war as a major concern. Khrushchev announced in 1956 that "war was no longer inevitable."[54] But since then the position did not change, as is evident from the stand taken by Gorbachev and the new edition of the CPSU Programme, which says that the survival of mankind was a major question for the rest of the twentieth century. The 27th Congress of the CPSU, in its new edition of the Party's programme states, "The Soviet State and its allies do not seek military superiority and will not allow the military-strategic parity existing on the world scene to be changed." The joint Statement of Ronald Reagan and Mikhail Gorbachev, after the Geneva summit in November 1985, recognised (a) that in the present world there can be no military superiority and (b) that in a nuclear war it is hard to imagine a scenario in which there will be victors and vanquished.

The Soviet Union had always tried to maintain its stand that it will not let the strategic parity to be disturbed, but at the same time an alternative had to be found out. The Warsaw Pact Powers had insisted that it would not be very appreciating if NATO tried to spread its tentacles by bringing other nations under its fold. It had been found that Gorbachev had in a number of occasions reiterated his stand on preserving strategic parity. In his Report to the 27th Congress of the CPSU, while describing the earlier period as Stagnation, he praised strategic parity that was achieved during the Brezhnev period. In a reception speech at Warsaw, given in honour of the participants in the meeting of Top Party and State Leaders of the Warsaw Treaty Countries, Gorbachev said, that 'we will not allow the military-strategic parity to be upset.' This, however, showed that the Soviet Union's idea of national security was quite against what the Western scholars call them to be.

Throughout the sixties and seventies, Soviet spokesmen emphasised mutual security and the impossibility of a victory in a nuclear war. Given this position under the impact of western doctrines of limited war, they had prepared to fight one.

Taking note of the contradictions in the contemporary world, the Political Report of the 27th Congress of the CPSU focussed on the global tasks in the wake of the global dimensions of contradictions. It said, "Analyses of yet another group of contradictions-those on the global scale, affecting the very foundations of the existence of civilisation-leads to serious conclusions." These referred to the ecological crisis and exhaustion of resources.

During Gorbachev's visit to India in November 1986, he said, "The USSR and India were of the opinion that the experience at the Reykjavik[55] Summit demonstrated that given a constructive and realistic approach, far reaching agreements for nuclear disarmament could be achieved."

Under *Perestroika*, various issues that were never discussed before, like, issues of force structure and strategy came out in the open. The Institute of World Economy and International Relations and the Institute for the Study of the United States and Canada and the Institute for Europe had started discussing them. Gorbachev's *"New Thinking"* had brought about a reduction in the role that the military played in decision making on Soviet defence and national security policy. The military had gone along with Gorbachev's insistence on the production process since this would become the basis of getting quality goods as components of new weapon system.

Off the coast of Malta in a Soviet ship named the Maxim Gorky, U.S. President George Bush and Soviet leader Mikhail Gorbachev met within weeks of the fall of the Berlin Wall to discuss the rapid changes in Europe. Bush expressed support for Perestroika and other reforms in the Eastern bloc, and both men recognised the lessening of tensions that had defined the Cold War. No agreements were signed at the summit, but to some it marked the end of the Cold War.

Another important aspect of military policy in the USSR was the military reforms in the country during the Gorbachev Era. The need for military reforms was dictated by a number of factors, like the national significance of the army for the country, the goals of education in the process of military service and the preparation of the citizen soldier, the structural transformations in society, and the requirements of a dependable armed defensive defence taking account of the level of actual danger of war. The military reform included a transition to a regular army staffed on a professional, volunteer basis. The reform suggested that the army should be made absolutely professional. There should be real participation of the whole of society in the implementation of military policy and the role of the CPSU should be determined by the USSR Supreme Soviet. The reform also suggested for a fundamental reorientation of the organs of administration of the Defence Ministry and other ministries connected with defence. The reforms would also take care of humanising the Army and changing the position of the serviceman.

The armed personnel in USSR had articulated the problem of nationalities' impact on the Army in Latvia and Estonia in the Baltic, in Armenia, Ukraine and also in Khirgizia. But the Latvian Commissar said that it was impossible to have a Latvian Army, thus the Army would remain an inter-ethnic entity. But there were other views as well. Many thought that in the wake of the withdrawal of the Soviet troops from the East European countries, the Baltic States should remain neutral. In Uzbekistan, however, the Supreme Soviet had been concerned with the employment opportunities, social care and working facilities.

There were few other matters as well which needed discussion. The top brass of the Soviet Army was comprised of the war veterans from the Second World War, whereas the Soviet officer corps had gained new experience in the Afghan War. The impact this would have on the Soviet army especially in the wake of perestroika was not clear. The question that arose time and again was the relation between the party and the army. Various new institutions and new procedures were taken up in order to ease out the relationship. But one aspect on which both the party and the army agreed was the concept of combat readiness, which again had two aspects-human and technological. The technological aspect was taken care of by the introduction of science and technology in the weapons system. It was suggested that the formation of military platform, ad hoc groups, media etc would inculcate greater participation that would in turn help in straightening party-army relationship. Perestroika and glasnost, it was considered was instrumental in bringing about this change in the Soviet military.[56]

Lenin and Gorbachev

There are a number of instances to show that actually Gorbachev had in a number of occasions treaded the path shown by Lenin.[57] Both Lenin and Gorbachev have had the opportunity to steer the Soviet Union from the same kind of economic stagnation. Lenin had tried to get over the same by emphasising on electrification after War communism, while Gorbachev had tried to improve the situation in the Soviet Union by following Acceleration or what later came to be known as *Perestroika*. Lenin too faced the problem of non-cooperation from the Western powers as had been faced by Gorbachev. Gorbachev had taken the path of socio-economic development on the basis of science and technology, which he did within the framework of On the other hand 'Lenin New Economic Policy suggested a tax in kind, administrative reorganisation, managing the fuel, food, transport crisis, along with decline in cloth and industrial production'.

During Lenin's time the emphasis was on rehabilitating and reconstructing by emphasising on first providing for infrastructural facilities and then basic necessities. During the period of Stalin the emphasis was on production of means of production themselves. As a result of industrialisation resources in the Eastern region of the country was tapped, which included Northern, Central Industrial Southern, Volga, Urals, Caucasian, Western Siberia, and Turkistan. This was an expansion of the Plan of Electrification which Lenin took up. Maurice Dobb shows how this shift to the eastern region of the country, had taken place after the Second World War. Even in this article Gorbachev repeated his stand that Lenin had an innate ability to read the situation in any country right and to address the issue immediately[58]. Thus one needs to grasp Lenin's concept of socialist society well and then apply it to contemporary Soviet Union. 'We should get rid once and for all of the view of socialism as if it were levelling out, negating personality, of the notion of socialism as a certain minimum: the minimum of material benefits, the minimum of justice, the minimum of democracy. We should implement a contemporary model of society ensuring for all its members civilised living standards and multiform opportunities to meet spiritual and cultural needs.

"It is necessary to determine these criteria. What is truly socialist and what is truly alien to the very idea of socialism:

It is necessary to rid socialism of everything pseudo socialist, distorted and deformed in the period of the personality cult, command system, stagnation, and restore the truly."[59]

Lenin's emphasis on electrification as key to acceleration of the Soviet economy marked the shift from steam power to electrical power. It also involved the management of town and country relationship in order to have resource mobilisation. Once the industrial infrastructure was built, Stalin emphasised on the resource mobilisation through managing town-country relationship (collectivisation) in order to apply the available know-how to industrialisation. During Khrushchev period, economic instruments were used to increase production and emphasis was laid on agricultural production and on consumer goods with industrial growth registering reasonable success. The Khrushchev era was also marked by the Soviet Union's breakthrough in missile and rocket technology that ushered the space age and strategic implications of that breakthrough was perceived by the US in cold war terms.

'For Lenin the concept of Soviet power was not set up once and for all: it was perpetually developing real democracy and social justice, without which communism would be impossible. In fact Lenin regarded electrification as a basic component of future society.'[60]

It was found that the changes that started with Perestroika did actually pay off. The economy started to show signs of improvement. In 1987, gross national product grew 3.3 per cent. The growth of the volume of industrial output was 3.8 per cent. Over the three years from 1985 to 1987 the average annual growth rates were: as regards national income-3.3 per cent, the gross national product-3.9 per cent, and industrial output-4.2 per cent, the output of consumer goods 4.7 per cent.[61] The gross agricultural output in average annual count grew 1.9 per cent, the commissioning of the fixed assets-3.5 per cent, of housing-3.6 per cent.

In the field of labour productivity, between 1981 to 1984 the country obtained 86 per cent of the national income due to it. Between 1985 to 1987 it was 96 per cent. In 1987 the whole increase was ensured through labour productivity. In the first quarter of 1988 year labour productivity in industry grew 5.4 per cent, including at enterprises working on conditions of full cost-accounting and self-financing-6.6 per cent. In the building industry-this growth was 8.9 per cent, and of those who work on conditions of full cost-accounting-9.8 per cent. This Gorbachev considered as serious progress.

In 1985 the renewal of the machine building products was 3 per cent, and in 1987-9.1 per cent, which is a three-fold increase. In the area of housing over ten million families have received better housing conditions in the last three years, i.e. after Perestroika was initiated.

Even the trade turn-over had grown 13 per cent. And it is apt to note, that over the past three years the sale of alcoholic drinks has declined by more than a half. But there was another side to the story as well.

Gorbachev's new system bore the characteristics of neither central planning nor a market economy. Instead, the Soviet economy went from stagnation to deterioration. At the end of 1991, when the union officially dissolved, the national economy was in a virtual tailspin. In 1991 the Soviet GDP had declined 17 per cent and was declining at an accelerating rate. Overt inflation was becoming a major problem. Between 1990 and 1991, retail prices in the Soviet Union increased 140 per cent.

Under these conditions, the general quality of life for Soviet consumers deteriorated. Consumers traditionally faced shortages of durable goods, but under Gorbachev, food, wearing apparel, and other basic necessities were in short supply. Fuelled by the liberalised atmosphere of Gorbachev's glasnost and by the general improvement in information access in the late 1980s, public dissatisfaction with economic conditions was much more overt than ever before in the Soviet period. The foreign-trade sector of the Soviet economy also showed signs of deterioration. The total Soviet hard-currency debt increased appreciably, and the Soviet Union, which had established an impeccable record for debt repayment in the earlier decades, had accumulated sizable amount to be paid as debt by 1990.

In sum, the Soviet Union left a legacy of economic inefficiency and deterioration to the fifteen constituent republics after its break-up in December 1991. In conclusion it could be said that if Gorbachev had made all the right moves why is it so that the existing socialist countries could not remain intact. What made the governments of all these existing socialist countries to crumble almost at the same time and under what pressure? Mandel in his book had stated that the Gorbachev had provided a way of coming out of the political and economic problem in these countries especially the U.S.S.R., but was silent when it came to moral-ideological degradation.[62] He did not simply provide an answer to this particular problem. Then, what could be the answer? Was it this moral-ideological degradation that no one witnessed and therefore did not address?

References

1. Raymond E Zickel ed., *Soviet Union: A Country Study*, 2nd Ed. Federal Research Division, Library of Congress, Washington D.C. 1991.

2. War Communism: economic policy applied by the Bolsheviks during the period of the Russian Civil War (1918–20). More exactly, the policy of War Communism lasted from June 1918 to March 1921. The policy's chief features were the expropriation of private business and the nationalisation of industry throughout Soviet Russia, and the requisition of surplus grain and other food products from the peasantry by the State.

3. New Economic Policy (NEP): the economic policy of the government of the Soviet Union from 1921 to 1928. Various measures like the return of most agriculture, retail trade, and small-scale light industry to private ownership and management

while the state retained control of heavy industry, transport, banking, and foreign trade were taken u p. Money was reintroduced into the economy in 1922 (it had been abolished under War Communism). The peasantry were allowed to own and cultivate their own land, while paying taxes to the state. The New Economic Policy reintroduced a measure of stability to the economy and allowed the Soviet people to recover from years of war, civil war, and governmental mismanagement.

4. Alec Nove, *Stalinism and After*, George Allen and Unwin Publishers Ltd, London 1975, p. 25.

5. *Ibid.*

6. Leszek Kolakowski, *Main Currents of Marxism, Vol. 3*, Clarendon Press, Oxford, 1978.

7. Jan F. Tricia, David D. Finley, *Soviet Foreign Policy*, The Macmillan Company Press, New York, 1968.

8. Aleksai Nikolayevich Kosygin (1904–1980): Soviet statesman and Premier of the Soviet Union (1964–80). He was a competent and pragmatic economic administrator rather than an ideologue.

9. Khozraschet: A system of self-supporting operations, applied to such individual enterprises as factories, encompassing a wide range of activities and a management process, involving a large number of individuals in Russia.

10. Nikolai Victorovich Podgornyi (1903-1983): Soviet statesman and Communist Party official. Podgorny's first government appointment came in 1939, as deputy people's commissar of the food-processing industry in the Ukraine; he was promoted in 1940 to deputy commissar of the Soviet food-processing industry. His first important Communist Party appointment was as first

secretary of the Kharkov regional party committee (1950–53), and he soon rose to first secretary of the Ukraine party committee (1957–63). He became a full member of the Politburo in 1960, and he was later promoted to secretary of the Central Committee of the Communist Party of the Soviet Union (1963–65).

Podgorny became involved in a power struggle with Leonid Brezhnev, who had become party first secretary in 1964. The apparent loser, Podgorny relinquished his secretaryship in 1965 and was given the less-influential post of chairman of the Presidium of the Supreme Soviet from 1965 to 1977. Podgorny enhanced his position of ceremonial head of state and travelled widely, but real power was in the hands of Brezhnev, general secretary of the Communist Party. On May 24, 1977, as a result of his resistance to Brezhnev's wish to hold both the party secretaryship and the Presidium chairmanship, Podgorny was ousted from the Politburo and "relieved" of his duties as chairman of the Presidium, with Brezhnev assuming the latter title. Thereafter Podgorny lived in retirement in Moscow.

11. Raymond E Zickel (Ed.), *Soviet Union: A Country Study*, 2nd Ed. Federal Research Division, Library of Congress, Washington D.C. 1991.

12. Mikhail S Gorbachev; *Perestroika: New Thinking for our Country and the World*; William Collins Sons and Co. Ltd, London, 1987.

13. *Ibid.*, p. 20.

14. *Ibid.*, p. 22.

15. Mikhail S Gorbachev; *Restore Lenin's Image of Socialism*, Mainstream, Vol. 26 No. 32; Perspective Publication, New Delhi, 1988.

16. Abel Aganbegyan, *New Directions in Soviet Economics*, New Left Review, No. 169, The New Left Review Ltd., London, May-June 1988.

17. Raymond E Zickel (Ed.), *Soviet Union: A Country Study*, 3rd Ed. Federal Research Division, Library of Congress, Washington D.C. 1998.

18. Chernobyl Disaster: accident at the Chernobyl nuclear power station in the Soviet Union, the worst in the history of nuclear power generation. The accident occurred on April 25–26, 1986, when technicians at reactor Unit 4 attempted a poorly designed experiment. Initially, the Chernobyl accident caused the deaths of 32 people. Dozens more contracted serious radiation sickness; some of these people later died. Between 50 and 185 million curies of radionuclides escaped into the atmosphere—several times more radioactivity than that created by the atomic bombs dropped on-Hiroshima and Nagasaki. This radioactivity was spread by the wind over Belarus, Russia, and Ukraine and soon reached as far west as France and Italy. Millions of acres of forest and farmland were contaminated; and although many thousands of people were evacuated, hundreds of thousands more remained in contaminated areas. In addition, in subsequent years many livestock were born deformed, and among humans several thousand radiation-induced illnesses and cancer deaths were expected in the long term.

19. General Agreement on Tariffs and Trade (GATT): set of multilateral trade agreements aimed at the abolition of quotas and the reduction of tariff duties among the contracting nations. When GATT was concluded by 23 countries at Geneva, in 1947 (to take effect on Jan. 1, 1948), it was considered an interim arrangement pending the formation of a United Nations agency to supersede it. When such

an agency failed to emerge, GATT was amplified and further enlarged at several succeeding negotiations. It subsequently proved to be the most effective instrument of world trade liberalisation, playing a major role in the massive expansion of world trade in the second half of the 20th century. By the time GATT was replaced by the World Trade Organisation (WTO) in 1995, 125 nations were signatories to its agreements, which had become a code of conduct governing 90 per cent of world trade.

20. Mikhail S Gorbachev, *op. cit.*, p. 84.

21. Joan Frances Crowley, Dan Vaillancourt; *Lenin to Gorbachev: Three Generations of Soviet Communists*; Harlan Davidson Inc., Illinois, U.S.A. 1989.

22. Mikhail S Gorbachev, *op. cit.*, p. 98.

23. Quoted in Rakesh Gupta, *Perestroika: transition with Participation*, International Studies, Vol. 27, No.1, Sage Publications, New Delhi, 1990, p. 2.

24. Milovan Djilas; *The New Class An Analysis of the Communist System*, Frederick A. Praeger, New York, 1957.

25. *Ibid.*, p. 39.

26. David L. Sills (ed.); *International Encyclopaedia of Social Sciences, Vol. 15*, The Macmillan Company and the Free Press, New York, 1972.

27. Fedor Burlatsky, *The Gorbachev Revolution, Mainstream, April 25*; Perspective Publication; New Delhi; 1987.

28. Boris Kagarlitsky; *Perestroika: The Dialectic of Change'; New Left Review, No. 169*; The New Left Review Ltd. London; May-June 1988.

29. Rakesh Gupta; *From Alienation to Participation; Mainstream,* Perspective Publishers; New Delhi; July 16, 1988, p. 32.

30. Robert Rozhdestvensky, *Gorbachev Spoke the Truth: Imparted Shock Therapy; Mainstream,* Perspective Publisher, New Delhi, November 26, 1988.

31. Vladimir Mytarev, *Soviet Economy: Fruitless Half-measures, Mainstream,* Perspective Publisher, New Delhi, December 10, 1988.

32. *op. cit.*, p. 114.

33. Mikhail S Gorbachev, fn. 14.

34. Joan Frances Crowley, Dan Vaillancourt; *Lenin to Gorbachev: Three Generations of Soviet Communists*; Harlan Davidson Inc.d Illinois, U.S.A.; 1989.

35. Hederick Smith; *The New Russians*, Random House, New York, 1990, p. 161.

36. Robert Maxwell (ed.); *M. S. Gorbachev: Speeches and Writings*; Pergamon Press; Oxford; 1986.

37. Quoted in Rakesh Gupta; *Soviet Policies in the Eighties*, Patriot Publishers, New Delhi, 1987.

38. Robert Maxwell (ed.); *M. S. Gorbachev: Speeches and Writings*; Pergamon Press; Oxford; 1986; p. 233.

39. *Ibid.*

40. *Ibid.*, p. 101.

41. Rakesh Gupta, fn. 36.

42. Mikhail S Gorbachev, *op. cit.*, p. 84.

43. Robert Maxwell (ed.); *M.S. Gorbachev: Speeches and Writings*; Pergamon Press; Oxford; 1986.

44. Rakesh Gupta, fn. 36, p. 104.

45. INF: Intermediate Range Nuclear Forces.

46. Rakesh Gupta; *Vision of a Changing Equilibrium; Mainstream*, Vol. XXVII No. 24, Perspective Publishers, New Delhi, March 11, 1989.

47. Mikhail S Gorbachev; *Reality and Guarantees of a Secure World, Mainstream*, Perspective Publishers, New Delhi, September 26, 1987, p. 10.

48. Rakesh Gupta, *Defense, Security Scenario*; World Focus Vol. 12, No. 9-10, Hari Sharan Chhabra, New Delhi, Sept-Oct, 1991.

49. Lobov was a Soviet Army General.

50. Ogarkov was Soviet Army General.

51. Moiseyev was Soviet Army General.

52. Rakesh Gupta, fn. 36.

53. Anastas Ivanovich Mikoyan (1895–1978): Old Bolshevik and highly influential Soviet statesman who dominated the supervision of foreign and domestic trade during the administrations of Joseph Stalin and Nikita S. Khrushchev.

54. Georgy Maksimilianovich Malenkov (1902–1988): prominent Soviet statesman and Communist Party official, a close collaborator of Joseph Stalin, and the prime minister (March 1953–February 1955) after Stalin's death.

55. Reykjavik Summit: In November 1985 in Geneva, Switzerland, Mikhail Gorbachev and Ronald Reagan met for the first time to discuss issues such as SDI and the reduction of nuclear weapons. However, after meeting, tensions still remained due to fighting in Afghanistan and Central America.

After months of postponement a mini-summit was organised in Reykjavik, Iceland, to open communications further. Here, the two leaders again discussed SDI at length but also made progress toward agreements to reduce ballistic missiles by 50 per cent and a "zero option" agreement in Europe–meaning there would be no more intermediate-range missiles in Europe.

While no agreement was signed in Reykjavik, both leaders felt that the meeting was a success and opened the way for further progress.

56. Rakesh Gupta, *Political Stability and Civil-Military Relations Under Gorbachev*, Lancer International, New Delhi, 1991.

57. Rakesh Gupta, fn. 36, p. 32.

58. Mikhail S Gorbachev; *Restore Lenin's Image of Socialism*, Mainstream, Vol. 26, No. 32, Perspective Publication, New Delhi, 1988.

59. *Ibid.* 1988.

60. Yevgeni Yevtushenko; *The Right to be Unconventional, Mainstream*, Perspective Publication, February 7, 1987.

61. Mikhail S Gorbachev; *Restore Lenin's Image of Socialism; Mainstream*, Vol. 26, No. 32, Perspective Publication, New Delhi, 1988.

62. Ernest Mandel; *The Future of Gorbachev's U.S.S.R.*, Verso, London, 1989.

5

Summary and Conclusion

We concentrate on the idea of change in the writings of Karl Marx. Marx tried to focus as to why this change became so important. Marx had concentrated on the concept of change because change could only bring about a better life for all the people of the world. While analysing the concept of change Marx realised that change could only be brought about by means of a revolution and thus the concept of change is intimately linked with the concept of Revolution, exploitation and alienation. The writings of the other Marxists like Lenin, Karl Kautsky, Rosa Luxemburg and others have debated on the idea whether revolution can or is the only means that could bring about change in the capitalist system. For many a change could only be brought about by reform and definitely not through revolution. They agreed on the basic need of revolution, except Kautsky and Bernstein.

But as we discuss the idea as to how Marx was bent upon bringing about change in the system we also should keep it mind that for him the change would be towards Communism–a better world and between the world he lived in and Communism there would be a transitional phase that would be referred to as socialism.

Marx brought together the issues of alienation, exploitation and revolution. There is a third section in the chapter which also deals with the question of bringing about socialism in Russia. Although Lenin always felt that Russia was in a situation to bring about socialism in the country, which he had discussed in most of his writings like, Capitalism in Russia and others yet, there were a number of scholars who felt otherwise. Isaac Deutscher and others have also condemned the idea that Russia could at all be considered for bringing about socialism. According to them socialism could have been more successful had it been brought about in a developed Western country rather than in Russia.

Nevertheless it could be pointed that Socialism for Marx and his followers was only a transitional phase with an aim of attaining something even better in the world. Yet, it cannot be denied that socialism was indeed a definitive stage.

Though socialism is a transitional phase, Marx did not consider it in detail. Mao said that continuous revolution should take place even under socialism. Two years later this concept was broadened and a few things were asserted.

(a) Socialist society is a society in period of transition and is full of "contradiction and struggle"

(b) Antagonistic classes remain in socialist society, and consequently, the dictatorship of the proletariat remains for the entire period of socialism;

(c) The aim of class struggle in a socialist society is seizure of power;

(d) The class struggle is spearheaded against the members of the exploiting classes, against the bourgeois in the party;

(e) The fundamental question of the revolution-the question of power-is being resolved in the course of the Cultural Revolution.

The concept of continuous revolution denied the society social harmony, which is the new basis of enlargement of democracy. According to many scholars Mao had reduced Marxism to mere class struggle. Mao and his followers had at another level, also rejected the constructive aspect of socialism.[1]

The problematique of alienation in the then existing socialist countries of Eastern Europe such as Czechoslovakia, East Germany, Hungary and Poland as they tried to transit from socialism to something beyond and its inability to do so, no text discusses those either written by Marx, Engels on Lenin.

The implementation of Socialism in the East European countries, its initial successes in the post World War–II years, followed by the stagnation under the effect of Stalinisation, attempted reforms and the subsequent Soviet backlash and the eventual collapse of the system starkly raised the issue of transition in this context. It is shown that the system that evolved in these countries was long influenced by Stalinisation, till long after de-Stalinisation took place in the Soviet Union itself. This resulted in stagnation and stifled all attempts at reforms and adaptation of the system within the socialist framework to meet the local requirements and ground realities. It is also shown that the policies of the Governments of these countries were overly influenced by the political leadership of the Soviet Union. Intimately the politics and economics of these respective nations were linked. Marxist theorisation was missing in terms of new national and internal dialectics.

In the case of Czechoslovakia, there is unambiguous evidence of the genuine grass-root support for Socialism in the post-World-War-II years. But by 1948, the effects of Stalinisation began to be felt. Successive purges in all levels of society by Gottwald and Novotny left Czechoslovakia sterile and devoid of intellectual growth. Czechoslovakia's impressive economic growth in the post war years stagnated to the point that by 1962 the third Five-Year Plan had to be abandoned.

The first attempt at reform came in 1968 during the period known as Prague Spring. Pressures from the weakness of the economy and that of the regime, as well as pressures from the Soviet Union in the direction of de-Stalinisation led to a liberal regime under Dubcek.

The extent of liberalisation was unacceptable to the leadership of the Soviet Union and liberalisation was reversed within a year following military intervention by Warsaw Pact forces in the context of international revolutionary process marked by conflict with NATO at the U.S. at its head. New dialectics of change were needed.

Post Dubcek, stagnation intensified, at least superficially. Because of the forcible suppression of the reforms, there was a slow growth of an underground dissident movement; an undercurrent gaining strength with the growing discontent with the regime.

Thus when the scene was politically suitable once again for reform, due to the advent of Glasnost and Perestroika in the Soviet Union, the quantum of change forced on the system by dissident demands was too great for the system to handle and the traumatic implosion led to the disbanding of Socialism in Czechoslovakia. Given the successes of the West even Dubcek could not survive for too long.

The situation in Czechoslovakia had a close parallel in Hungary. The post-World-War-II reconstruction of Hungary saw Rakosi apply the Soviet economic model without consideration for indigenous problems of Hungary. The inappropriate application of the Soviet model led to popular dissatisfaction with material shortage, decline in agricultural output and mounting foreign debt.

Attempts at taking remedial measures during the 1956 uprising by Imre Nagy were brutally overthrown by Soviet military intervention. Nagy was replaced by Janos Kádár, who recognising the need for reform, yet aware of Soviet antipathy to Hungary charting an independent socio-political and economic course for itself, set up a system popularly known as "goulash communism'. A certain degree of reform was introduced in the otherwise unchanged Soviet model.

Consequently the inherent contradictions and inefficiencies of the system remained. The popular dissatisfaction led to the growth of a dissident movement, which eventually overthrew the Socialist regime.

The pragmatic reforms of Kádár, though insufficient and in the long run ineffective in saving the Socialist system, nevertheless were instrumental in making the transition less traumatic for Hungary. The issues at stake were was the leadership scientific, was way of life better, was the standard of living improving.

East Germany was a different case. The defeat of Germany, followed by division of the country between the Allied countries led to a political vacuum, which was filled by the Socialist Unity Party (SED) at the behest of the Soviet Union. The subsequent confiscation of properties of former Nazi Party members and sympathisers and redistribution of land was viewed as imposition on a defeated country rather than a deliberate move towards Socialism. Under the SED regime, the economic growth was higher in East Germany than the other Eastern Bloc countries. But compared to West Germany, a country with which a natural comparison can be drawn, the economic condition was fairly bleak.

This was compounded by the problem that attempts at reforms in East Germany were less radical as compared to what could have been necessary to prevent stagnation. The spirit of nationalism kept rocking socialism which expressed in Helsinki accords and Hanecker's pro-West policies.

The effect of Stalinisation, which was never lifted from East Germany, left its mark on the intellectual output of the country. As only SED members, obedient, submissive and compliant to Soviet dictat, could hold critical posts, the ability of the party to adapt Socialism to local and ground realities was effectively suffocated. With the increasing dissatisfaction of the populace with their condition vis-à-vis their Western counterparts, the SED came to be looked on as the tool of a conquering power.

Thus when the control of the Soviet Union was loosened by Glasnost and Perestroika, the SED, inexperienced in charting an independent course and lacking the support of the masses, was unable to deal with the transition and the implosion wrecked both the state and the party at the same time. Further the conservative and the Socialist Party of FRG never treated GDR as an equal.

The events in Poland were in a different direction. Unlike the case in other East European countries, the collectivisation of land was carried out more slowly, in order to avoid antagonising the rural populace. The phase of de-Stalinisation took place comparatively more quickly after the death of Stalin. However, the imposition of the centrally planned economy as well as the system of emphasising the growth of heavy industry and neglecting the consumer sector led to the worsening of living conditions as compared to that in Western Europe.

Attempts at reform within Poland were made several times, primarily during the 1970's. The Polish economy had registered economic growth hyphenated by successive periods of economic stagnation. Poland's economy adopted the Five-Year plans after the Soviet model of economic planning, and measures were taken to isolate the Polish economy from the international economy and trade. Like any other East European country Poland too was affected by Stalinisation. But among the most interesting feature of Poland's politics under the socialist rule was the Solidarity movement. It was the first full-blown trade union movement to have taken place in any East European country under the leadership of Lech Walesa, which left a long lasting impact in the political life of Poland. In the Polish crisis of the 1980s the role of the Catholic Church that was popular among peaseves cannot be ignored.

The political history of Soviet Union, in the 70 plus years, under communist rule, is intriguing. A country which was largely backward rose to be one of the two most powerful nations of the world, under the communist rule. Its economic growth had been hyphenated by periods of economic stagnation, moral degradation, etc, One of the major aspects on which the chapter focuses is the impacts of Stalinisation and its evil effects that crippled all spheres of Soviet system-socio-political-economic. The degradation that started then was reversed to a certain extent by Khrushchev's de-Stalinisation, and later by Brezhnev. But the deterioration in certain spheres continued.

It was only after Gorbachev, that a certain conscious effort was made to address all the issues together. Gorbachev's perestroika involved the society, politics, economy, army, administration or bureaucracy, foreign policy-almost everything. He tried to bring about more openness in the media as well. Gorbachev wanted to take up all these measures in order to achieve two ends-to bring about a change in the lives of the Soviet people and in the larger perspective to be able to transit from existing socialism and beyond. He showed remarkable concern for humanity by and large. Gorbachev called for nuclear disarmament on a number of occasions. This call of his was dependent on the thought that nuclear wars are not the alternative and it actually does not take nations anywhere. He was in this repeating Khoushchev Gorbachev reinterpreted history, socialist practice, Leninist theory and current powerless to regulate a socialistic humanist agenda by incorporating the spiritual, scientific, political and economic needs of a new socialist middle class.

Although there were broad problems with socialism that engulfed all the nations of the world, yet, there were quite a few of them that were indigenous to the nations themselves. Thus in order to understand that let us take a look at these countries one by one.

Czechoslovakia

In Czechoslovakia problems emerged as early as in the 1967, when protests took place against the regime of Novotny. Novotny was replaced by Alexander Dubcek, as first secretary of the party. Dubcek's reform measures were again too much for the Soviet government to accept and it is alleged that the Russians tried to split the Czechoslovak Communist Party leadership with the aim of throwing off Dubcek. The Soviets were quite often accused of interfering in the affairs of the then existing socialist countries.

It is also argued that the party tried to control everyday affairs of the Czechoslovak state.' The aim of the Party is not to become the 'universal' manager of the society, to tie down every single organisation, every step in everybody's life by its directives. Its mission is, above all, to stimulate Socialist activity, to show the way and the real scope for Communist perspectives and by personal example all working people'.[2]

According to Andrej Korbonski[3], the quick and complete collapse of the regimes in 1989 was due to the simultaneous disintegration of all their basic levels of decision-making. Owing to their nature, to the strong interrelationship of their individual parts, the communist regimes probably could not have ended in any other way. 'Still the surprising quickness of the collapse was, for a time at least, the source of collective euphoria.'[4] Its unexpected consequence was that all the post communist governments felt obliged, without the benefit of thorough discussions, of taking quick decisions in three crucial spheres which determine the nature of all political systems: the constitutional, the economic, and the socio-cultural.

The developments in Czechoslovakia, Jiri Musil writes, are almost a textbook example of the importance of timely settled basic constitutional agreements for the transformation of post communist societies. In this respect the principal problem in Czechoslovakia has been the relationship between two other macro regions, Bohemia and Moravia, does not pose comparable dangers, though it too tends to divert attention and siphon off energy from economic reform and the building up of civil society.

East Germany

In East Germany, the administrative-centralist structures of direct political domination over the economy turned increasingly against the economy as these conditions continually reproduced themselves and became entrenched[5].

There had been nationalisation of production that led on the one hand, to a monopolisation of the function of proprietor by the state, which itself was outside of the real production process. On the other hand, the workers, who were officially the social proprietors of the means of production, in reality did not dispose over them. This meant that the producers were unable to determine themselves the aims of production and thus were unable to fulfil the functions of proprietor.

The separation between proprietor and producer, between definition of ends by the state and the realisation of ends by the enterprise, left real production, according to some, "without a master" and the producers without responsibility and without interest, which is tantamount to mass de-motivation.

The economy was thus placed in a position of simultaneous subordination to the state administration, legitimised by party ideology. The state deteriorated into an instrument of power of the ruling class and into an executive instrument of the party apparatus, which was itself a part of the state. Thus the party became a prisoner of its own state decisions. The plan became a power instrument of political management instead of an instrument of economic regulation in the hands of the producers. State controlled planning was complemented by a centralist distribution of resources with the help of balance sheets. As the complexity of the economy grew and the division of labour increased, it became less and less amenable to centralist management. The swelling of the administrative apparatus, the instruments of state control, and the plan indices did not increase the effectiveness of central management, but they did entail a growing loss of the controlling function of money as the right to goods freely chosen. Personal relations, the administration of scarcity, and acts of barter acquired a growing weight compared to market-oriented innovative action.

The performance-inhibiting formal unity of economic and social policy principle, proclaimed in the GDR in 1971, was based more on external political factors and outmoded traditions of the labour movement than on a scientific knowledge of the requirements of social development. Its fetishism with equality, security, and welfare gradually curtailed the performance principle and at the same time gave rise to increasingly greater non-realisable economic requirements.

The soft revolution from below and the top-level leaders' fear of the consequences of the brutal measures of suppression that were standing ready, ultimately made the "turn" possible and allowed the party under Honecker's heir Krenz, to place its hope in *dialogue*, as the presumably more successful strategy of asserting power. This new strategy had already been called for and prepared by segments of lower-level party organisations. Thus the alienation of the top power apparatus from the base in higher education, institutions, and firms was obvious. Even in the security services, Honecker's general line was not undisputed, so that there was no full clarity of whether the army, the military state security troops, and paramilitary units would remain loyal in case of a possible and prepared state emergency. This is one of the reasons why the top and regional SED leaders did not resort to the use of persuasive means of force as the ultimate argument on October 9, 1989. Another reason was that the consequences of a violent suppression of the demonstration, in which more than 70,000 participated in Leipzig, exceeded the powers of imagination of any power conscious party functionaries, who in the mean time have become less rigid.

Another essential factor in the deep crisis of the party was the power struggle over succession to the gravely ill

Honecker. The general Secretary seems to have feared that the crown prince Egon Krenz might grab the crown prematurely. During the internal holiday phase, Honecker divested his chairman of his powers, and appointed the Economic Secretary Mittag his acting party head. However Mittag underestimated the grave situation, paid no attention to the obvious signals from the various party districts and from the security apparatus, and was therefore not capable of a clear course. But in Honecker's absence the Politburo could not make any thorough-going decisions. The Party thus, in the end drifted along without a leader.

In mid-October 1989, the way was cleared in the German Democratic Republic for fundamental political and economic reforms. When the question was posed as to what type of economy should be created, the expected answer was either "planned economy" or "market economy." Basically, however, such a categorisation was ultimately superficial and not sufficient for true understanding.

For a long time, the GDR was, however, analysed as a stable and unshakeable bulwark of late Stalinism in Europe. In the 1970's and early 1980's, the Evangelical Church and a few smaller groups had begun to voice demands for the observance of human rights. The final act of the Helsinki accords, which the GDR also signed, played an important role here as well, as the critics could appeal to it in their demands. Nonetheless, the state apparatus remained master of the situation. But oppositional groups had never before defined themselves as opponents of the system. Rather, they initially placed their stakes on a peaceful and, for a long time, also on an internal transformation of socialism, and the reforms of the Soviet Union in 1987, in particular, had an inspirational effect. The self confidence of the courageous small oppositional groups was strengthened when they noted a certain uncertainty in the state application of sanctions, i.e., in the persecution of the critical demonstrations precursory to Honecker's visit to the Federal Republic.

Poland

The high level of frustration in Polish society has been pointed out by S Nowak (1979)[6]. More recent studies have shown that the level of frustration and anxiety and sense of danger was greater in the 1970s than it was in the 1960s. One indicator of the level of anxiety in a society is the suicide rate. During the 1970s the suicide rate grew steadily in Poland, the first decline being recorded in 1980.[7]

The 1970s cannot be viewed as a particularly repressive period in Poland.[8] In comparison with Stalinist times–if we restrict ourselves to post-war history–this was a period of relative liberalisation of the system, of greater openness to the outside world and increased contacts with the West.[9] There was no intensification of terror, police invigilation, social conflict, or manifestation of hatred. And yet the institutional system functioned so that the people faced external coercion on an increasing scale. This was based on 'pressure based on violence of some other kind', as Ossowski has defined it in his distinction between coercion based on direct physical violence and that which is not. That is to say, the state monopoly of the basic institutions of public life deprived the individual of the opportunity of changing a situation which he or she did not accept and of substituting another. The lack of such organisations as free trade unions and the frequent violations of the rule of law meant that people saw their situation very clearly as being one from which there was no way out, and where there was no way of defending themselves against possible threats. This sense of being locked in was aggravated by an inability to control events at grass root level, a lack of self management and the blocking of spontaneous activity both within and outside the enterprise.[10] It must be borne in mind here that regardless of the form of pressure used, external coercion places the individual in a situation in which he or she is obliged to act in a way which is at variance with his or her opinion.

Martial law was imposed in Poland on 13 December 1981. This meant an intensification of external coercion[11].

The Poles were subjected to a pressure which Ossoewski would have defined as being based on direct violence, using such penal sanctions such as death, corporal punishment and imprisonment. This pressure was designed to serve several purposes.

Physical coercion helped to end resistance and to break up sit-ins of the workforces of many enterprises who were protesting against the de-legalisation of Solidarity, the internment of its leaders and the suspension of all independent social organisations representing the interests of various social groups.

The threats or actual use of physical coercion made it possible to paralyse communication. This was done by disconnecting telephones, banning any permanent move to another town, imposing curfews, carrying out personal searches in the streets and at home, closing virtually all the editorial offices of daily newspapers, magazines and publishing houses.

Food prices were drastically raised in the second month of martial law. The threat of recourse to physical coercion prevented a repetition of the social protests which had occurred in 1976 and 1980 in response to such rises.

Physical coercion in the shape of internment, interrogation, searches and trials eliminated all forms of symbolic support for the ideas of Solidarity.

In addition to physical coercion, the authorities also applied economic coercion. This involved either dismissal from employment of Solidarity activists, or the imposition of compulsory work through, for example, the militarisation of certain enterprises and institutions. The price rises, which pauperised the overwhelming majority of society and large families and old-age pensioners in particular, themselves constituted a form of economic pressure.

During the first few months of martial law this wholesale use of actual or potential physical violence, the suspension of many basic civil rights and the economic coercion intimidated virtually the whole of Polish society. This fear and existential danger was associated with the blocking of all those needs and values which had started to be met on such a vast scale in 1980-1 for the first time since the People's Republic had come into being. For martial law had resulted in the suspension or dissolution of all those organisations which had come into being in 1980-1 in order to express and defend the different interests of various groups of Polish society. This physical restraint was therefore associated with the extreme frustrations which were caused by this situation of severe relative deprivation. As many studies have shown the withdrawal of certain privileges aroused greater stress and is the source of more dangerous frustration than deprivation which is not preceded by the experience of having a specific need satisfied.

There were demands for authentic rather than manufactured participation. Having succeeded in the early revolutionary period in harnessing the population to accomplish a variety of tasks associated with the process of constructing the socialist order, the East European regimes failed, by and large, to provide adequate outlets for the mobilised and socialised masses to express their preferences and articulate their demands. Although they engaged in impressive institution-building efforts during the first decade or so of their rule, the respective governments forced these institutions to play a one sided role as instruments or generating support rather than presenting demands or giving advice.

The end product of the two crises–distribution and participation-was a serious challenge to the legitimacy of the system. The concept of legitimacy is not easy to define but in a simplified form it may be seen as denoting voluntary acceptance of a government or a policy by the majority of the population, which viewed them as inherently 'good' or 'right', either because of the way in which they had come into being or because they had succeeded in fulfilling popular expectations. In this context it is useful to distinguish between a 'derivative' and a 'fundamental' legitimacy crises.

Apart from the ones already stated there were also crises arising out of identity and penetration. If we accept the above definitions, it may be argued that in the early 1960's, on the eve of the first wave of economic reforms, just about every country in Eastern Europe was experiencing at last developmental crises. For Poland it was the crises of distribution.

Hungary

Hungary also had its own spate of problems. The Kolkhozes turned out to be inefficient and the reason behind it was traced to be psychological factors. An outstanding characteristic of the Hungarian peasant is his individuality. Usually peasants tried to concentrate their effort on the plots of land left to them, rather than to participate actively in the work of the kolkhoz. The changes in Hungary were certainly part of a structural crisis in Eastern European Economies, a crisis manifest in the ability of the socialist economic mechanism to restructure, to keep up with the 'micro-chip' revolution.[12] The Polish and Hungarian situations are identical in their calls for economic reform; they differ with regard to the political role of the church and the weight of the opposition movement. The current HSWP leaders are indebted to Kadar's successful compromise of the 1960's and 70's for the absence of Solidarity like mass movement in Hungary.

The answers to the question as to why socialism fell in Hungary are partly to be found in the remote past, in the origin of Kádár's regime and in the way that system was put together after the revolution in 1956, and partly in the very particular circumstances of the mid-1980's when the system ran out of steam and cried out for a new infusion of energies, but this could not be arranged because of the way it had been put together. Crucially, Kádár's own role as a conservative innovator who could not move with the times when the need arose requires particular scrutiny.

After 1956, Kádár had to re-establish his power, reorganise the Communist Party, that had fallen apart in the revolution, break down the resistance of the population, end the general strike and liquidate the institutions that the revolution had generated. He could not be too fussy about the means and he did not have much of a choice either. By the early 1960s, Hungarian society was thoroughly cowed down.

One may assume that future studies to be written about the peculiar features of the Eastern European transition to liberal democracy will rediscover evidence to prove that a uniform state-socialist model never existed, and that individual countries deviated to a significant extent from the basis theoretical model. Differences in their transitions to democracy were also determined primarily by these deviations, above all, by substantial differences between the internal power structures of individual party states, and by differences in the ways in which Eastern European countries became 'normalised' and consolidated.

In Hungary, just as in other Eastern European countries, the dramatic change in the external environment enabled factors within the country to play a decisive role in formulating the system. For the first time since 1948, an opportunity presented itself to suggest openly a change in the model, and for the first time it became possible to make a fundamental change in the power structure. While previous Soviet leadership groups almost instantly sanctioned any deviation from the basic model by way of direct and indirect pressure and interference, and primary objective of the Hungarian leadership was not to upset social peace in Hungary.

During the first part of the transition, Hungarian domestic political events followed the shifting power considerations in Moscow.

Another fundamental and peculiar feature of the 1988–89 Hungarian events was the fact that while the potential scope of internal political activities significantly increased, at least, in so far as the East was concerned, the country's sovereignty, its ability to chart the direction in which its own development takes place plummeted to a minimum. The phenomenon was linked primarily to the dangerous acceleration of indebtedness repayable in dollars. Hungary faced a pressure from both East and West.

From among the internal conditions for change, disintegration of the party state, and with that the emergence of open conflict within the political and economic elite, played the central role in Hungary. The above described changes in the external environment played a role in the disintegration in the party state. The latter was highly unfavourable from the standpoint of the inflexible and obsolete structure of the Hungarian economic system. Series of liberalising, decentralising and centralising government policies which followed in close sequence served only to deteriorate the condition of the economy. The drying up of external resources needed to sustain the economy heightened internal tensions in an economic system. Kádár's soft authoritarian system tried to sustain a monopoly of power in harmony with the maintenance of social peace by providing solid economic prosperity to citizens. It was hardly transparent and difficult to control even from the top. Although the alternative of 'hardening up' the system–i.e. a return to the Ceausescu or Husak type 'raw authoritarian' model–was brought up repeatedly by the party. Subsequently, towards the end of 1988, at a time when the transition had already started, Grósz's Party leadership made a weak attempt at reversal. By that time the party state had already fallen.

The rifts within the various elite prepared the ground for the second condition of transition, notably for the establishment of an informal alliance between reform Communists and the organised forces of civil society. The most important leaders of the democratic opposition were not invited to the conference. Later, this fact played a role in the division of autonomous political forces.

The third condition of change was to take the lid off the authoritarian system, i.e. to attain and defend the political rights of civil society. From early 1988, small groups of intellectuals–jurists, sociologists, historians, philosophers and others established increasingly large number of autonomous political groups organised the struggle against repeatedly renewed restrictive legislative proposals.

The fourth condition for transition was the accompaniment of a radical change in the political orientation of society. In contrast to the rest of the European countries, mass movement did not topple the old system in Hungary, and in the course of the Hungarian transition, it was not so much the mass support enjoyed by the Opposition but rather the passive rejection of the old system that played the decisive role. On the occasion of March 15 national holiday in the course of which far more people appeared at the celebrations organised by the Opposition. Above all the reburial of the 1956 revolutionary leaders in June served as such as assessment. Despite the above mentioned sising up of strength, political organisation within civil society was rather low, throughout the transition period. Even in September 1989, when an agreement was reached to call free elections, the ratio of the adult population organised as part of the autonomous political organisation did not exceed 1 per cent.

The second phase of political transition (March–October 1989) was characterised by negotiations between the state party and the opposition. The significance of the phase is also indicated by the fact that a number of social scientists call the Hungarian transition 'negotiated revolution.' It was at that time that the process of law making dictated by the state party could be stopped and the Opposition succeeded in making parliament pass only those laws to which the Communist Party and the opposition had previously agreed.

The third phase of the political transition lasting until the free election (Oct '89–April '90) was already characterised by the participation of the society. During the weeks after the partial signing of the pact on 18th September, the AFD carried out a signature campaign for the settlement of the still outstanding issues and subsequently the plebiscite of 26th November, which sharply marked the split between the radical and the moderate opposition. In the meantime, the old HSWP ceased to exist at the October Party Congress and it was replaced by the significantly lighter Hungarian Socialist Party (HSP).

It is tempting to blame history. One view in this vein maintains that historical stages cannot be jumped, that socialism was imposed too early and society will have to go back through a bourgeois phase and learn the positive 'citizen' values of bourgeois society. The analysis presented above suggests that these are evasions, that the crisis must be located squarely in socialism, or at least a particular type of socialist model, and that the forces at work are not the hidden forces of history or a silent bourgeois revolution, but the system of the owners, managers and workers of that socialism's economic system.

But the question still remains as to why did existing socialist regimes collapse? Gorbachev had only tried to revolutionise the system on the basis of Lenin with his Perestroika, but failed in his attempt to do so. Marx and Engels had only given broad outlines as to how one should without explaining the details of it, leaving it to the times to fill up the gaps. What they had visualised was that the material conditions of the state will wither away and a society of free individuals will come in where men will govern things instead of things governing men. This transition could not be worked out despite stages of socialism, people's state, developed socialism or Gorbachev's developing socialism. The other East European countries also faced the same problems. They did not have anyone to look upto. As they opened up to the West these countries became all the more incapable of handling the problems as a result of it, and in the process they also collapsed, apart from the fact that these countries had their own indigenous problems in handling socialism in their countries. The issues which remained problematic in one country did not match with the issues in the other countries. A new middle class, on meritoracy new phase of national identity, new issues of economy in the context of globalisation, persistence and penetration of religious lineages, imaging freedom, prosperity and spiritual well-being cases of nuclear accidents, the gender issues in socialist states had now passed through the stage of periodic crises into socialist crisis in general. Recordination of Marxian-Lenist concepts was the need of the hour, while flush capitalism over took it all to turn back the wheels of humanity.

References

1. Rakesh Gupta, *Soviet Policies in the Eighties*, Patriot Publishers, New Delhi, 1987, pp. 2-3.

2. Kurt Weisskopf, *The Agony of Czechoslovakia*, Elek Books Limited, Great Britain, 1968, pp. 180-189.

3. Andrzej Korbonski, *The Politics of Economic Reforms in Eastern Europe: The Last Thirty Years*, Soviet Studies, Vol. XLI, No.1, January 1989, pp. 1-19.

4. *Ibid.* pp. 1-9.

5. Karl Cordell art : *Political Change In The GDR: The Role Of The Evangelical Church, International Relations, Vol. 10,1990-91*, David Davies Memorial Institute Of International Studies, England.

6. Jadwiga Koralewicz, *Changes in Polish Social Consciousness during the 1970s and 1980s: Opportunism and Identity*, from *Crisis and Transition: Polish Society in the 1980s*; Berg Publishers Ltd. Oxford; 1987, pp. 3-4.

7. Jarosz calculated on the basis of Central Statistical Agency data that the first decline in the Polish suicide rate for thirty years occurred in 1980.

8. Jadwiga Koralewicz, *Changes in Polish Social Consciousness during the 1970s and 1980s:*

Opportunism and Identity, from *Crisis and Transition: Polish Society in the 1980s*; Berg Publishers Ltd. Oxford; 1987, pp. 4-5.

9. *Ibid.*

10. For a discussion of the changes in institutional and organisational structures and the power system as the main source of coercion, see Panków (1982a). It seems that the period under consideration was marked by the increased significance of controlled processes in institutional and organisation structures for the processes taking place in the class and stratum structures of society. The spontaneous restructuration which was observable in the late 1950s and the 1960s was of a limited nature. Since people at the two levels of social structure were unable to meet their basic needs, small groups played the main supporting and compensatory role for individuals.

11. Jadwiga Koralewicz, '*Changes in Polish Social Consciousness during the 1970s and 1980s: Opportunism and Identity*', from *Crisis and Transition : Polish Society in the 1980s;* Berg Publishers Ltd. Oxford, 1987, pp. 15-17.

12. Nigel Swain; *Hungary's Socialist Project in Crisis*; New Left Review, 1989, pp. 173-178.

Bibliography

Books

1. Adam Schaff, *Marxism and the Human Individual*, McGraw Hill Book Company, New York, 1970.
2. Alec Nove; *Stalinism and After*; George Allen & Unwin Publishers Ltd.; London; 1975.
3. Bela Balassa; "The Hungarian Economy in the Communist Era" in Robert Finley Delaney (Ed.), *This is Communist Hungary*; Henry Regnary Company Chicago; 1958.
4. David L Sills (ed.); *International Encyclopaedia of Social Sciences Vol. 15*; The Macmillan Company & Free Press; New York; 1972.
5. David S Mason; *Public Opinion and Political Change in Poland, 1980–82*; Cambridge University Press; London; 1985.
6. Della Volpe; *Rousseau and Marx*; Laurence & Wishart; London; 1978.
7. E.H. Carr; *1917: Before and After*; Macmilan; London; 1969.
8. *Encyclopaedia of Marxism and Communism Vol. 7.*

9. Eric Solsten (Ed.); *Germany: A Country Study 2nd Edition*; Federal Research Division, Library of Congress; Washington DC; 1996.

10. Ernest Mandel; *Beyond Perestroika–The Future of Gorbachev's USSR*; Verso; London; 1989.

11. *Experiences, Results, Prospects: The Role of the Masses in the Development of Socialist Society*; Panorama DDR; Grafischer Grossbetreif Volkerfreundschaft; Dresden; 1977.

12. Frederick Engels; *Anti-Duhring: Herr Eugen Duhring's Revolution in Science*; Foreign Languages Publishing House; Moscow; 1954.

13. Galia Golan; *Reform Rule in Czechoslovakia: The Dubcek Era 1968–1969*; Cambridge University Press; 1973.

14. Geoffrey Hosking; *The Beginning of Independent Political Activity in Post-Communist Societies*; 1995.

15. Georg Lukács; *History and Class Consciousness: Studies in Marxist Dialectics*; Merlin Press; London 1967.

16. George Kolankiewicz & Paul G Lewis; *Poland: Politics, Economics and Society*; Printer Publishers; London & New York; 1988.

17. George Mikes; *The Hungarian Revolution*; Andre Deutsch; London; 1957.

18. Glenn E Curtis (Ed.); *Poland: A Country Study 3rd Edition*; Federal Research Division, Library of Congress; Washington DC; 1994.

19. Hederick Smith; *The New Russians*; Random House; New York; 1990.

20. Howard Selsam, David Goldway, Harry Martel; *Dynamics of Social Change*; International Publishers, London; 1970.

21. Ihor Gawdiak (Ed.); *Czechoslovakia: A Country Study 3rd Edition*; Federal Research Division, Library of Congress; Washington DC; 1989.

22. *Introducing the GDR*; Panorama DDR; Grafischer Grossbetreif Volkerfreundschaft; Dresden; 1976.

23. Isaac Deutcher; *Stalin: A Political Biography*; Penguin; London; 1968.

24. Isaac Deutcher; *Trotsky Vol. 1–3*; Oxford University Press; London; 1963.

25. Isaac Deutscher; *Unfinished Revolution: Russia 1917 to 1967*; Oxford University Press; London; 1967.

26. Jadwiga Koralewicz, *Changes in Polish Social Consciousness during the 1970s and 1980s: Opportunism and Identity*, from *Crisis and Transition: Polish Society in the 1980s*; Berg Publishers Ltd. ; Oxford; (1987),

27. James D White; *Lenin: The Practice and Theory of Revolution*; Palgrave Publishers; New York; 2001.

28. Jan F Tricia, David D Finley; *Soviet Foreign Policy*; The Macmillan Company Press; New York; 1968.

29. Jean Ellenstein; *The Stalin Phenomenon*; Lawrence & Wishart; London; 1976.

30. Joan Frances Crowley, Dan Vaillancourt; *Lenin to Gorbachev: Three Generation of Soviet Communists*; Harlan Davidson Inc; Illinois; 1989

31. Karen Dawisha; *Eastern Europe: Gorbachev and Reform: The Great Challenge*; Press Syndicate of the University of Cambridge; USA; 1988.

32. Karl Kautsky; *Selected Political Writing*; Macmillan; London; 1983.

33. Karl Marx & Fredrick Engels; *The Communist Manifesto*; Martin Lawrence; London; 1930.

34. Karl Marx, 'The German Ideology', *Collected Works, Vol. 5*, Progress Publishers, Moscow, 1976.

35. Karl Marx; 'A Contribution to the Critique of Political Economy' in *Collected Works Vol. 16*; Progress Publishers; Moscow 1980.

36. Karl Marx; "Theses on Feuerbach"; *Collected Works Vol. 5*; Progress Publishers; Moscow; 1976

37. Karl Marx; *Civil War in France*; Lawrence & Wishart; London; 1941.

38. Karl Marx; *On Britain*; Foreign Languages Publication; Moscow; 1953.

39. Karl Marx; *The Class Struggle in France 1848-50*; Progress Publisher; Moscow; 1965.

40. Kurt Weisskopf, *The Agony of Czechoslovakia*, Elek Books Limited, Great Britain, 1968.

41. Kurt Weisskopf; *The Agony of Czechoslovakia '38/ '68*; Elek Books Ltd.; Great Britain; 1968.

42. Leszek Kolakowski; *Main Currents of Marxism Vol. 1-3*; Clarendon Press; Oxford; 1978.

43. Lucio Colletti; *From Rousseau to Lenin: Studies in Ideologies and Society*; Oxford University Press; Oxford; 1976.

44. M R Myrant; *Socialism and Democracy in Czechoslovakia 1945-48*; Western Printing Services Ltd; Cambrige University Press; Great Britain; 1981.

45. Maurice Cornforth, *Dialectical Materialism Vol2*, Lawrence and Wishart, London, 1953.

46. Michael Reiman; *The Birth of Stalinism: The USSR on the Eve of the Second Revolution*; IB Tauris & Co. Ltd.; London; 1987.

47. Mikhail Gorbachev; *Perestroika: New Thinking for our Country and the World*; William Collins Sons and Co. Ltd.; London; 1987.

48. Mikhail Gorbachev; *Speeches and Writings*; Pergamon Press.; Oxford; 1986.

49. Milovan Djilas; *The New Class: An analysis of the Communist System*; Frederick A Praeger; New York; 1957.

50. Miroslav Hroch, "Nationalism in Central and Eastern Europe" in Anthony D Smith, *Nationalism: Concepts in Political Science, Vol. 2.*

51. Oscar Lange & Fred M Taylor; *On the Economic Theory of Socialism*; Tata McGraw Hill Publisher Company; New Delhi; 1976.

52. P K Sundaram (Ed.); *Wither Czechoslovakia: Essays and Documents on Czechoslovak Crisis*; Dawn Publishers; New Delhi; 1969.

53. P.N. Fedoseyev et.al.; *Karl Marx: A Biography*; Progress Publishers; Moscow; 1973.

54. Paul Bellis; *Marxism and the USSR*; The Macmillan Press Ltd.; London; 1979.

55. Perry Anderson; *Considerations on Western Marxism*; NLB; London; 1976.

56. Philip Windsor & Adam Roberts; *Czechoslovakia: 1968 Reform, Repression and Resistance*; Northumberland Press Ltd.; Great Britain; 1969

57. Rakesh Gupta; *Political Stability and Civil-Military Relations Under Gorbachev*; Lancer International; New Delhi; 1991.

58. Rakesh Gupta; *Russian Military Doctrine*, Occassional Paper, Institute of Defence Studies and Analysis, New Delhi, 1984.

59. Rakesh Gupta; *Soviet Policies in the Nineteen Eighties*; Patriot Publishers; New Delhi; 1987.

60. Raymond E Zickel (Ed.); *Soviet Union: A Country Study 2nd Edition*; Federal Research Division, Library of Congress; Washington DC; 1991.

61. Rosa Luxemburg; *Imperialism and the Accumulation of Capital*; The Penguin Press; London; 1972

62. Rudolf L Tökés; *Hungary's Negotiated Revolution: Economic Reform, Social Change and Political Succession*; Cambrige University Press; Great Britain; 1996.

63. Rudolph Barho; *The Alternative in Eastern Europe*; NLB; USA; 1978.

64. Santiago Carrillo; *Euro Communism and the State*; Lawrence & Wishart; London; 1977.

65. Stephen Burant (Ed.); *Hungary: A Country Study 2nd Edition*; Federal Research Division, Library of Congress; Washington DC; 1990.

66. Tom Bottomore; *Dictionary of Marxist Thought*; Blackwell Publishers; London; 1983.

67. Vladimir Illich Lenin; "Economics and Politics in the Era of Dictatorship of the Proletariat" in *Collected Works Vol. 30*; Progress Publishers; Moscow; 1965.

68. Vladimir Illich Lenin; "Imperialism: The Highest Stage of Capitalism" in *Collected Works Vol. 22*; Progress Publishers; Moscow; 1964.

69. Vladimir Illich Lenin; "State And Revolution" in *Collected Works Vol. 25*; Progress Publishers; Moscow; 1964.

70. Vladimir Illich Lenin; "The Development of Capitalism in Russia" in *Collected Works Vol. 3*; Progress Publishers; Moscow; 1960.

71. Vladimir Illich Lenin; "The Immediate Task of the Soviet Government" in *Collected Works Vol. 27*; Progress Publishers; Moscow; 1965.

72. Vladimir Illich Lenin; "The Tax in Kind" in *Collected Works Vol. 32*; Progress Publishers; Moscow; 1965.

73. Vladimir Illich Lenin; "Two Tactics of Social Democracy in the Democratic Revolution" in *Collected Works Vol. 9*; Progress Publishers; Moscow; 1961.

74. Vladimir Illich Lenin; "What is to be Done" in *Collected Works Vol. 5*; Progress Publishers; Moscow; 1961.

75. Vladimir Shlapentohli; *Soviet Ideologies in the Period of Glasnost: Response to Brezhnev's Stagnation*; Praeger Publishers; New York; 1988.

76. *What is Life Like in the GDR: Living Standards and the way of Life under Socialism*; Panorama DDR; Grafischer Grossbetreif Volkerfreundschaft; Dresden; 1977.

Articles

1. Abel Aganbegyan; "New Directions in Soviet Economics"; New Left Review; No. 169; New Left Review Ltd.; London;1988.

2. Adam Przeworski; "Political Support for Economic Reforms in Poland"; Comparative Political Studies; Sage Publication Inc.; London; 1996.

3. Alex Pravda; "Poland 1980: Premature Consumerism to Labour Solidarity"; Soviet Studies

Vol. XXXIV No. 2; Carfax Publishing Company; United Kingdom; 1982.

4. Anatoly Dobrynin; "Revolutionaries Cannot Trail Behind Life"; Mainstream; Vol. 26, No. 31 Perspective Publications; New Delhi; 1988.

5. Andrzej Korbonski, 'The Politics of Economic Reforms in Eastern Europe: The Last Thirty Years', Soviet Studies, Vol. XLI, No. 1, January 1989

6. Andrzej Korbonski; "The Politics of Economic Reforms in Eastern Europe: The Last Thirty Years"; Soviet Studies; Vol. XLI, No. 1; Carfax Publishing Company; United Kingdom; 1989.

7. Andrzej Paczkowski; "Communist Poland 1944-1989: Some Controversies and a Single Conclusion"; The Polish Review; Vol. XLIV, No. 2; The Polish Institute of Arts and Sciences of America; New York; 1999.

8. B.N. Arora; "Lenin: The Stuff He Was Made Of"; Mainstream Vol. XLI No. 18; Perspective Publication; New Delhi; 2003.

9. Barnabas Racs; "The Parliamentary Infrastructure and Political Reforms in Hungary"

10. Bela Kádár; "What We Inherited"; Soviet and Eastern European Foreign Trade; M.E. Sharpe Inc.; New York; 1990-91.

11. Bogdan Mroz; "Poland's Economy in Transition to Private Ownership"; Soviet Studies, Vol. 43; Carfax Publishing Company; United Kingdom; 1982.

12. Boris Kagarlitsky; "Perestroika: The Dialectic of Change"; New Left Review; No. 169; The New Left Review Ltd. London; 1988.

13. Boris Kagarlitsky; "The Intelligentsia and the Changes"; New Left Review; No. 164; The New Left Review Ltd. London; 1987.

14. Fedor Burlatsky; "The Gorbachev Revolution"; Mainstream Vol. 25, No. 32; Perspective Publication; New Delhi; 1987.

15. Fred S Oldenburg: "The October Revolution in the GDR–System, History and Causes"; Eastern European Economics, Vol. 21; M.E. Sharp Inc; New York; 1990-91.

16. Gábor Révész; "How the Economic Reforms Were Distorted"; Eastern European Economics; Vol. 27; M.E. Sharpe Inc.; New York; 1989.

17. Goran Therborn; "Dialectics of Modernity: Of Critical Theory and the Legacy of Twentieth-Century Marxism"; New Left Review; No. 215; The New Left Review Ltd. London; 1996.

18. Irwin Collier; "GDR: Economic Policy during the Honecker Era"; Eastern European Economics; Vol. 21; M.E. Sharpe Inc.; New York; 1990-91.

19. Jens Hölscher; "Economic Dynamism in Transition Economies: Lessons from Germany"; Communist Economies & Economic Transformation; Vol. 9, No. 2; Carfax Publication; Great Britain; 1999.

20. Jerzy Szacki; "Polish Democracy: Dreams and Reality"; Social Research; Vol. 58, No. 4; New School for Social Research; New York; 1991.

21. Jiri Musil; "Czechoslovakia in the Middle of Transition"; Daedelus; Vol. 121; American Academy of Arts and Sciences; Boston; 1992.

22. Jiøina Šklová; "What Did We Lose Afetr 1989"; Social Research; Vol. 63, No. 2; New School for Social Research; New York; 1996.

23. Karl Cordell; 'Political Change in the GDR: The Role Of The Evangelical Church', International Relations, Vol. 10, 1990-91, David Davies Memorial Institute of International Studies, England.

24. Karl Cordell; "Political Change in the GDR: The Role of the Evangelical Church" International Relations, Vol. 10; David Davies Memorial Institute of International Studies; England; 1990-91.

25. Katalin Botos; "Financial Aspects of Agricultural Policies in Hungary"; Soviet Studies, Vol. 42, No. 1; Carfax Publishing Company; United Kingdom; 1990.

26. Len Goldman; "Commentary on the Recent Events in the German Democratic Republic"; Capital and Class, No. 1940-42; Conference of Socialist Economists; London; 1990.

27. Mikhail S Gorbachev; "Reality and Guarantees of a Secure World"; Mainstream Vol. 26; Perspective Publication; New Delhi; 1988.

28. Mikhail S Gorbachev; "Restore Lenin's Image of Socialism"; Mainstream Vol. 26 No. 32; Perspective Publication; New Delhi; 1988.

29. Nigel Swain; 'Hungary's Socialist Project in Crisis'; New Left Review, 1989, No: 173-178

30. Nigel Swain; "Hungary's Socialist Project in Crisis"; New Left Review; The New Left Review Ltd. London; 1989.

31. Norbert Zmijewski; "Vicissitudes of Political Realism in Poland: Tygodnik Powszechny and Znak"; Soviet Studies; Vol. 43, No. 1; Carfax Publishing Company; United Kingdom; 1991.

32. P.G. Hare & P.T. Wanless; "Polish and Hungarian Economic Reforms–A Comparison"; Soviet Studies

Vol. XXXIII, No. 4; Carfax Publishing Company; United Kingdom; 1981.

33. Rakesh Gupta; "Crash of Socialist Polity in the GDR"; The Indian Journal of Social Science; Vol. 4, No. 1; Sage Publications; New Delhi; 1991.

34. Rakesh Gupta; "Defence, Security Scenario"; World Focus Vol. 12 No. 9-10 ; Hari Sharan Chhabra; New Delhi; 1991.

35. Rakesh Gupta; "Disarmament Meet: US Thwarts Consensus"; Mainstream Vol. 26 No. 38; Perspective Publication; New Delhi; 1988.

36. Rakesh Gupta; "From Alienation to Participation"; Mainstream Vol. 26 No. 40; Perspective Publication; New Delhi; 1988.

37. Rakesh Gupta; "Perestroika: Transition with Participation"; International Studies; Vol. 27, No. 1; Sage Publications; New Delhi; 1990.

38. Rakesh Gupta; "Vision of a Changing Equilibrium"; Mainstream Vol. XXVII No. 24; Perspective Publication; New Delhi; 1989.

39. Ranko Petrovic; "The German Problem in a New Historical Context"; Review of International Affairs; Vol. 40, No. 930-53; FPI RTY International Politics; Yugoslavia; 1989.

40. Robert Rozhdestvensky; "Gorbachev Spoke the Truth: Imparted Shock Therapy"; Mainstream Vol. 26; Perspective Publication; New Delhi; 1988.

41. Stephen E Medvec; "Poland and Czechoslovakia: Can They Find They Need Each Other?"; The Polish Review; Vol. XXXVI, No. 4; The Polish Institute of Arts and Sciences of America; New York; 1991.

42. Tamara Deutscher; "Poland–Hopes and Fears"; New Left Review, No. 125; The New Left Review Ltd. London; 1980-81.

43. Thomas Saalfeld; "Germany: From Dictatorship to Parliamentary Democracy"; Parliamentary Affairs; Vol. 50; Hansard Society for Parliamentary Government; Great Britain; 1997.

44. Valerie Bunce; "Peaceful versus Violent State Dismemberment: A Comparison of the Soviet Union, Yugoslavia and Czechoslovakia"; Politics And Society; Vol. 27, No. 2; Sage Publications; London; 1999.

45. Vladimir Mytarev; "Soviet Economy: Fruitless Half Measures"; Mainstream Vol. 26; Perspective Publication; New Delhi; 1988.

46. Yegor Yakovlev; "Four Days that Shook the World"; Mainstream; Vol. 26; Perspective Publication; New Delhi; 1988.

47. Yevgeni Yevtushenko; "The Right to be Unconventional"; Mainstream Vol. 25, No. 21; Perspective Publication; New Delhi; 1987.

48. Zhores Medvedev; "Innovation and Conservativeness in the New Soviet Leadership" New Left Review; No. 157; New Left Review Ltd. London; 1986.

Index

E